BEST BACKROADS of Florida

Volume 2
Coasts, Glades, and Groves

Douglas Waitley

Pineapple Press, Inc.
Sarasota, Florida

Inquiries should be addressed to:

Pineapple Press, Inc.
P.O. Box 3889
Sarasota, Florida 34230

www.pineapplepress.com

Library of Congress Cataloging in Publication Data

Waitley, Douglas.
    Best back roads of Florida. Douglas Waitley.
              v.   cm.
    Contents: v. 2. Coasts, glades, and groves
    ISBN 1-56164-232-0 (v. 2)
1. Florida—Tours. 2. Automobile travel—Florida—Guidebooks. 3. Scenic byways—Florida—Guidebooks. I. Title.

F309.3.W325 2000
917.5904'63—dc21

                                                    99-045354

First Edition
10 9 8 7 6 5 4 3 2 1

Design by *Osprey Design Systems*
Text and Cover Composition by Shé Sicks

Printed in the United States of America

To Jeff: May the song of the road always be his.

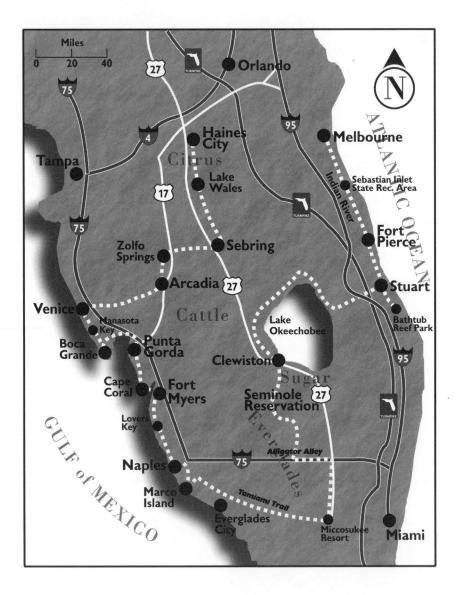

Contents

Introduction

The Lure of the Backroads

Backroads have an essence that main roads lack. This essence is a mysterious quality that some may call tasty unpredictability, which is part of their appeal. Backroads often have curves where none are really required. They have bumps in the least expected places. They go up and down on what seem to be whims. Backroads are like children—capricious, petulant, playful. As you get to know them, you'll find they have personalities, each road its own.

Backroads are territorial. Because most of them do not go very far,

Backroads delight in curves, as does this byway along the Indian River Lagoon.
The trees are Australian pines, hated as exotics by environmentalists,
but graceful shade trees nonetheless.

1

they grasp the land they pass through like a gator grabs a catfish. There are sandy beach roads and humid swamp roads and fragrant citrus roads. Some roads are sweet on sugarcane, while others prefer to romp through cattle pastures. The road traipsing north from Naples is enamored with glitzy, high-rise condos. The one proceeding west from Stuart is content with a canal.

But there is more to the lure of backroads. Each has poignant stories. There are happy tales of young couples in horse-drawn carriages heading to the village dance. There are grim chronicles of discouraged Seminoles when this was a wilderness trail. There are sagas of immigrant farmers, of itinerant preachers, of disgraced politicians, of crooks on the lam. Where do you hear these stories? At the old gas station with the repair garage. At the mom-and-pop restaurant with the pressed-tin ceiling. At the dusty crossroads where you ask directions when you really don't need to know.

The Art of Backroads Driving

Many people don't realize that there is an art to driving the back-

Backroads, like this beach-access pathway on the Gulf of Mexico, often lead to enjoyable hideaways. The spiked plants are sea oats.

roads. They view them as obstacles to be passed over as quickly as possible. But a true backroads driver knows you must deal with them on their own terms. They resent being hurried. If you try to rush, they'll just make the curves sharper and the bumps more frequent. They may even throw in a few cattle trucks just for the sport of it. Certainly you'll find the small towns dustier. And the people will clam up or maybe even provide you with obtuse answers when you ask about the directional sign you missed as you passed that cattle truck.

Backroads like to be stroked. You should proceed slowly to let the roads know that you respect them for what they are. You must accept the fact that when you get on a backroad, you're not really going anywhere. The road exists for itself. So settle into an easy-going, country mode. If you do, you'll get to know and enjoy the backroads.

Now that a relaxed mood is on you, join me as we set out to explore the southern portion of Florida. We're going to do a lot of turning and slowing and stopping. We're going to be curious. We're going to ask questions with an attitude of respect and wonderment.

A word about fishing licenses: the state's laws on who needs one and under what circumstances are rather complex. But the licenses themselves are relatively inexpensive and easy to obtain. A three-day nonresident's freshwater license costs only $6.50, and a seven-day license is $13.50. A Florida resident's minimum purchase is a twelve-month license, which costs $13.50. The rules concerning saltwater fishing (which includes the Indian River Lagoon) are different. Licenses, as well as information as to when they are needed, can be obtained by calling toll-free 888-347-4356. Have your credit card ready.

Every backroad has its special setting and unusual stories. So start your engine. The beckoning road awaits.

Icons

 Directions while driving

 Bridge and road tolls; admission fees

 Walking trails and paths

 Restaurants

 Bike rentals, trails

 Swimming areas

 Photo opportunities

 Fishing

 Hotels, motels, bed and breakfasts

 Boat rides, cruises

 Canoe rentals

Boat ramp

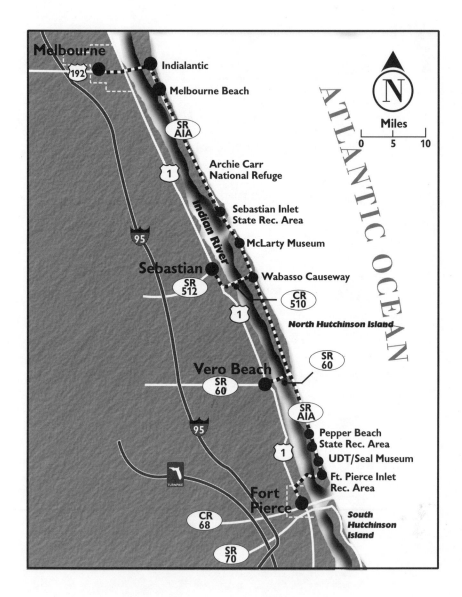

The Treasure Coast
Melbourne Beach to Ft. Pierce • 65 Backroad Miles

The Song of the Road: Overview

This exploration begins at Melbourne, from which a causeway spanning the Indian River leads to a narrow barrier island fronting the Atlantic Ocean. Here, at the village of Melbourne Beach, you can stroll onto the Indian River pier, a favorite place for fishermen and bird-watchers. From the pier, Ocean Boulevard leads to an Atlantic beach ideal for swimming. During midsummer nights, giant sea turtles frequent the coast. Thus it is not surprising that most of the beaches for the next fifteen miles south have become a national wildlife refuge. At the Sebastian Inlet State Recreation Area, you can enjoy a walk onto the windswept jetty, a prized location for anglers or those who enjoy watching birds wheeling in the salt-misted air. You can also rent boats at the park, snack beside the dunes, or swim along the more than three miles of beaches.

Just south of the inlet is the McLarty Museum, where relics of the doomed Spanish treasure fleet of 1715 are on display. These displays vividly recreate the tale of a wild hurricane and a lost fortune in gold and silver. A movie shows how American treasure hunters recovered some of this fabulous wealth—and tells about the untold millions that still await discovery.

Cross over to the mainland at the town of Sebastian and visit Mel Fisher's famous museum—storehouse for a significant portion of the recovered Spanish treasure—or relax at Captain Hiram's Restaurant, from which a sightseeing boat can transport you on a scenic voyage along the Indian River. Then it's back to the barrier island, where you may want to visit Disney's very un-Mickeylike Vero Beach Resort, with lodgings and restaurants directly on the ocean. Next is a stop at the impressive UDT/SEAL Museum, where you'll learn the exciting story of the daring Underwater Demolition Teams that trained here under live fire during the Second World War. Much of their equipment is on display. The exploration ends at the Ft. Pierce Inlet State Recreation Area, where you can swim, surf, or take a nature walk through a mangrove wetland.

On the Road Again

From downtown Melbourne take the US 192 causeway across the Indian River lagoon, which is almost a mile and a half wide at this point. Turn south onto the barrier island's first street, Riverside Drive.

The Pelican Pier: Melbourne Beach

After passing some beautiful homes that, unfortunately, obscure the river, you'll reach Melbourne Beach, where the road goes along a waterfront bristling with piers. The largest of these is the city pier, which reaches several hundred feet into the river. Tropical birds often strut along the wooden planks, and squadrons of pelicans skim the river. Pelicans, singly and in groups, make spectacular, high-level dives into the water. Fishing is good from the pier, so you might want to unlimber your rod and try your luck.

The pier has been an institution at Melbourne Beach since the first one was constructed in 1889 by a railroad company to accommodate visitors aboard the ferryboat from the mainland. The company had rails but no locomotives. So it simply loaded tourists, freight, and mail

A fisherman spirals his net into the Indian River Lagoon at Melbourne Beach. Cast nets are legal in salt water.

Melbourne Beach has several quaint restaurants.

into a horse-drawn car that rattled over the rails a quarter mile to the middle of town where the freight and mail debarked. The tourists generally continued another quarter mile to the Atlantic beach.

Although the rails and, of course, the weary nag have long since been retired, you can still follow Ocean Boulevard along the railroad's former route. As you do, note Dijon's Restaurant, which was once the popular Dixie Inn. Farther on is the city hall, a modest building serving the quietly modest community of around thirty-five hundred people.

Ocean Boulevard ends at SR A1A and the beach. Here Boomerang's Restaurant offers functional food before picture windows fronting the ocean. The facilities at the public beach, although minimal, do include the essential port-a-potties. A sign posted beside the wooden walkway leading to the beach informs people that this area is frequented by sea turtles, which are protected by federal, state, and county laws. Anyone who disturbs nesting females, the eggs, or the emerging hatchlings is subject to fines that can reach $20,000! There is also a sign on the tall streetlamp nearby announcing that it is a "turtle light" and will be turned off between May 1 and October 31 in order not to disturb the nesting or hatching process. So now you know: you're in Turtle Country.

Turtleville, U.S.A.

Sea turtles have become almost an obsession along this part of the

The sand is clean and the water fine at Melbourne Beach.

coast, where more than twenty-eight thousand endangered logger-head, leatherback, and green turtles make their nests among the dunes. Civilian turtle protectors scour the area during summer nights to make sure the lighting and molestation restrictions are observed. Police are called in for serious offenses, and the law is astonishingly severe. For example, to remove and sell turtle eggs can result in a five-year prison term!

This mobilization to protect such reclusive creatures is truly amazing. Over the years many people have dedicated themselves to this project. Perhaps the most influential was Archie Carr. In 1967 he wrote what has become a classic in the field, *So Elegant a Fish: A Natural History of Sea Turtles*. In his honor, much of the seashore for the next fifteen miles has become the Archie Carr National Wildlife Refuge.

Archie Carr spent his childhood along the Gulf and Atlantic coasts, where his parents taught him to love and respect nature. In the 1930s he studied zoology at the University of Florida. Upon graduation, he spent four years as a naturalist in the uplands of Honduras before being offered a position at his *alma mater* teaching a new subject called ecology. Somewhere along the line he became interested in sea turtles, but he quickly found that almost nothing was known about them, aside from the flavor of their eggs and the pleasure of green turtle soup. Carr was particularly fascinated by the turtles' uncanny ability to swim over vast distances, then return to the tiny segment of beach where they were born in order to lay their eggs.

Carr conducted many experiments trying to learn this migratory secret. First he injected tiny magnets into some of the hatchlings. But he was mortified to find that the magnetic field could be read only from a proximity of two inches. Next he attached radio transmitters on his turtles' backs. But the signals could be heard only during the brief time the turtles came up to breathe. So he tied the transmitters to four-foot-long helium-filled balloons painted bright yellow that rose sixty feet above the animal. He even put a tiny light on each balloon so an airplane could track it at night. But the helium leaked from the balloons before enough pertinent data could be accumulated.

Although Archie Carr failed to discover the sea turtles' navigational secrets, his curious mind was always active. "Archie knew more about Florida wildlife and wilderness than any other person, today or in times gone by," concluded his wife, Marjorie, in her introduction to selections from Carr's writings published in 1994, seven years after his death.

As you drive south from Melbourne Beach along A1A, watch for signs indicating the Archie Carr National Wildlife Refuge. It consists of four strips of beach along A1A but there are no formal entrances. Each strip had to be purchased piecemeal by state, county,

Turtles lay eggs along these protected beaches.

and private conservation organizations in the hope that eventually they could be melded into a single unit. So when you find a sign, simply park in the sandy strip beside the highway and walk over the low dune to the beach.

Frankly, there is not much to see in the Refuge, yet that very fact is its glory. There are very few places along Florida's east coast where the shoreline appears much the same as it did before the advent of humans. On the low dunes, sea oats do the same rhythmic dances they have performed since the island was formed. Deep in the sand, ghost crabs rest in their cool, dark tunnels waiting for darkness when they do their sideways dances as they hunt for food along the shore. Meanwhile, somewhere out in that vast, inscrutable ocean, giant turtles paddle along faraway currents until the biological moment arrives when they must return to their ancestral nesting sites along these very sands.

Florida's most common sea turtle is the loggerhead, which is about three feet in shell length and can weigh up to four hundred pounds. But leatherbacks are far larger: they can reach a staggering eight feet in length and weigh nearly two thousand pounds. Adult sea turtles are well adapted to hold their own among the sharks and other hunters. Their jaws are powerful enough to crack open the shells of

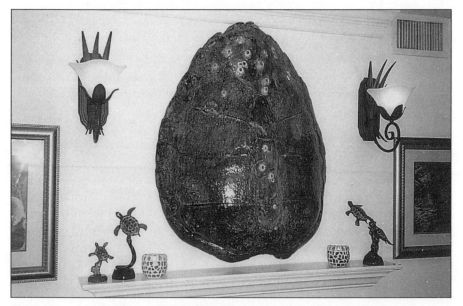

Sea turtles can be quite large, as this shell in a restaurant clearly shows.

clams, crabs, and the other mollusks upon which they feed. But they are nonaggressive, solitary animals that roam alone over hundreds, even thousands, of miles. Although they spend nearly their entire lives in the open water, they follow some instinctive pathway that may be related to ocean currents or to the earth's magnetic field—or to still-unknown factors—toward the very beach where they were born. They mate just offshore, then, during the night, the females pull their heavy bodies out of the water and lumber across the sand and up a dune. There, each turtle digs her nest and lays a hundred or so golf ball–size eggs. Her maternal instinct now satisfied, she covers the nest and returns to the ocean. She will never visit the nest again nor will she ever see her babies.

The hatchlings break out of their shells two months later. They emerge at night and begin a frantic dash toward the ocean, which they distinguish by the reflection of stars or the moon on its surface. But some are disoriented by electric lights and run in the wrong direction toward roads, where they will die. Those that head for the ocean must run a gauntlet of hungry raccoons and ghost crabs. Almost every baby turtle that reaches the water will eventually be gobbled up by fish. Out of a thousand eggs, it is estimated that barely one turtle will survive to adulthood. That is why the female lays so many.

Gazing out at the ocean, one may sense a strange, primordial attraction in the endless swells and sighs of the water. The rumbling waves soothe us, yet at the same time create an uneasy longing for something . . . we know not what. We wander the shores picking up the shells of dead creatures. We wonder at their lives but know we are far different from the fish and the globs of squirming matter that inhabited those seashells.

Our feeling for turtles is different because they are air breathers like us. Although at home in the ocean, they are linked to the land to which they must return if their species is to survive. Watching a female sea turtle emerge from the ocean is like seeing an apparition from the Triassic past—a past from which we ourselves may have descended.

You can see the turtles at the Carr Refuge during nesting time simply by strolling along the beach after dark in June or July. But for a far more rewarding experience, take one of the free turtle walks conducted by rangers from the nearby Sebastian Inlet park just down A1A. The walks are conducted four nights a week depending on the tides and turtle activity. A group of around twenty-five people meets at 8 P.M. for an hour-long orientation, then goes along the shore for the next hour or two. Although no flash photos are allowed, you can stand as close as one or two feet from the blasé turtle as she digs her nest and deposits her eggs. These walks are so popular that you should make your reservation in May (407-984-4852).

Activity Center: Sebastian Inlet State Recreation Area

The Sebastian Inlet is well worth the $3.25 per car entry fee. The park is on both sides of the man-made inlet through which boats travel between the Atlantic and the Indian River. For many tourists the most popular attractions are on the north side, where nearly everyone walks out on the jetty protruding far into the Atlantic. Although the jetty's primary purpose is to shelter the inlet, it has become a major fishing and bird-watching destination. Birders can usually spot pelicans, anhingas, egrets, herons, wood storks, white ibis, and double-crested cormorants. Fishermen catch snapper, black drum, redfish, and snook. The fishing is so good that the official State Parks Division booklet calls Sebastian "the premier saltwater fishing location on Florida's east coast."

Excitement can also be found along the shore, where the surf often runs high. Indeed, several national surfing tournaments are held here every year. The park provides changing rooms as well as showers to remove the salt water after your swim. Fishing is fun from the shore, for the tarpon run big along here—thirty to

A fearless wood stork waits for fishermen's castoffs on the long pier at the Sebastian Inlet.

eighty pounds is not unusual. Once in a while someone snags a tarpon in the 120-pound range. Then the fight begins. You have to play the fish skillfully so it doesn't break your line. "I fought one for fifteen minutes," said a fisherman. "When it finally broke off, I realized I was a half mile down the beach."

You can rent fishing equipment for $9.50 for a half day at the bait and tackle shop adjacent to the concession facility. The shop also sells the required three-day saltwater fishing license to non-residents for $7. The concession offers light breakfasts and lunches, and there are picnic tables both inside and outside.

People hankering to get out on the water can rent canoes and kayaks for $12 and $14 for a two-hour paddle on the calm waters of the Indian River. Powerboats are also available, beginning at $29 for a half day. Those who prefer less strenuous but more educational tours can board the Inlet Explorer, where a park ranger's narrative enlivens the two-hour trip ($15 for adults and $10 for kids under 12) past the Indian River's Pelican Island, the nation's first wildlife refuge.

The Story of a Hurricane

Although Sebastian surfers enjoy the high waves that develop in the aftermath of Florida's frequent hurricanes, no resident takes these storms lightly. Such was the case when meteorologists began tracking a tropical depression early in September 1999. It grew in size and intensity as it moved across the Atlantic directly toward Florida. When winds reached 75 mph, the storm was named Hurricane Floyd and warnings were issued throughout the state by television, radio, and newspapers.

As Floyd's core winds reached 150 mph, the storm was approaching Category One—subtitled "catastrophic"—the most fierce of hurricanes. With Floyd still on a collision course for central Florida, more than a million people were ordered to evacuate the coastal areas. This was especially difficult for residents on the barrier islands as the few bridges over the Indian River became clogged with traffic. With the hurricane bearing down on them, some people feared that the high winds would catch them on a bridge, so they turned around and decided to brave the storm in their homes. State officials, fully occupied otherwise, could do nothing to prevent this, and as the last of the cars crossed, they closed the bridges, leaving the remaining islanders completely on their own. They were in extreme danger. A hurricane of Floyd's magnitude could easily have sent

Relentless Atlantic winds have sculpted these bushes.

storm-surge waves crashing over the island, carrying away everything in their path.

But at the last moment Floyd veered northward, which might have saved the lives of those who chose to stay. Even though the powerful hurricane remained forty miles at sea, peripheral winds lashed out at near-hurricane strength. These winds drove against the shore, where they picked up debris and carried it out to sea. One log began slamming into the Sebastian Inlet's north jetty, battering eighty feet of thick, reinforced concrete pillars beyond repair. That portion of the jetty was closed off and remains so today.

The Golden Disaster: The Wreck of the Spanish Treasure Fleet

People nowadays do not properly appreciate the science of hurricane prediction. Modern early-warning techniques have allowed most people ample time to prepare for such storms. But throughout the ages such storms arrived with barely any advance notice. Such was the case in 1715 when an eleven-ship Spanish treasure fleet approached this area.

The weather had been fair when the ships caught the wind and sailed from Havana. Their holds were crammed with gold and silver as well as a cache of specially crafted jewelry for the queen of Spain herself. The ships also carried nearly fifteen hundred passengers—

men, women, and children—all eager to see their beloved homeland once more. The good weather held as the fleet passed through the Florida Straits and began skirting the coast.

But on July 29 the sky took on a strange milky haze that made the experienced seamen uneasy. Toward evening a line of squalls appeared along the eastern horizon. Soon ocean swells began rocking the ships. General Don Juan Esteban de Ubilla, in charge of the fleet, gave the order to lay on all canvas in the hope of outrunning whatever was approaching. But the wind was erratic, and by dawn the fleet had traveled only a few miles.

That morning the air was clammy and the sky grew ever darker. By mid-afternoon rain began and the wind picked up. It was clear that something bad was going to happen, so canvas was taken down and the hatches closed. As the seas grew rougher, the passengers, now confined below decks, began to pray. Toward dusk the hurricane struck. The wind snarled over the ships, lashing them with rain and hammering them with crashing waves. Timbers groaned and split. Then seawater began spurting into the interiors. There was no way to escape. With each monstrous wave, more wood splintered. Masts broke in two and thudded against the decks. Cannons were torn loose and battered against the bulkheads.

By midnight the ships were helpless with the ferocious winds driving them toward the shore. As the mountainous waves crested, then drew back, the vessels' hulls began slamming against the ocean bottom. At last the timbers could stand no more. One by one the hulls broke open, hurling the passengers, crew, and cargo into the thrashing waves.

As the hurricane screamed on the next day, seven hundred people had drowned and the remains of the eleven ships with their fabulous treasures were strewn along the ocean shallows for many miles. The survivors stumbled ashore at nine points along what was then known as the "Palmar de Ais," or palm grove of the Ais Indians, but is now part of Orchid and Hutchinson Islands. General Ubilla was among the dead, so Admiral Francisco Salmon took over. Wary of marauding pirates, Salmon constructed a fortified camp a couple of miles south of the Sebastian Inlet and gathered all the survivors there. The camp was large, extending from the ocean to the Indian River. Shelters were built from the wreckage that littered the beach. For supplies, they were fortunate to retrieve important items from the *Urca de Lima*, about twenty miles down the coast. The *Urca*, one of the smaller ships, had miraculously remained afloat—until a following storm sent her to the bottom with the others. For food they caught flounder and mullet and gathered oysters and clams. The Ais, traditionally friendly toward the Spanish, brought them sea grapes, palmetto berries, and the hearts of cabbage palms.

Fortunately, several longboats had been salvaged from the *Urca,* and with these Salmon sent for help from St. Augustine and Havana, where church bells tolled mournfully the entire day. Relief ships were dispatched and eventually the civilians were evacuated. The Spanish military brought in divers to salvage what they could of the treasure. The principal ships had gone down in water shallow enough so the divers could attach lines to the chests that were unbroken. Slowly, recovered gold and silver began to accumulate on the beach.

But it had not taken long for word of the wreck to reach the English ruffians who frequented the tough waterfront of Jamaica. Soon three hundred sea dogs piled aboard a pair of ships commanded by a grizzled roustabout named Henry Jennings. When Jennings and his men hit the beach near the Sebastian Inlet, they rousted the sixty Spanish guards, loaded their ships with as much booty as they could hold, then sailed off for debaucheries in Jamaica, where it is rumored even the British governor, Lord Hamilton, enjoyed a share of the loot. Two months later, after the Spanish had recovered more treasure, Jennings and his rowdy comrades once more relieved them of a sizable portion. Despite the setbacks, the Spanish did manage to salvage a significant portion of the treasure before another storm dislodged the wrecks, covering them with sand so they could no longer be found. After the Spaniards left, memories of the lost fleet began fading and finally vanished.

The Modern Treasure Hunters

Two centuries later American beach-walkers began discovering ancient, encrusted Spanish coins washed up on the shore. In 1950 an Ohio businessman named Kip Wagner borrowed an Army-surplus metal detector and started methodically scanning the beaches around the Sebastian Inlet. Within a few months he had accumulated forty coins, most tarnished silver, but a few bright gold! Convinced there were a lot more out in the shallows, Wagner organized a salvaging team. Recovery was slow at first, but when they were joined by Mel Fisher, a one-time chicken rancher turned professional treasure hunter, things began to happen.

The hoped-for strike came in late spring of 1964. Using scuba gear, Fisher's divers discovered a secluded underwater trench that glowed with a pavement of gold coins. When the divers surfaced, their gloves stuffed with the precious metal, the crew shrieked with excitement. All day the divers descended into the grotto. By the time darkness forced them to stop, they had collected over a thousand coins. It was, wrote Robert Burgess and Carl Clausen in *Florida's Golden Galleons*, "the biggest haul that they, or, for that matter, any other 20th-century salvager had ever made in Florida." When Fisher's crew recovered nearly that many coins the next day, Wagner began worrying that such a flood of doubloons would seriously debase their price on the world gold market. But it did not.

Although they tried to keep the location of the treasure secret, word got out. Gold seekers "came in droves," wrote Burgess and Clausen, ". . . amateur and professional treasure hunters, cranks, con men, crooks, and the curious." Nearby Ft. Pierce became flooded with them and the city fathers were delighted to advertise the area as "The Treasure Coast." Nor did they try to squelch stories of suddenly rich salvagers flipping doubloons in Ft. Pierce bars to see who bought the drinks. Still more treasure was found. In a single day the following year, ten thousand pieces of eight were recovered.

But gradually, as the most accessible locations were mined, the haul lessened. Within eight years Wagner's company was bankrupt. By then, Mel Fisher had moved his operations to the Keys, where he discovered a new source of wealth in the *Atocha*, wrecked in 1622.

A number of decades have passed since the initial treasure was located. Although millions of dollars in gold, silver, and precious jewels have been removed, a considerable fortune still remains. Thus in 1993, when a local optometrist and amateur diver went out with a crew just south of the Sebastian Inlet, he chanced upon what he called an "underwater jewelry store." Included were nine intricately designed gold rings, two five-foot-long solid gold chains, and a pair of gold rosaries probably last touched by fervently praying nuns in 1715. Possibly the most amazing part of this story was that this most recent haul was found in just eight feet of water barely a hundred yards offshore. After the state got its twenty percent, most of the remainder—estimated at nearly a million dollars—was put on temporary public display at Mel Fisher's Treasure Museum in the town of Sebastian.

This formidable Spanish cannon is one of the exhibits at the McLarty Museum.

The Gateway to Treasure: The McLarty Museum

The McLarty Museum, a few miles south of the Sebastian Inlet, now occupies the site where the Spanish survivors of the tragic wrecks had gathered. For an admission of just $1 per person (kids under six are free), you can see exhibit cases showing such personal items as carved dice, pewter dinner plates, and porcelain that had been carried all the way from the Orient only to spend more than two centuries on the ocean bottom. Also on display are fascinating old coins—most worn from use—with the coat of arms of eighteenth-century Spain. There is even a menacing ten-foot-long iron cannon, which, when hauled from the depths, was still loaded with bar shot meant for British pirates.

The museum also has a short movie entitled "Treasure: What Dreams Are Made Of," featuring recent interviews with divers who have found Spanish coins. "For all the millions that have been recovered," one treasure hunter says, "untold millions remain. . . . There are several wrecks that we haven't found yet."

You can see where some treasure may lie by taking the boardwalk at the rear of the museum through a seagrape forest to the beach. Here a platform shaped like the prow of a wrecked ship points toward the ocean. Listen carefully and you might hear the crunch of galleon timbers and see in your mind's eye the ships breaking apart.

Chests filled with the wealth of the Indies sink with the battered hulls. Some are still beneath the waves. Are you tempted?

The Spanish Royal Treasury, Sebastian Branch

Although the McLarty Museum is well worth a visit, to really see what masses of treasure look like you must drive five miles farther along the beach to the Wabasso Causeway (CR 510), which crosses the Indian River. Then proceed five miles back north on US 1 to the town of Sebastian. Here, at 1322 on US 1, is the Mel Fisher Museum, loaded with so much Spanish treasure there are video cameras, an alarm system, and a guard on permanent duty. Gold, silver, and precious gems fairly drip from the display cases. One highlight is a set of two earrings and two brooches containing four hundred diamonds that alone are worth $1.2 million! Another is a golden, five-inch religious cross studded with seven brilliant emeralds. Although Fisher died a few years ago, his daughter continues as the museum director. Admission is $5 for adults, $1.50 for kids six to twelve, and free for younger children. The museum is open Monday through Saturday from 10 A.M. to 5 P.M. and Sunday 12 P.M. to 5 P.M.

Just north of the museum, at 1580 US 1, is Captain Hiram's Restaurant, offering casual dining on the Indian River as well as boats that leave on two-hour, $15-per-person tours of the Indian and Sebastian rivers. Sunset cruises pass Pelican Island to watch thousands of birds return to their roosting sites. Cruise times vary according to the season, so call 561-589-4345 for current times. Next to Captain Hiram's is a brand new, three-story overnight lodging called, somewhat illogically, the Key West Inn. Rooms start at $79 to $99, depending on the season. For reservations call 800-833-0555.

Now head back south on US 1. Although Sebastian's population is around fifteen thousand, there is no real downtown. Main Street is simply US 1. The Chamber of Commerce is here; and next to it is the historical museum, whose doors flutter open ever so briefly on Tuesday and Wednesday between 11 A.M. and 2 P.M. There is a smattering of commercial buildings. But that's about it. The settlement never was much, having been started mainly as a fishing village a hundred or so years ago. But the link with the ocean was not good, because the Sebastian Inlet (which had been dug by hand as early as 1886) quickly refilled with sand, as did a second channel nine

The food is good and the view excellent at Hiram's Restaurant in the town of Sebastian.

years later. So did a third in 1921! It was not until just after World War II that the inlet was permanently opened. By then the fishing industry had long since swum off to other parts.

Incidentally, the town's name—as well as its treasure—recalls its Spanish past. Castilian sailors, filling their casks with fresh water from the river three miles north of Captain Hiram's, named it in honor of St. Sebastian, killed by the Romans for refusing to renounce his Christian faith.

Continue south on US 1. If you had passed by here in the 1920s you would have gaped at a huge mound fifty feet high and as large as a football field. This was Barker's Bluff, a gigantic accumulation of oyster shells and human debris left by a vanished tribe of Native Americans. The bluff could have been a valuable source of knowledge about these people, but times were different then and the archaeological treasure was dumped over the county as road bedding.

At the Wabasso Causeway turn east. Part way across you'll come to a side road leading to the Environmental Learning Center. Although it is oriented toward school children, it has a considerable amount of environmental literature as well as an elevated walkway through a mangrove forest—all free. But, hikers, be forewarned:

mangroves are more like overgrown shrubs than proper trees and their thick matting of leaves hugs the heat and moisture, making a delightful environment for mosquitoes.

The Case of the Hiding Grapefruit

As you cross back over the Indian River, you might wonder just where the vaunted Indian River grapefruit has gone. Well, it has forsaken its namesake home to take up residence along Interstate 95 to the west. But right here along the Indian River is where the fruit got its start. Watch for a street sign indicating Michael Creek Road at the eastern end of the causeway. It was the Michael family, headquartered south down the road, who turned much of Orchid Island into one huge grapefruit grove. The Michaels had a long pier into the river from which an endless procession of steamboats picked up the fruit during harvest season. Grapefruit, as opposed to oranges, thrived in this damp, poorly drained soil, where the coquina limestone supplied a rich source of calcium. The Indian River grapefruit had thin skin and a high sugar content, making it very popular. The eldest Michael became known as the "Dean of Citrus."

Today the Indian River grapefruit thrives in equally damp soil along Interstate 95, where the land is cheaper and transportation facilities much better. The industry is centered in the three adjacent counties of which Vero Beach, Ft. Pierce, and Stuart are the seats. Ft. Pierce's St. Lucie County alone produces more than twenty million boxes annually, enabling the town to proclaim itself the "Grapefruit Capital of the World."

The Jungle Trail: Dining on Fish Guts

Immediately past Michael Creek Road is a street sign announcing the four-mile, southern segment of the Jungle Trail. This was Orchid Island's original road punched through the trees in the 1920s. It has not changed much since then, but don't let the fact that the Trail is merely graded sand and shell fragments deter you. Except in bad weather it is quite passable. So follow it south along a narrow channel of the Indian River. This is almost as wild and desolate an area as when a group of twenty-four wretched shipwreck victims was detained here at the Ais village of Jece in 1696.

The group was in extreme danger from the Indians, who would have killed and eaten them had they realized they were English, enemies of their friends, the Spanish. Most prominent among them was Jonathan Dickinson, who was traveling from Jamaica to Philadelphia with his young wife, Mary, and their six-month-old son, who was still nursing. Also among the survivors were Dickinson's ten slaves, two other passengers, and nine crewmembers.

A fierce storm had wrecked their ship near Jupiter, sixty miles to the south. After having been stripped and harassed by the local tribe, they began their trek north along the beach, hoping to reach Charleston, more than five hundred miles distant. A chill November wind blasted them, and they had nothing to eat except green cocoplums and sea grapes, which tasted so horrible they could barely swallow them.

When they got as far as Vero Beach, they were met by the chief of the Ais, who spoke to them in broken Spanish. Their lives were saved when one of the crew answered him with the few Spanish words he knew. The chief led them to his village, a collection of trash and palmetto huts that was, nonetheless, the capital of this portion of the coast. The Indian River was on one side and a mangrove swamp thick with flies and mosquitoes on the other. The huts were barely four feet from ground to roof, and when it rained the water was knee-deep. The Ais, not quite sure the sandy-haired group was really Spanish, treated them with indifference and would not even give them food. Thus they had to content themselves with garbage such as the "gills and guts of fish picked off the dung-hill," to quote Dickinson.

Despite the hardships, the Dickinson party did make it to Charleston, although it would take them three torturous months. Dickinson became a wealthy Philadelphia merchant and eventually the city's mayor. He published his recollections of the harrowing experience, and today *Jonathan Dickinson's Journal* is a classic account of life on the Florida coast in the days when the Indians ruled.

There is no trace of Jece, nor of the Ais tribe, except the account Dickinson left to us. But the river and the trees remain, as does the sense of remoteness. When you reach A1A, take it south. You'll no longer be traveling along the beach, and landscaping hides the expensive homes and resorts that now occupy the choice scenery. One of these unseen villages—Indian River Shores—has one of the highest median home sale prices ($425,000) in the entire state.

In five miles you will reach Vero Beach Oceanside, consisting mostly of an upscale little shopping strip with boutiques, art shops, and unique gift stores. Immediately south on A1A is Disney's beautiful Vero Beach Resort, a group of buildings constructed to convey a

Victorian air. The public is invited to Disney's three restaurants, including the Green Cabin Room, which serves light meals and offers a commanding view of the Atlantic. This is the very place where Mel Fisher and his divers salvaged fifteen hundred silver coins from what was designated the Sand Point Wreck. You're also invited to spend a night at the resort, provided you have a couple of hundred dollars to spare.

Vero Beach

Before continuing south on A1A, cross over the Indian River on the Seventeenth Street (SR 656) bridge to the main part of Vero Beach, a thriving town of almost twenty thousand and the Indian River County seat. Once on the other side, take US 1 a few blocks north to Twenty-first Street. Follow Twenty-first west over the Florida East Coast Railroad tracks to Fourteenth Avenue, which is the heart of town. Near the corner is the Chamber of Commerce, where you'll find a good assortment of informative leaflets.

The town was named for Vero Gifford, who settled here with her husband in 1888. But nothing much happened around the mosquito-ridden place until Herman Zeuch of Davenport, Iowa, decided that, with proper drainage of the nearby swamps, the bugs could be controlled and the land used by farmers, such as his Iowa neighbors. Thus in 1912, Zeuch organized the Indian River Farms Corporation. When the standing water was eliminated, the town of Vero began to prosper.

Another big event in Vero's history took place eight years later with the erection of a wooden bridge across the Indian River. On opening day a noisy procession of Tin Lizzies inaugurated the trip over to Orchid Island. But the celebration was dampened when a rainstorm flooded out both the merrymaking and the island's crude roads, leaving the crowd stranded until the water drained into the sand. Once access to the Atlantic shore was established, the word "beach" was added to Vero's name.

A block from the Chamber of Commerce is the Citrus Museum, at 2140 Fourteenth Street. Open Tuesday through Friday between 10 A.M. and 4 P.M., it has informative exhibitions on the tasty Indian River grapefruit. The admission price of merely $1 is also tasty.

Vero Beach has recently joined Florida's Main Street Program and is in the process of bringing new life to a downtown that had declined over the years. A major accomplishment was the recycling

The old movie theater at Vero Beach has been rehabilitated and put to a new use

of the original Indian River Court House, across from the Citrus Museum, into a modern office building.

The jewel of the renovation is the town's old theater building on Fourteenth Street. It has been skillfully recycled into the Theatre Plaza complex of offices and shops. The auditorium itself awaits an operator before renovation will begin. The old theater had a drama of its own. Some say that Vero Beach formed its own county in 1925 because locals wanted to see movies on Sundays but were prevented by a St. Lucie County ordinance (enforced when the sheriff drove up from Ft. Pierce).

Now drive north on Twenty-first a few blocks to where it merges with US 1. Continue north on US 1, passing over the Main Relief Canal, which drains the former marshes. Just over the bridge is Aviation Boulevard, where you should turn left. As you head west, you'll skirt the New Piper Aircraft plant, where Piper planes are parked on the tarmac connecting with the Municipal Airport. These planes are similar to the one flown by John F. Kennedy Jr. on a tragic evening in July 1999.

Kennedy had had his pilot's license for just fifteen months when he bought a Piper Saratoga and came to Vero Beach for training. He lived in the airport dormitory, where he kept mainly to himself. Nonetheless he was cordial to his federal examiner, John McColgan. "I put him through his paces," McColgan said, "and he passed everything with flying colors." But, McColgan noted, Kennedy had a visual pilot's rating, which licensed him to fly only when he could see the world outside his cockpit.

On the day of the accident, Kennedy was heading to a cousin's wedding in Massachusetts. He had meant to make the short flight to Martha's Vineyard during daylight and left Manhattan for the Fairfield, New Jersey, airport in plenty of time. But the Friday afternoon traffic was extraordinarily heavy, and it took his sister-in-law, Lauren Bessette, and him twice as long as the usual forty-five minutes to reach the airport. There they were met by John's beautiful wife, Carolyn. After leisurely buying a few bananas as a snack, the three boarded John's Piper Saratoga and took off. By now the sun had set and the blood-red sky was darkening fast. Although the weather was fair, it was a questionable time for a person with only a visual rating to take off. But there was a wedding to go to and Kennedy had, what a friend called, "this incredibly fine-tuned sense of [living] on the edge."

After flying for about thirty minutes over the ocean, Kennedy was approaching Martha's Vineyard and began to descend. It was almost pitch black now, and the island lights that he expected to see were obliterated by a thick summer haze. In the haze he could not tell where the horizon was. An uneasy feeling must have swept over him, for at this point radar shows that he made a sharp right turn and began to ascend, apparently hoping to get above the haze. But he must have became completely disoriented, for he tipped his wing and entered into what pilots call a "dead man's spiral." As the Piper began plummeting downward at nearly one hundred feet a second, the strong G-forces pressing against them would have warned Kennedy, Carolyn, and Lauren that they were facing disaster, but there was no way to pull out. Their terror would have lasted twenty or thirty seconds before they crashed into the water, where their bodies were later found still strapped into their seats, upside-down in a shattered piece of fuselage nearly 120 feet below the surface.

Questions immediately centered on the plane. Piper was just recovering from bankruptcy and could not afford any scandal that reflected the safety of its aircraft. When an investigation revealed that the plane was functioning perfectly just prior to the crash, the company breathed a sigh of relief. So did Vero Beach, for the revived Piper had become one of the area's largest employers.

The New Piper is a very efficiently run and distinctly public-oriented company. It offers ninety-minute tours of its manufacturing plant on Tuesdays and Fridays at 10 A.M. and 2 P.M. This is a rare experience to see airplanes being assembled. To ensure you'll be included, it's best to call in advance (561-567-4361, extension 5).

Continuing west on Aviation Boulevard, you'll pass the Municipal Airport, which is all that remains of a gigantic Navy training field that throbbed with military aircraft during the Second World War. Shortly you will come to Dodgertown, long-time winter home of the Los Angeles Dodgers. In March and early April the Big Leaguers train here and play exhibition games against other Grapefruit League teams. Spectators are delighted to watch the stars up close. On game days tickets cost $11 for anyone, big or small, who occupies a seat. Tickets can be purchased on the day of the game, but if you want to be certain of getting in, call in advance (561-569-6858) after February 1. The Dodgers play seven days a week, and game time is usually at 1 P.M. Don't despair if you're not there in early spring, because during the off-season you can cruise around the grounds and past the motel-like residences where the players reside (off-limits when the Big Leaguers are here). Someone with a sense of whimsy had the streetlights fashioned in the shape of baseballs. The Vero Beach farm Dodgers play a regular night-game schedule season from late April until the end of August. Tickets for these games are only $4 for adults and $3 for children. Later in the year National Football League teams sometimes work out here to adapt to hot weather, which Vero Beach obligingly furnishes in abundance.

A Watery Spanish Ghost

Now drive back to Orchid Island and take A1A south once more. Soon you will cross onto North Hutchinson Island, although a sign may be your only clue. The island was named for James Hutchinson, who had a farm across the river back in the days when the Spanish claimed all of Florida. But Hutchinson found himself bothered by the Seminoles, so he got the Spanish to give him the uninhabited island. Before Hutchinson could do anything with his new grant, however, he drowned in an Atlantic storm. Later, when Florida became part of the United States, the American government recognized the Spanish land grant and Hutchinson's name remained on the island upon which he probably never lived.

In a few miles you'll reach the Pepper Beach State Recreation Area, where there is free parking. Pepper Beach is popular with snorkelers and scuba divers because just two hundred yards offshore are the sunken remains of the *Urca de Lima*, the Spanish supply ship that was such an important aid to survivors of the 1715 treasure fleet tragedy. The ship, which lies in ten to fifteen feet of water, has been declared an Underwater Archaeological Preserve and is marked by buoys. Divers are welcome to moor here and explore the relic, which consists of portions of the hull as well as a few cannons. It is a weird experience to see the ancient timbers quavering in currents that have engulfed them for almost three centuries. Non-divers must content themselves with walking north about one thousand paces from the park boundary and scanning the water for the bobbing white buoy. Once, centuries ago, this beach was littered with wreckage. Survivors used the two longboats from the *Urca* to go for help at Havana and St. Augustine. They were among those who ultimately gathered near what is now the McLarty Museum to await rescue.

The UDT/SEAL Museum is a fascinating place to visit.

The Daring Frogmen

PAY
TOLL
AHEAD

Beside Pepper Beach is the UDT/SEAL Museum, open Tuesdays through Saturdays from 10 A.M. to 4 P.M. and Sunday from 12 P.M. to 4 P.M. Admission is $4 for adults, $1.50 for kids six to twelve, and free for younger children. UDT stands for Underwater Demolition Teams. These daring individuals, also known as "frogmen," performed some of the Navy's most dangerous and vital tasks during World War II: the destruction of cement and steel beach invasion obstructions in the face of withering enemy fire.

Many of the volunteers at the museum are actual former frogmen. It was from some of them that I gathered firsthand information about the vigorous training they endured here. "We lived in tents on South Hutchinson Island across from the Ft. Pierce Inlet," a veteran told me. "There were about three hundred of us. Neither North nor South Hutchinson had any civilians at this time because there were still large swampy areas where mosquitoes bred in horrible numbers. The training was very intensive. We were urgently needed in the Pacific, where a succession of island invasions was moving Americans to within striking range of Japan. I was here for ten weeks, during which I had only a single weekend liberty."

The men had to master a variety of tasks connected with their job of reconnoitering the enemy beach to learn the location of the obstructions and of returning later to blow them up during the actual invasion. Although enemy gunners were almost sure to be shooting at them during the reconnaissance phase, it was during the invasion that the danger was the greatest. by then the warships and carriers were there and the battle was in full fury.

Since rubber boats would be used, the men constantly worked with them, negotiating the tricky currents of the Ft. Pierce Inlet and the crashing surf of the North Hutchinson beaches. "We were at it even during the night," recalled another veteran.

During the demolition phase, the frogmen would be let off from small launches a hundred yards from shore. "Then we had to swim to the beach obstructions pushing ahead of us a twenty-pound knapsack of high explosives. During training, in order to simulate these actual battle conditions, attack planes would zoom in from the base at Vero Beach, firing live bullets along the dunes just as if the enemy was entrenched there. Sometimes it got too real, when they mistakenly sprayed the water near us, for they were in training too."

Through it all the frogmen learned to work calmly yet quickly as they attached their explosive charges to the obstructions put up by the Navy Seabees. When they were combat-ready, they were sent to the South Pacific, where the bullets were aimed at them and death was real.

When the war ended, the base was closed and the Navy moved out, leaving North Hutchinson Island littered with bullets, shrapnel, and other wartime debris. Even some of the underwater obstacles remained. It was not until many years later that the government agreed to pay for the cleanup.

The SEALs were organized later in response to the needs of the Vietnam War. They were a more covert operation because amphibious landings played little part in these hostilities. Although the SEALs were based in Coronado, California, much of their training was similar to that of the World War II frogmen. Because the frogmen were so secret a force, little remains of their activities. It is SEAL memorabilia, therefore, that predominates at the museum. Most of the major equipment can be inspected on the grounds. This includes landing craft, river patrol boats, and swimmer delivery vehicles. Inside are weapons, underwater gear, and demolition apparatus. A small theater shows videos of the arduous training and dangerous operations these men went through.

After visiting the museum, walk across the parking lot to the beach. Quiet today, it once resonated to the roar of Navy fighter planes, the deadly rattle of machine guns, and the thunder of the frogmen's explosives.

If you want to contemplate the scene in leisurely luxury, drive a mile farther south on A1A to the Radisson Beach Resort, where Carmen's Restaurant offers fine dining overlooking the ocean. For lighter repasts there is Watercolors Café. If you care to stay at the Radisson, courtyard rooms cost between $80 and $120, and oceanside rooms between $140 and $170, depending on the time of year. For reservations, call 800-333-3333.

There is a reef about twenty yards offshore from the resort where tropical fish glide among rocky ledges that are hardly  over eight feet beneath the surface. You can enjoy the reef even if you don't stay at the resort, because the beach is public. Lobsters up to fourteen pounds also make their homes here. Unfortunately for them, they appeal to the human palate. So catching them is a popular sport between August and March. They have no claws, but their spiny tails can be unpleasant, so use a net, wear cotton gloves, or let someone else do it for you.

The Ft. Pierce Inlet State Recreation Area is a quarter mile beyond the Radisson. Frogmen once planted so many explosive charges around what is now the parking lot that it is still known as Dynamite Point. The park offers swimming, surfing, fishing, and a twenty-minute, self-guided nature trail through a dune hammock composed mainly of cabbage palms, sea grapes, and wax myrtles topped by a canopy of live oaks. There are restrooms and showers for beachgoers.

The Jack Island Preserve forms a separate section of the park. Here a mile-long trail leads through a completely different riverside plant community composed of mangrove trees and salt marshes. The path leads to an observation tower overlooking the Indian River. You'll also see one of the dikes Florida constructs around its marshes in order to control the salt mosquitoes that so plagued settlers in earlier times.

Although admission is just $3.25 per car, this park does not have the same facilities as those at the Sebastian Inlet. There are no boats to rent, no fishing equipment available, and no on-site food vendor.

Since there is no bridge over the inlet, A1A makes an abrupt westward turn at this point. It crosses the Indian River to US 1 and the town of Ft. Pierce, where the next exploration begins.

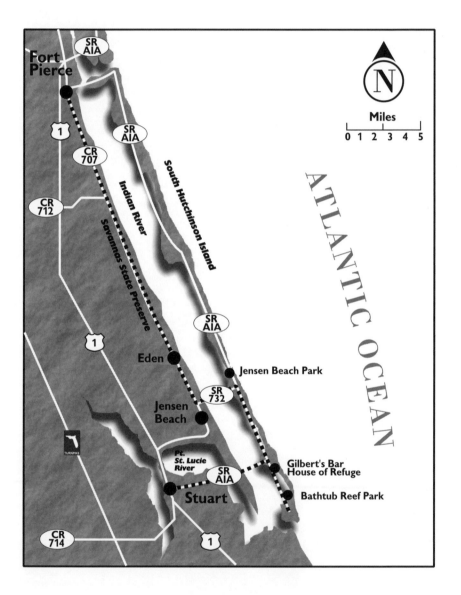

Along the Indian River

Ft. Pierce to Stuart • 38 Backroad Miles

The Song of the Road: Overview

The Indian River is a 156-mile-long lagoon nestled between the mainland and a string of barrier islands. It is a scenic and ecological waterway like no other in North America. This exploration begins at the Harbor Branch Oceanographic Institution at Ft. Pierce, which is the best place to gain an understanding of this unique ribbon of water. The Institution's skilled guides conduct river tours aboard comfortable pontoon boats.

Next you'll drive south to downtown Ft. Pierce, where, from a sheltered viewing stand, you can watch scores of wild manatees, otherwise known as sea cows. Ft. Pierce has completely redone the surrounding waterfront, allowing you to stroll along pathways and through parks and visit the casual restaurants overlooking the marina. From here you can also take a walking tour of the rejuvenated downtown.

Heading south from Ft. Pierce along the Indian River, you'll be on one of Florida's most satisfying drives. At the site of Eden you may want to pause to read the experiences of young Lucie Richards, who grew up here with her parents, brothers, mosquitoes, and snakes. Then it's across the Indian River on a scenic causeway to the Jensen Beach Park, where you can swim in the sparkling Atlantic or just enjoy a snack at the concession area overlooking sand, sea oats, and rumbling surf.

Now the route leads along the Atlantic Ocean to the House of Refuge, perched atop a rocky bluff. On display are relics of the days when the building served as a shelter for sailors shipwrecked on this treacherous coast. The oceanside road continues down a finger of land to Bathtub Reef, an unusual geological formation that forms a sheltered lagoon ideal for calm-water swimming. This area was frequented by Pedro Gilbert, a vicious pirate whose escapades once bloodied this now-peaceful coast.

Then it's west over the St. Lucie and Indian River bridges to Stuart, the "Sailfish Capital of the World." The little town is justly proud of the shops and cafés along refurbished Osceola Street. If it's dinnertime, you might want to stop at the Dockside Restaurant, where spacious windows offer appealing overviews of the St. Lucie River.

On the Road Again

This exploration begins at the Harbor Branch Oceanographic Institution, four miles north of downtown Ft. Pierce on US 1. Harbor Branch is an internationally respected science and educational center whose underwater investigations, sometimes done in conjunction with the National Geographic Society, have appeared as feature television programs. It offers two ninety-minute educational tours. On one, you'll be shown selected areas of the five-hundred-acre campus for $6 ($4 for kids 6 through 15). On the other, you'll sail on the Indian River with an environmental expert for $16 ($10 for kids). Call 800-333-4264 for departure times. (When I was there, no food was being served. If you're going to arrive near lunchtime, bring your own food or call ahead to see if the policy has changed.)

If you take the campus tour, you'll see some of the Institution's three dozen aquaculture sheds. When I was there, in one shed they were raising two billion clams especially adapted for maximum survival. In another, aqua-farmers were learning about shrimp culture. For this enterprise Harbor Branch was offering shrimp "seeds" to qualified individuals for as little as $10 per thousand. During this tour you'll probably come across schoolchildren of all ages because the Institution is involved in bringing the importance of the aquatic environment to the awareness of the public.

Before this tour is over, you'll pause in front of the little yellow submarine that was used during the Institution's early years. When it was operational, two to four scientists and their equipment were jammed into it, and it was lowered nearly a quarter mile beneath the water. There it would remain for most of a day. Had a catastrophe occurred, the people onboard would have been beyond outside aid. It was an experience that attracted only devoted scientists—or lunatics, which some say are one and the same.

If you're lucky, one or more of Harbor Branch's oceangoing ships will be docked in the channel. Probing the world's waterways from the Caribbean to the Java Sea, they are among the world's most advanced research vessels. To reach the loneliest of depths, they carry submersible vehicles larger and far more sophisticated than their little yellow grandfather. But researchers still have to travel down in them.

The Harbor Branch Oceanographic Institution did research in this early-model, submersible vehicle.

From within their cramped quarters, these researchers peer into the inky water surrounding them by means of a 3-D laser imaging apparatus invented by Harbor Branch scientists. When they want to gather plant or animal specimens, they use the sub's robotic arms.

A River Alive

The river tour begins at the channel in back of the main building. The pontoon excursion boat is not much compared to the sleek research ships, but it's just what you'll need for a comfortable, leisurely excursion on the Indian River. Once in the mainstream you'll find the river extending north and south farther than you can see. But it is not actually a river, for it has no source, no mouth, and no particular current. It's a lagoon—once part of the Atlantic, but now largely cut off from it by a series of barrier islands that began as sandbars. You feel as if you're in a world apart. The shores are forested. The river mingles the colors of the sky and clouds as the sun's rays tint each wavelet. Liquid gurgles against the hull, almost as if the river were talking.

The Indian River is a unique place. Its unusual brew of salt and fresh water has created one of the most diverse ecosystems on earth. Within its watery depths are seven hundred species of fish—four that breed only in the lagoon. Some of the gamefish, such as tarpon and bass, are large. One man recently caught a thirty-eight-pound snook

The Indian River lagoon is a broad waterway with numerous spoil islands.

using only a fly rod. These can be hooked from piers as well as from boats. There are also more than three hundred species of birds. They are everywhere, often nesting in the trees, where their droppings whiten the branches. "I took some Northerners out on a chilly day near Christmas," the tour guide chuckled, "and there was so much guano that they were convinced it was snow."

The river throbs with sounds other than those made by humans. Besides the cries and cackles of birds, there are the more subtle sounds that only the denizens of the lagoon can hear. The guide told how one night, when he and a researcher lowered a microphone over the side, they listened in on the love songs of mating fish. "It actually resembled music," he said. "You can't believe the activity beneath the surface." To demonstrate, he filled a glass with clear river water. But when he put a drop or two under a magnifier, we saw dozens of micro-creatures speeding through the liquid as rapidly as gnats in a wind. "They're plankton," he told us. "Although they're among the lowest forms of life, they are also among the most vital in the intricate food chain that all the other animals depend on."

The tour boat went past many small islands. "They were all formed out of dredgings from the Intracoastal Waterway," the guide said, referring to the deepened boat channel that runs for nearly one thousand miles along the East Coast from Key West to Chesapeake Bay. Because the average depth of the lagoon is only three feet, there are several hundred of these "spoil islands." Far from being eyesores, they support a rich growth of vegetation that has attracted a wide variety of birds including great egrets, cormorants, blue herons, and brown pelicans, most of which you can see from the tour boat. There are also small animals, such as raccoons and rabbits, which have made a one-way trip over from the mainland. These islands, washed by the Indian River and shaded by graceful Australian pines, make ideal picnicking and camping sites.

On the way back to port you may be accompanied by a group of dolphins, for there are an estimated eight hundred of these air-breathing mammals in the lagoon. Some three hundred are known personally to the scientists, who have identified them by their slight color variations and the shapes of their dorsal fins.

Dolphins travel in pods of up to nine individuals. Many are mothers and their young, who remain together until the youngsters are around three. They communicate by means of whistles—distinct to the individuals. A researcher recorded more than seventeen hundred of these whistles from a large group of dolphins gathered off the coast of Scotland to catch salmon. It's not exactly a language, but it's moderately close to it.

But don't get overly sentimental about dolphins just because they are dutiful family animals and have that "do-good" Flipper smile. They are predators who live on live food. The males congregate in roughneck gangs that kidnap females, whom they bite and thump, then mate with. Nonetheless there is something undeniably appealing about dolphins as they speed just below the surface, then leap into the air with what must be sheer exuberance. We relate to them as we do to no other water creature. We can imagine ourselves coursing with them through their fluid world, gliding almost effort-lessly among the bending sea grasses, snatching up a juicy squid or two before streaking to the surface. We break the plane that divides water from air and soar into a universe of sunshine. Then we descend once more into a familiar environment where water wraps protec-tively around us.

Yes, an excursion on the Indian River Lagoon is an experience you shouldn't miss.

Beanpot Backus

Now drive south on US 1 to Ft. Pierce. When you reach Avenue C, turn east over the Florida East Coast Railroad tracks to

Memorial Park, where there is a beautiful vista of the Indian River with the gentle arc of the A1A bridge in the distance. On the south, the park is defined by Moore's Creek and the city marina; on the north, by the Amphitheater; and on the west, by the venerable Seven Gables House, which has been converted into the Visitors Center. Beside it is the A. E. "Bean" Backus Gallery, displaying the engaging pictures done by this hometown painter and member of the Florida Artist Hall of Fame.

Backus, perhaps influenced by the Indian River, was fascinated by the interplay of colors. His pictures show Florida scenes in hues even more vivid than actual, for, as he once said, "an artist is one who can exaggerate to make something more real." He loved various shades of red, which to him was the "mother color." He apparently believed palms were the most graceful of trees, for almost all his paintings have them. His brushstrokes even tend to follow the direction of the wind on their fronds. Waterscapes were his special love, with billowy, peach-hued clouds, arching palms, and quiet waters dappled with the colors of sky and plants.

Backus spent almost all his eighty-some years shuffling around Ft. Pierce. He began life in a small house beside the Indian River, where his family called him "Beanpot" for some obscure reason known only to them. By the 1930s he was painting movie posters for the Sunrise Theater on Second Street. Here the famous fan-dancer, Sally Rand, appearing at a stage show, was so enraptured by a Beanie poster of her that she took it with her when she left.

After spending time in the Navy during World War II, Bean bought the worn, old building on Moore's Creek that his father had formerly used as a boat shop. The place leaked in so many places that the containers he placed to catch the rainwater sounded like a calypso band. Bean didn't care, for he was an indifferent housekeeper. Thus when a paint can tipped over on the top of his refrigerator, he was so charmed by the drip pattern that he kept it. When friends asked him why he didn't maintain a neater home, he replied that then the kids wouldn't come. He loved children and had art classes for them as well as for adults.

He also loved Patsy Hutchinson, a twenty-four-year-old blond beauty two decades his junior. They had five years of married happiness, marred only by two miscarriages. After Patsy died during heart surgery in 1955, Bean never remarried. Although chums claimed that a party didn't begin until good-time Backus arrived, he could not quell a loneliness that may have contributed to his inordinate love of liquor. Despite occasional binges, however, Backus became such a popular artist that his paintings were snatched up almost as soon as he completed them. Just to get enough pictures for exhibitions, he had to borrow his own paintings from purchasers. Fortunately today an impressive collection of Backus's gorgeous Florida landscapes is on display at the museum, which is close to his former studio on Moore's Creek. Although the museum was built in 1961, the modest artist refused to allow it to be named in his honor. Death stilled his objections in 1990. The museum is open from mid-September to early March from 10 A.M. to 4 P.M. Tuesdays through Saturdays 12 P.M. and to 4 P.M. on Sundays. As for the admission price, it's affordable—free.

The Ugliest Mermaids

Just south of the Backus Museum in Memorial Park is the Manatee Observation and Educational Center, one of the town's most popular attractions. Here, from a long, covered platform, onlookers can watch manatees lumber about in the warm water of Moore's Creek between November and April.

Manatees are gentle, air-breathing mammals—distantly related to

This overlook of Moore's Creek on the Ft. Pierce waterfront gives a good view of congregating manatees.

elephants—who have adapted to life in the water. They are large, sluggish, and supremely ugly, yet men on the old sailing vessels who sighted them from a distance hungrily converted them into beautiful mermaids. Manatees' main joy in life is chomping water plants, including the pesky water hyacinths. Grazing near the surface, they are unable to avoid the knifelike propeller blades of motorboats. As a result, most manatees have been cut—many so badly that they have died, causing their numbers to plummet dangerously in recent years. Now, because conservation groups have so effectively publicized their predicament, manatees have become something of a *cause célèbre* in Florida. In fact, Ft. Pierce built the observation platform because so many people started coming to Moore's Creek to see them.

The Tragic Tale of Kimberly Bergalis

There is a plaque in Memorial Park to the memory of Kimberly Bergalis, who lived her twenty-three short years in Ft. Pierce. She was a beautiful young woman who contracted AIDS during a routine visit to her dentist. Although she was horrified at the prospect ahead of her, she made it her mission to get legislation requiring all health-care workers to be tested for the AIDS virus. Her activities were written up in newspapers across the country, and she appeared on television interview shows. But her disease progressed quickly, taking the most virulent course. "I have lived to see my hair fall out," she lamented, "my body lose forty pounds, blisters on my sides." Yet she kept up her campaign and often wore a T-shirt proclaiming "You Can't Sink a Rainbow." In her last days, although she was growing weaker and sicker, she made a grueling nineteen-hour train trip with her parents to Washington, D.C., to testify before Congress for the passage of the Bergalis Testing and Disclosure Bill. Satisfied that her terrible suffering had served a purpose, she returned to her sickroom in Ft. Pierce, where she died shortly before Christmas in 1991. Her bill was rejected.

The Passing Pageant from Cobb's Verandah

From Memorial Park, walk south beside the Ft. Pierce Marina to the Tiki Bar, where you can enjoy a repast or merely something cool if you prefer. Across the street, at the corner of Indian River Drive and Avenue A, is the P. P. Cobb Building. The town got its start here in 1875 when Ben Hogg constructed the frame building as a

The Cobb Store has been a Ft. Pierce fixture from the earliest days.

trading post. Because Hogg depended on boats to bring him goods from as far away as Jacksonville, he built a long pier from his front door into the Indian River. But Hogg evidently found the humdrum life of a storekeeper too tame, for he soon sold out to a pair of New Englanders who turned the store into an oyster cannery. The smelly area around it became known as Cantown. One of the cannery workers was young Peter Cobb, who somehow scraped together the funds to buy the building, converting it back into a general store, much to the relief of the townsfolk.

The P. P. Cobb establishment became the focal point of early Ft. Pierce. The store had about everything on its sagging shelves and bulging bins. Do you need a cooking pot or an iron frying pan? Go to Cobb's. Need thread or needles or buttons for the young'uns' shirts? Cobb'll have it. Waiting for a letter from friends or lovers? Cobb will have that too, for he was also the postmaster. And as for gossip—well, if you can't learn the latest shenanigans at Cobb's, then it hasn't happened yet.

Cobb apparently enjoyed it all and remained a fixture at Ft. Pierce for nearly half a century. He was a tall, thin man with a sparse mustache and a manner in his early bachelor years that many young ladies found appealing. But their hopes were in vain, for he never married. As he grew older, he began wearing a pair of spectacles that rode low on his nose. He especially loved children, one of whom was little Beanie Backus. "Mr. Cobb had a great big barrel of candy," Backus remembered, "and would let us reach in and get all the candy we wanted after we paid. He was always so quiet and gentle."

Peter Cobb thrived, and over the years his pier grew longer. Eventually Ricou & O'Brien's wholesale fish house sprouted at the end. Steamboats were always pulling in or out, and the wail of their whistles was as much a part of the town as the warbling of the mockingbirds.

Ft. Pierce also thrived. During the 1920s it became the trading center for the prosperous surrounding region. Cobb must have watched in amazement as ornate, Mediterranean-style buildings replaced the original wooden structures. At about this time he saw the first automobile kicking up the dust on the town's unpaved streets. Soon thereafter sweating convicts began laboring on the Dixie Highway, the first paved road of any length that anyone had ever seen. Dixie's red bricks ran directly in front of the store. Now Cobb began serving soda pop to motorists from as far away as Michigan, which was hardly in the U.S.A. Most were on their way to Miami, and some must have confided to him about how rich they'd become from the land boom. He saw many of the same people chugging slowly back after the devastating real estate crash of 1926.

As the years rolled on, Peter Cobb, now white-haired, relaxed ever more often on his store's verandah. Eventually the auto traffic on the Dixie Highway dwindled as the road was displaced by US 1, just west of the town's central business district. Then one day the steamboats were no more, their place taken by trucks and autos and by the huge oil-burning freighters that rode the Atlantic. By the time Cobb died in 1943, German submarines were cruising the coast, blasting the freighters and dousing the pristine beaches he had once known with gummy oil and splintered wreckage.

P. P. Cobb's store is still a landmark on Ft. Pierce's waterfront. Although the exterior looks much like it did in Cobb's day, the interior has been modernized into offices and is not open to the general public. The pier where steamboats once unloaded fish has been displaced by Avenue A, and the site of Ricou & O'Brien's warehouse is now occupied by the Ft. Pierce Marina. The river area south of the former pier became a parking lot.

Footloose in Old Ft. Pierce

During the 1970s and 1980s, the downtown deteriorated as outlying commercial developments lured shoppers away. Eventually three-fourths of the downtown's buildings were empty, and the area took on an air of decay and discouragement. But in the mid-1990s, after Ft. Pierce joined the Florida Main Street Program, community spirit was reborn. As a result of $15 million in redevelopment work, the downtown was reborn. Now almost all the buildings have tenants and optimism is everywhere. Plans are in the works to construct a four-story, Mediterranean-style building that will include retail stores, residences, offices, and an eighty-room hotel overlooking the Indian River.

To see the transformed town center, walk west from Cobb's on Avenue A. Once, horse-drawn wagons carrying heavy barrels of fish groaned down the street over a pair of rails extending from Cobb's pier to the East Florida Railroad freight yards several blocks west. Partway along, the wagons halted at an icehouse to have the barrels packed for the trip to northern markets. (They were re-iced at Jacksonville and other points further along the route.)

In a block you'll come to Second Street, the downtown's main thoroughfare. The sidewalks are paved with recently installed rust, charcoal, and tan bricks laid in an attractive crosshatched pattern. Many of the old buildings have been, or are being, renovated. One of the most significant is the Sunrise Theater, which recently received a state grant for $270,000. In 1926, when the Sunrise was completed, vaudeville was at its height, and many comedians performed their delightfully silly acts on its full-size stage. During the 1930s, Bean Backus painted movie posters in a cramped studio on the second floor. Plans call for the theater to open once more for live performances.

Kitty-corner across Second Street was the St. Lucie Courthouse, an imposing structure with a domed rotunda. But styles change and in the early 1960s the old courthouse was replaced by a more functional building. Two decades later the spectacular Civic Center Addition went up beside the courthouse. Sheathed with tinted glass and polished granite, the Addition is a pleasure to behold. But inside, grim guards and electronic metal detectors remind one that the new age is not always better than the old.

Boston Avenue is on the far side of the Civic Center. By walking a block east on Boston, you'll be back at Indian River Drive, the former Dixie Highway. On the south corner is the Governor's House, former home of Daniel McCarty. He was elected in 1952 and died from complications of pneumonia and heart problems the following year. Yet during his short term he managed to earn a reputation for stonewalling civil rights. Across the street is the eerie Boston House, residence of a ghost who mysteriously ascends the stairway when shadows gather in the afternoon. "If you are standing on the third floor," an eyewitness from the historical association told me, "you'll hear sounds coming up the staircase. The stairboards seem to bend as the footfalls move right past you. It's really weird. I can't explain it. No one knows what it is . . . or was."

Walking a block north on Indian River Drive, you'll pass the former Ft. Pierce Hotel. Now rehabbed into an office building, it was once a welcome stopover for weary travelers on the Dixie Highway. The hotel had a spacious entrance hall, with a wall decorated with Backus paintings. They were done when the artist was in his mid-teens, and he later described them as "god-awful things." Fortunately for his memory, they were eliminated during the remodeling. Continuing two blocks farther north, you're back at Cobb's.

The Engaging Indian River Drive

From downtown Ft. Pierce, take the Indian River Drive (CR 707) toward Jensen Beach, fourteen miles south. This is one of Florida's most delightful backroads. When first built, it was just a bumpy path paved with oyster shells. In places the road was so close to the river that Cobb's delivery wagon once hit a caved-in portion and toppled into the water.

A mile south of Ft. Pierce the road passes Old Fort Park, where the original Fort Pierce stood. The commander and namesake was young Colonel Benjamin Pierce, whose brother would one day become president of the United States. Although the Second Seminole War was raging, duty at the fort was pleasant, for the river provided a bounty of fish and waterfowl. "We all began to grow fat on this good living," wrote one soldier in 1838. "Every day our clothes became tighter." The fort was constructed of pine logs that rotted away after the war. We know of its location only from the discovery of brass army belt buckles carelessly discarded so many years ago but invaluable today.

In 1906 "Beanpot" Backus was born in the tiny house still standing at 2203 Indian River Drive a mile and a half or so beyond Old Fort Park. The family owned a small sailboat in which they loved to race along the river. Each Fourth of July, Pa Backus would load a

This drive between Ft. Pierce and Stuart is a highlight of a visit to the Indian River country.

big-snout cannon on his horsecart and fire it off in front of every house on the road.

During the 1920s, the road was paved and became part of the famed Dixie Highway. In an era when most Florida roads were merely ruts in the sand, this brick thoroughfare was a wonder. It was, in effect, America's first interstate motorway, running from the upper Midwest to Miami. Because it was built as close to the river as possible in order to facilitate transportation of bricks and supplies to the work crews, it precluded the later construction of homes, much to the frustration of developers, who seem to have a special gene that demands lining all scenic waterways with buildings. The wide lagoon stretches eastward to distant Hutchinson Island, from which the tops of a few high-rise apartments poke above the vegetation. Road signs warn that driving over thirty-five miles per hour will result in a fine of $120. No matter, for most of the cars are driven by leisurely locals going to and from their residences. There is nothing here to attract travelers—nothing commercial, that is—except a beautiful expanse of water shimmering between the trees.

The Indian River Lagoon seems so permanent that it is difficult to realize that its survival as a viable ecological system is threatened by changing water conditions. Originally a large percentage of the lagoon's replenishment was provided by freshwater tributaries flowing in from the outlying marshes. But as these streams were deepened to drain the marshes, they began transporting high concentrations of decayed plant matter and general muck that harmed the lagoon. In addition, as more and more people settled in the area, runoff from lawn fertilizers, auto oil, and a host of other pollutants caused further deterioration of the lagoon's water quality. This resulted in algae blooms, followed by the thinning of seagrass beds and a precipitous decline of certain fish and shellfish populations.

Although ecologists warned that the Indian River was dying, it wasn't until the 1980s that serious efforts began to bring the lagoon back. Today much of the waterway's restoration is coordinated by the Indian River Lagoon National Estuary Program. Representatives of business, agriculture, fishing, and private citizenry have become active in promoting concern for the lagoon. One of their most visible successes has been the widespread sale of Indian River Lagoon license plates. The revenue goes into a restoration trust fund. This money, combined with contributions from various federal, state, and local agencies, has resulted in programs to control polluted runoff waters and to redirect flood-control canals into retention areas rather than directly into the lagoon. Now the river is regaining its clarity and the sea grasses are starting to come back. Clams, oysters, and blue crabs are slowly returning, as are such prized game fish as tarpon and red drum.

When you come to the Midway Road (CR 712) turn west, leaving the Indian River Drive temporarily. Within a few blocks you'll pass over a sandy ridge occupied by the East Florida Railroad tracks. Just beyond, the road descends into a long, narrow wetland that extends in a north-south direction for nearly a dozen miles. The ridge was once an Atlantic Ocean sandbar and the wetland was a lagoon much like the Indian River. The area is still in the process of filling in, with some places dry enough to support pines, some marshy enough for cattails, and others still open water.

A portion of this land has been set aside as the Savannas Recreation Area, with its entry off a mile-long sand road that gives an excellent view of the wetland. It costs $1 per car to enter the park itself, where there are rental canoes for $3 an hour or $8 for a half day. For anglers, the waters have been well-stocked with bass.

Continuing south on Indian River Drive, in two miles you'll pass through a lightly populated area called Ankona. It was here during the Spanish era that James Hutchinson had a farm. Constant harassment by the Seminoles, who claimed the land was theirs, caused Hutchinson to obtain a grant to the island across the river that still bears his name.

The Girl from Eden

Today the twin cylinders of the Florida Power and Light plant sprout on Hutchinson Island. From this plant, high-tension wires, supported by a series of grim towers, drape across the river. One can imagine the consternation they must cause to people with homes facing them. However, these same people are undoubtedly glad for the services electricity provides. As with many things, it's a give-and-take situation.

Such matters were no concern for nineteen-year-old Lucie Richards when she first sailed down the river in 1880. She wrote to a girlfriend in New Jersey:

> The river was wide and green and so clear I could look down and see fish. The mullet were jumping five or six feet and splashing on their sides. Some would jump and land and then jump again two or three times as though they were showing off for their fish friends. A school of porpoises passed us by, rolling along, and sometimes one of them would clear the water. For the first time since I left home a calm settled over me and I thought, What a beautiful, peaceful place. We will surely be happy here.

But Lucie's perception of the uninhabited area altered when she stepped ashore with her father and older brother. "This is not the Eden I expected, but a wild and primitive place," she wrote. Although there were two primitive palmetto huts that her father had thrown up earlier, ". . . everywhere else was jungle with tall palm trees with tops like feather dusters poking out above the rest. The whole place seemed so menacing I wanted to go back out in the middle of the river and feel safe again." Among the menaces were scorpions that could lurk anywhere. And snakes—so many, in fact, that Lucie had to watch her every step.

Lucie and her family settled on the water rather than inland, for the river was a prized highway that offered communication with the outside world. The river became such an active migration route that Lucie's father built a dock and a small hotel to handle the constant stream of visitors.

After they were halfway settled, Lucie's mother arrived with two more of Lucie's brothers. She had been reluctant to come, and her reluctance was not lessened when a snake crawled over her foot. Lucie's brother also found a snake as long as a coach whip in his bed! The men killed the snakes when they could and once even had Lucie cook a rattler for dinner. This upset Lucie, to whom the snake seemed to writhe in the frying pan. "I would not have stayed in the house," she confided to her friend, "if it had not been for the mosquitoes."

Mosquitoes may have been the most troublesome of all the torments—even after her father and the boys constructed a proper house out of ship wreckage found on the Atlantic side of Hutchinson Island. There was only one way to keep the voracious little critters from sucking them dry when darkness came: fill the house with smoke. It was a disagreeable solution, but they tried to make the best of it. "Harry has put up four swings on one of the timbers of the house," Lucie wrote, "so evenings we make a big smudge and we sit and swing in the smoke and sing."

While singing helped, they did not know many melodies, and soon the same verses became stale. "Be sure to bring some new songs," she urged her younger brother before he joined them. Soon neighbors moved in with a piano and more songs, and Lucie commented to her friend that "we are always singing."

Sometimes other pleasurable moments came unexpectedly. One quiet evening a boatman whose boat was tied up at the dock brought out his cornet. His melodies ran like liquid over the placid water. "I never heard anything so sweet," Lucie wrote. "He plays well—and the quiet and dark contributed to the beauty of it all. I really shed some tears, it was so beautiful."

More people began to settle at Ft. Pierce, an easy sail north. "Hogg has his store running and they will have a school there," Lucie wrote happily. Of course, Hogg's stock was limited, and when Mother Richards bought fabric with which to make shirts and frocks, they all had the same pattern. The activity at Ft. Pierce also brought Peter Cobb into Lucie's small world. One of her brothers, catching her making eyes at the handsome bachelor, teased her. But by 1882 there were other eligible young men around, so nothing came of the Cobb flirtation.

On Christmas that year everyone gathered for a party on

Hutchinson Island. "We took our lunch and spent the day on the beach," Lucie wrote. "The water was just fine for bathing." Afterwards the partygoers sailed to Ft. Pierce, where there was music and dancing and an outdoor picnic—with dinner served at a long table—where everyone laughed and frolicked.

During the next decade everything went well at the tiny settlement that was now called Eden. The menfolk turned the sand ridge behind the house into a large pineapple farm. The rich harvests were placed on carts and rolled over rails down the ridge to the pier. Here steamboats picked up the fruit and carried it to Ft. Pierce, where it was iced, then loaded onto freight cars and sent to northern markets. The Richards' home was soon expanded into the Eden Grove Hotel, where Lucie served as cook, maid, and greeter. Eventually she wed a neighbor and spent the rest of her seventy-four years at Eden, where she became one of its most prominent and vocal citizens.

Today there is nothing much at Eden. The Richards' house is gone, having burned a few years ago. The farm reverted to native plants in the early 1900s after the pineapple business was destroyed by freezes, fungus, and foreign imports. As for Eden itself, about all that remains are some private homes and a few street signs.

But Lucie Richards has not been forgotten, for the letters she wrote over a period of eight years have been gathered together by a descendant, Raymond Richards Brown, and published as *Memories of Eden*. In them, this admirable, witty, and quite likable frontier lady lives once more.

The World's Pineapple Capital

A mile and a half beyond Eden is the SR 732 bridge leading to the sandy shores of Hutchinson Island. But before turning, you may want to see the little town of Jensen Beach (population about twelve thousand) just south of the bridge. It was founded by a Dane named, of course, Jensen, whose decision to settle there was influenced by Thomas Richards' cultivation of pineapples. Jensen and others were so successful that by the early 1890s they were shipping a million boxes of the fruit yearly, which enabled them to call their town the "Pineapple Capital of the World." Fish too was an important export, and soon Jensen became headquarters of the R. R. Ricou Fish Company, which boasted eight major fish houses from the Indian River to Key West. Ricou used the services of up to fifty boats. Some days Ricou's icehouse in Jensen packed more than two hundred barrels of fish. The town became so important that Henry Flagler graced it with what local boosters proclaimed was the finest railroad station on Florida's east coast.

But after the demise of the pineapple, the town fell on such hard times that John Jensen himself sold out and hustled down to Cuba, arriving just in time to be almost killed in a revolution. With the subsequent decline of fishing, Jensen's town settled into a graceful decay that is still apparent on the block-long drive down Ricou Terrace to the Florida East Coast tracks, then a block south to CR 732, which is the town's main street. Here the once-renowned train station stood, along with the bank, general store, barber shop, livery stable, and ice factory.

Splendor on the Beach

Now drive back to the SR 732 bridge and turn east over the Indian River. The road ends at A1A and Jensen Beach Park, a free, state-run facility with a pavilion offering snacks and breakfasts. The noteworthy ocean view from the picnic pavilion makes the food more than palatable. This is particularly true during one of the famous Atlantic dawns, when the wave-crests sparkle crimson. At low tide people with electronic metal detectors often swing slowly along the shore, hoping, perhaps, to come across Spanish doubloons from an ancient treasure ship that sank several miles up the coast.

The waters hereabouts hold other treasures for fishermen. Surf casters are nearly always flinging their lines into the cascading waves. Farther out are charter boats from nearby Stuart, which calls itself the "Sailfish Capital of the World." Experienced fishermen say that playing a sailfish is one of the supreme thrills of the sport. At one time, so many were caught that their numbers dwindled dangerously. Now, once they are landed and the bragging-rights photos snapped, the magnificent fish are released to be available for the next spinner of fish tales.

From Jensen Beach, drive south on A1A. Soon you'll pass an upscale Holiday Inn with many rooms facing the Atlantic and a public restaurant. Beyond is the Elliott Museum, featuring antique cars and period rooms and toys. It also includes the collection of Seminole artifacts accumulated by naturalist Hugh Willoughby during his epic trek across the uncharted Everglades in

The old beacon at Gilbert's Bar House of Refuge warned ships away from dangerous shoals.

1896–97. The gift shop sells Lucie Richards' *Memories of Eden* for $14.95. The museum is open daily between 10 A.M. and 4 P.M. Admission is $6 for adults and $2 for children six to thirteen.

Angels and Pirates

Continuing on A1A, in a mile you'll come to MacArthur Boulevard, where a sign points toward Gilbert's Bar House of Refuge 1.3 miles south. Follow MacArthur as it wends over the rolling fairways of Marriott's luxurious Indian River Plantation before passing into a subtropical growth of saw palmettos, sea grapes, and black mangroves. Here the road becomes a simple two-lane byway hardly qualifying as a boulevard. At the House of Refuge, the road squeezes between the Indian River and low dunes that border the Atlantic.

The House of Refuge at Gilbert's Bar dates from the 1870s, when the American government built a series of ten such shelters along Florida's Atlantic coast to serve as temporary residences for the victims of storms and hurricanes. As the only one remaining, the Gilbert's Bar refuge is of special historical interest. It is open daily from 10 A.M. to 4 P.M. Admission is $4 for adults and $2 for children six to twelve.

The Keeper's House is furnished much as it was when Hubert Blessey was in charge. Hubert, his wife, Susan, and their three children lived on the first floor, and up to twenty-four shipwrecked sailors could be wedged into the second floor. During emergencies, Blessey was expected to launch his rescue boat into the stormy sea and pick up whatever survivors he could find. This boat was stored in a separate building, which is now the visitors center and gift shop.

Lucie Richards stayed here for a week in 1882 while her father and a brother were gathering up recent wreckage to build their house at Eden. A family named Brown ran the establishment at that time, and the daughter, Anna, was about Lucie's age. The two of them had exciting times scurrying over the shoreline. "We walked down to one of the old wrecks," Lucie wrote. "It was almost buried in the sand now, but we could still climb around on parts of it. We pretended we were sailing on the high seas. . . . It was so nice to be with young people again and just play."

Anna also showed her the strange rocky formation just offshore now known as Bathtub Reef. Here the rocks form a semicircular barrier that creates a calm-water lagoon. This reef had more grim history than the girls realized. A half century earlier, it had been used by the notorious pirate Don Pedro Gilbert

Murder and Retribution

Don Pedro Gilbert claimed he was the son of a Spanish nobleman, although his last name hints that he may have had more than a trace of English seafaring blood. In any event, Gilbert somehow came into possession of a speedy, black-hulled schooner on which he mounted four mean cannons. After he scraped together a cutthroat crew, he chose this part of the coast for his base.

Gilbert built a watchtower hidden among the mangroves from which lookouts constantly scanned for approaching ships. When one was spotted, Gilbert would light a bonfire. To ship captains this indicated stranded sailors, so they would often approach to offer aid. If the tide was low and visibility poor, the ship would founder on the reef, where it would be boarded by Gilbert and his ruffians. After the crew had been murdered and the loot distributed, the pirates would be off to Port Royal, Jamaica, for general debauchery, returning to Gilbert's Bar when they needed to refresh their treasury.

But as grisly tales of Gilbert circulated, business slackened. So he turned to the African slave trade. Here he met trouble, for a British warship intercepted him, blew up his vessel, and took Gilbert and his men prisoner. They were transported in chains to Boston. There, in

1834, he was hanged—the last of the pirates who had long made Florida's waters so perilous. Nonetheless, his name lingered, for this long spit of sand and rock was known from then on as Gilbert's Bar.

Bathtub Reef is a mile south of the House of Refuge via winding, two-lane MacArthur Boulevard. It is a free public park with excellent swimming, especially for small children, who appreciate the calm water. The park has changing rooms as well as several informative plaques. One tells how the rocks—so unusual for Florida—were formed from sand and shell fragments cemented into tubes by a certain type of worm. A boardwalk leads to the sandy shore over a low dune feathered by sea oats.

Stuart's Second Coming

Now return to A1A and head west over two bridges. The first crosses the Indian River. Watch for turnoffs to the small islands formed from dredgings when the bridge was built. Here there are small parks with swimming and restroom facilities, as well as marvelous views of the river. The second bridge comes up almost immediately. It spans the St. Lucie River, named by the early Spanish in honor of a holy lady whose vow of virginity so frustrated a suitor that he turned her in to Roman authorities, who promptly executed her for the horrible crime of being a Christian.

The town of Stuart begins on the far shore of the St. Lucie River, which here runs parallel with the Indian River but soon bends westward. Continue west on A1A, also called Ocean Boulevard. In two and a half miles you'll come to the modern Martin County Courthouse. Next door is the older, former courthouse, which has been converted into the Cultural Center.

The first jail was beside the Cultural Center, and from here the sheriff and his deputies kept an eye on the wild little town. This was particularly difficult during Prohibition, when the secluded coves of the Indian and St. Lucie Rivers made ideal unloading points for rum smuggled in by speedboats from the Bahama Islands, just sixty miles distant.

At first, everyone except the sheriff and his deputies seemed to know about the shipments. But soon the lawmen were confiscating a goodly portion of the contraband. They were supposed to dump the booze in the surrounding forest, but suspicions grew that they were keeping the best for themselves. Thus it was decreed that they must smash all the bottles in the jailyard, where anyone could watch. This worked well, except for the groans of the onlookers as choice spirits spilled over the dirt, and for the odor of alcohol that made the town reek.

A block beyond the Cultural Center is what the locals call "confusion corner." This is the meeting of Ocean Boulevard, Colorado Avenue, the railroad tracks, and the Dixie Highway. By going a half block north on Colorado Avenue, one block west on Flagler Avenue, and two and a half blocks north on St. Lucie Avenue you'll be at a snug little park between the city hall and the St. Lucie River. Here you'll find the Riverwalk, a slightly elevated boardwalk running along the St. Lucie River almost as far as the US 1 bridge. There are benches, landscaping, and a pleasing view of the river. It was along here that Walter Kitching, one of Stuart's founding fathers, docked his floating emporium a hundred years ago.

Kitching's fifty-six-foot sailing vessel was stuffed with clothing, shoes, canned groceries, patent medicines, kerosene, and knickknacks of every size and shape. Indeed, Walt carried such a variety of items that he himself could not get into certain spaces once they were tightly packed, so he hired a cabin boy small enough to worm his way among the goods. When the lad, half-suffocated, found an item, he'd give a muffled whoop and Walt would haul him out by his feet. During his forty-day sojourns, Walt visited every settlement, shanty, and campfire on the river. He'd announce his approach by bellowing on a conch shell and always found the shore crowded when he tied up.

Although Kitching knew that the arrival of the railroad would end his floating days, he owned most of the land along the waterfront. So he talked crusty old Henry Flagler into bridging the St. Lucie River at this point and buying a strip of right-of-way at a juicy price. After the railroad bridge was completed, Kitching built a general merchandise store beside the freight station, which was almost due south of the modern Riverwalk. In this way the town of Stuart got its start. As for Kitching, this dapper Englishman prospered and eventually became president of the town's bank.

During the railroad era, the area around the boardwalk was far from the clean and tranquil place we find today. In those days scruffy fishing boats lined the dock. Even scruffier crews gutted their catches here, tossing the entrails into the St. Lucie. Then horse carts hauled the barrels of fish to the icehouse near the freightyard, where they were prepared for shipment north. Manure littered the waterfront and would remain there until rainwater washed it into the river. Over on Flagler Street, which ran along the tracks, pineapple farmers (sweaty from the fields) bargained loudly with shopkeepers like

The Heritage Museum occupies one of Stuart's oldest buildings.

Kitching or George Parks, who opened a store nearby for farm tools. Meanwhile their wives sought to obtain material to replace torn shirts or, perhaps, just little trinkets to somehow brighten their dingy shanties. Seminole men and squaws, often with papooses on their backs, would saunter about, hoping to trade animal pelts or fresh meat for steel knives or tobacco. Above it all, steam locomotives bellowed and snorted, sending cinders and sulfurous smoke drifting over everything and everyone.

From the waterfront, go back south two and a half blocks to Flagler Avenue, then right a half block to the Stuart Feed Supply store. George Parks, the first owner, and his Irish-born wife, Julia, lived on the second floor, where Julia gave birth to two of their children. The store is now a historical museum open Monday through Saturday between 10 A.M. and 3 P.M.

Nearby is the Dockside Restaurant, a prominent riverside landmark with a pair of huge sailfish displayed on the roof. Inside, large picture windows provide sweeping views of the river. It's open after 4 P.M. for full dinners only (closed Tuesdays). East on Flagler is the restored Lyric Theater, a picturesque relic of the 1920s.

The Florida East Coast Railroad is on the other side of the street, just where Henry Flagler laid the first tracks more than a hundred years ago. In those days the town was named Potsdam, and, as the trains pulled in, the conductors would call out "Pots-*damn*" to shock the proper Victorian ladies. To avoid such embarrassment, the town renamed itself Stuart—after the station agent, some say, after a local businessman, others insist.

During the 1970s and 1980s, downtown Stuart suffered the same decline experienced by most small towns. But in 1987 Stuart joined Florida's Main Street Program, becoming one of the first towns in this part of the state to do so. This program provided the impetus for merchants, building owners, and civic groups to form the Main Street Alliance, which laid plans for the downtown's resurrection. The Alliance was helped by the city, which modernized the utilities and installed vintage lampposts.

Now Stuart's fifteen thousand citizens are once more proud of their downtown, which consists mainly of the neighborhood around Osceola and Flagler Streets. And proud they should be, for the town won the Governor's Award for Urban Design a few years back.

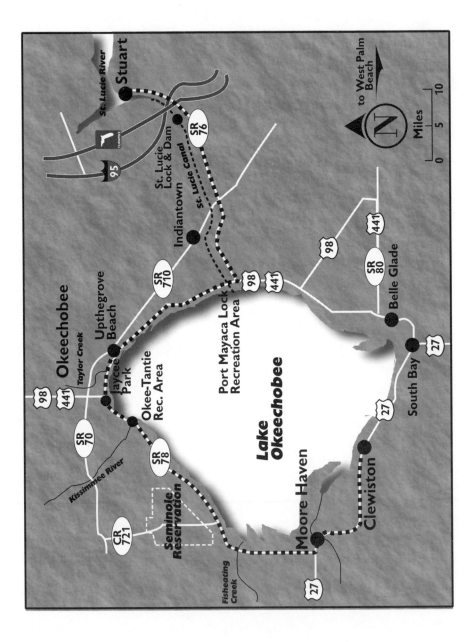

Okeechobee's Two Worlds

Stuart to Clewiston • 112 Backroad Miles

The Song of the Road: Overview

These backroads provide an exploration of Lake Okeechobee and its environs. Heading west from Stuart, you'll be traversing a region once dreaded as the Alligator Swamp. But a maze of canals was constructed to drain the area, allowing farmers to convert much of it into pasture and grapefruit groves. The major canal is the St. Lucie. It begins at a dam and locks, where there is an extensive park with good vantage points for watching water roaring over the dam and boats being raised and lowered through the locks. From here you can follow the canal to Indiantown, where, at the charming Seminole Country Inn, you'll hear the story of Wallis Warfield, who almost became the Queen of England. Continuing along the St. Lucie, you'll reach the Port Mayaca dam and earthworks, with its marvelous view of Lake Okeechobee, the second largest body of fresh water wholly within the United States. From there the way leads north along a low ridge paralleling the massive Hoover Dike, which encircles the lake. At the town of Okeechobee the cattle world begins. Florida is one of the nation's major beef producers, and the cattle auctions held in Okeechobee's livestock market are the largest in the state.

Now the road turns southwest as it continues to follow the lake. You can stop for a while at the Okee-Tantie Recreation Area beside Canal 38, also known as the Kissimmee River. Major portions of the river are being restored in what has been called the most ambitious such project in the history of the world. Okee-Tantie is also the site of an excellent restaurant as well as weekly bass fishing contests that have made Lake Okeechobee famous in the fishing world.

Continuing to follow the Hoover Dike, you'll pass through cattle country, where the grasslands extend farther than you can see. But by the time you reach Moore Haven, the cattle ranges will be replaced by equally vast sugarcane fields. At Moore Haven you can pause beside the broad Caloosahatchee Canal, an essential part of the Okeechobee Waterway, which connects the Gulf of Mexico (at Ft. Myers) with the Atlantic (at Stuart). Finally, you'll reach Clewiston on the southern shore of Lake Okeechobee. This is the heart of the sugar world, and Clewiston calls itself America's Sweetest Town. You can enjoy a fine meal at the Clewiston Inn, owned by the United States Sugar Corporation. The Inn also has overnight accommodations. Or you can partake of a not-so-fancy meal and even stay over at Roland Martin's Lakeside Resort, where boats by the score dock and bass stories by the ton are the topic of the day—and night.

On the Road Again

The first portion of this trip is along the twenty-four-mile St. Lucie Canal. Begin at the I-95/SR 76 interchange just outside of Stuart. Driving west on SR 76, watch for Lock Road, which comes up almost immediately. Turn right on Lock, and in a mile or so the road will end at an extensive park along the canal. The St. Lucie was completed in the early 1920s in order to provide a waterway between Lake Okeechobee and the Atlantic. Because Lake Okeechobee was sixteen feet above sea level, a dam was built to control the water flow. At the same time locks were constructed to allow boats and barges to be raised or lowered between the canal and the St. Lucie River. At the park you have free access to picnic tables on the canal banks. The picnic area has grills, and fishing is permitted. I'm told the fishing is good, so you may be able to catch your meal. But have burgers handy just in case.

Gateway to the Glades: The St. Lucie Canal

The St. Lucie is the vital eastern link of the Okeechobee Waterway, which runs for 152 miles across Florida via Lake Okeechobee and down the Caloosahatchee River to the Gulf of Mexico. This cross-Florida route was a significant factor during World War II, when freighters with war materiel used it to avoid the Nazi subs lurking off both coasts.

Be sure to take the walkway along the top of the dam and lock. The lock chamber is 250 feet long. If you're lucky, you'll be there when it is being flooded in order to raise a boat to the level of the canal. Then walk to the dam overlook. The view is most impressive during the winter, when the level of Lake Okeechobee is being lowered in preparation for summer rains. The water churning through the seven gates is a murky tan color with the fragrance of sewage. This is not surprising, for a portion comes from the feeder canals and ditches that drain former muck land. From here the liquid

Water from Lake Okeechobee churns through the St. Lucie Canal dam.

gushes into the Indian River Lagoon, where it contributes more pollution than all other water sources combined.

The Alligator Swamp

Now go back to SR 76 and continue west. This was once the detested Alligator Swamp. "Everywhere was water," wrote Lawrence Will, who saw it in its prime, ". . . a vacant scope of country fitten only for garfish, otters, and alligators." It was a "dismal, watery desert" where saw grass shredded a traveler's clothing. In 1838, during the Second Seminole War, a band of Miccosukee Indians was driven into this swamp, and, when the army finally rounded them up, they were near starving. The place was dubbed the "Hungry Land," a title still found on some road maps. But the St. Lucie Canal and its feeders drained this once-sour area, where rich harvests of grapefruit are now grown.

Stop beside a grapefruit grove and examine the soil. It is sandy with the tannish cast of decayed plant debris. Grapefruit trees here grow full and tall and bear the large, juicy fruit so characteristic of the Indian River varieties. Environmentalists lament the loss of wetlands, but farmers question how anyone can find fault with converting nonproductive land into acreage that benefits everyone.

The former Alligator Swamp ends where a tongue of land reaches down from the north. This rise is barely perceptible to travelers on SR 76, but in a region of low elevation it is enough to afford sufficient

Grapefruit trees bear bountiful crops in the drained Alligator Swamp.

dryness for the growth of the type of grasses that cattle thrive on.

The Drums Are Stilled: Indiantown

The first white settlers, Francis and Annie Platt, arrived in this area a hundred years ago to raise cattle. As others came, a village grew up. Francis secured the vaunted job of postmaster. And, since the village could not receive mail without a name, he selected the name "Annie," after his wife. Next, in order to facilitate the transportation of mail, Platt had a road (of sorts) constructed through the swamp to Stuart. Completed in 1902, the Stuart-Annie Road became the grand-daddy of SR 76.

Apparently Annie Platt was not that thrilled to have an isolated village and muddy road named after her, for two years later, she, her husband, and their young son sloshed off to Stuart, where there was a decent school. After it was concluded that the Platts and their son would never return, the village name was changed to Indiantown.

Indiantown is interesting enough to warrant a one-mile detour north on SR 710. The lofty bridge over the St. Lucie Canal gives a satisfying view of the fertile countryside. The Seminole Country Inn on SR 710 is a hidden jewel that you may want to visit for lunch or dinner or a stay-over. The rooms are clean and there's a swimming pool surrounded by a butterfly garden.

The inn has a story of its own. Plans were laid in 1924, when dour

Indiantown's exquisite Seminole Country Inn has memories of Wallis Warfield and her tempestuous love affair with the King of England.

old Solomon Davies Warfield built it as the social center for passengers and favored shareholders on the Seaboard Airline Railroad, of which he was president. Warfield saw a great future for Indiantown, both as a railroad center and as the county seat. Thus he spent more money on the building than its humble location seemed to warrant. This is readily apparent in the lobby, with its expensive pecky-cypress ceiling, striking brick fireplace, and finely polished wooden floor.

When the inn was completed two years later, Warfield decided to open it with a flare. Thus he invited his vivacious young niece, Wallis, to serve as hostess during the festivities. Uncle Sol knew Wallis could well handle the task of making celebrities feel at home, for she was a witty and lively young miss, yet she had a serious side and could play poker with a vengeance. When Uncle Sol's invitation arrived, Wallis was happy to oblige.

This in itself would not make much of a story were it not that Wallis would soon take off on a career that would stun the world.

The Duchess Who Shook the World

Five years after her brief appearance at Indiantown, Wallis met Edward, the Prince of Wales and heir to the throne of the British Commonwealth, which at that time included Great Britain, Canada,

South Africa, India, Pakistan, Australia, and various principalities scattered hither and yon around the globe. Edward was a capable young man who was also unbelievably handsome. The British held him in an esteem that bordered on reverence. But Edward found such adulation embarrassing, and when Wallis treated him with light-hearted camaraderie, he became completely taken with her. Soon they were inseparable, to the horror of Edward's ardent admirers, who hated Wallis not only for being non-British, which was bad enough, but also for having dumped two husbands along the way. The press made Wallis out to be a cross between a pushy social climber and a backstreet seductress. When Edward's father, George V, died in 1936, Edward was crowned king. But, as it became increasingly clear that there was no way Wallis would be accepted as his queen, Edward was faced with a choice: Wallis or the throne.

When Edward abdicated, a hurricane of public anger was unleashed. It was even worse than Wallis had anticipated. She began to receive death threats at the rate of nearly a dozen a week! About the only person delighted with the abdication was Adolph Hitler, whose plans for Nazi conquest of Europe now began to envision a re-crowned King Edward and Queen Wallis as his proxy rulers in a subdued Great Britain.

Wallis and Edward deemed it advisable to disappear from public life until the passions cooled, and scuttlebutt has it that the Seminole Inn was one of their sanctuaries. Although the death threats eventually ended, Wallis became a *persona non grata* in England. And although Edward was eventually granted the title of Duke of Windsor, along with the governorship of such inconsequential British possessions as the Bahama Islands and, later, Bermuda, King George VI, his own brother, never received him nor allowed him to settle in England. Despite the harshness of what amounted to exile, Edward and Wallis, now the Duchess of Windsor, lived a long and happy life together.

Anyone driving down Indiantown's main street does not have to be told that the settlement has fallen rather shy of Uncle Sol's expectations. Except for the Seminole Inn, the downtown seems to consist mainly of low-priced businesses that cater largely to the Guatemalan citrus workers who comprise a significant portion of the town's population of fifty-five hundred. However, west of the commercial strip is an active marina. Indiantown also has an airport that boasts, somewhat quixotically, the longest unpaved runway in the entire U.S.A.

From Indiantown go back south on SR 710, also called Warfield Highway, which will mean something to you now. Turning west on SR 76, you'll see the boat masts at the Indiantown marina across the canal. But you'll not see much more since the mound left over from the canal's construction blocks the rest. Citrus groves line the highway. During the late fall and winter, there will probably be fruit-picking crews with ladders. There are very few commercial buildings along the highway, and, thankfully, virtually no billboards.

Charlemagne of the Swamp: Fingey Conners

After ten quiet miles you'll see the old water tower that marks Port Mayaca on Lake Okeechobee. SR 76 ends at the impressive Port Mayaca dam and lock, framed by the US 98/441 high-rise bridge over the canal. But drive south (away from the bridge) a few hundred yards to a turnoff that will put you on the old Conners Highway. Park beside the time-mellowed mansion and hear the almost forgotten tale of "Fingey" Conners.

Conners was a self-made man whose fists and boisterous mannerisms made him boss of the tough longshoremen of Buffalo, New York. The broken fingers he suffered during one of his many fights gave him the nickname of "Fingey." Over the years he turned his aggressive temperament to the rough-and-tumble conflicts of the business world. Gradually his bold ventures brought him a fortune.

Conners arrived in Florida in time to witness the opening of the canal between Lake Okeechobee and West Palm Beach in 1917. Entranced, even obsessed, with the potentialities of the lake, he bought virtually the entire town site of Okeechobee from the Florida East Coast Railroad, which had just entered it from the north. Because the settlement was inaccessible by land from the south, Conners decided to construct a fifty-two mile highway from the Palm Beach Canal along the lake to the village of Okeechobee. He considered irrelevant the little detail that much of the route was through swamp. So road-building equipment was assembled, laborers hired, and work begun.

The problem of the swamp actually proved to be minor, for Conners was able to use dredgings from the West Palm Beach and St. Lucie Canals for the base of his roadbed. This was topped with a thick layer of crushed limestone taken from the bottom of the St. Lucie. Then oil was spread over the surface. Tollgates were installed, marked by great wooden arches that spanned the roadway. As soon as the highway was completed in 1924, Conners invited everyone to join the motorcade from Palm Beach to the ribbon-cutting ceremony at the town of Okeechobee. Oh, by the way, they'd be expected to pay the $1.50 toll.

The turnout was impressive: more than two thousand tin lizzies and assorted gasoline contraptions participated in the thrilling trek. Conners greeted the crowd with a mixture of booze, barbecue, and oratory that few would ever forget. One well-fed speaker compared Conners to Charlemagne, which everyone agreed was, if anything, an underestimation of good old Fingey. Even after the hangovers were gone, traffic continued to flow, adding constantly to Conners' bulging coffers until he died five years later.

The City That Never Was: Port Mayaca

After the Conners Highway came through, big plans were made for Port Mayaca. Conners sold the land hereabouts to some hotshot developers who worked up blueprints for a large marina, two golf courses, and a maze of streets and home lots around artificial lakes with enticing names such as Opal and Topaz. Work was actually begun on an ornate administration and sales building. But with the Florida real estate crash of 1926, these plans sank into the swamps, from which they have never emerged.

A Watery Dilemma

Now take US 98/441 north. After going over the St. Lucie Canal, watch for the single-lane road leading to the Port Mayaca Lock Recreation Area. The road ascends the Hoover Dike, a massive, thirty-four-foot-high embankment running around the entire lake. The view of Lake Okeechobee from the top is rewarding, but don't be surprised that you can't see across it. Okeechobee is the second largest body of water wholly within the continental United States (only Lake Michigan is larger). To the Indians, Okeechobee meant "Big Water." It occupies a large, saucer-shaped depression about thirty miles in diameter. Yet despite its size, the lake is surprisingly shallow, with an average depth of barely thirteen feet.

Actually Okeechobee is hardly a lake at all. It's more a wide place in the sheet of water that flows gently in a wide swath southward to Florida Bay, creating, in the process, the vast sea of grass called the

Everglades. Engineers turned it into a lake by walling it in rather than simply letting it ooze over its southern margin.

But don't minimize the power of Okeechobee just because it's not a full-fledged, deep-water lake. No major body of water in America has ever exploded with such murderous ferocity as did Okeechobee when, during the hurricane of 1928, mountains of water crashed over Belle Glade and other communities a few miles south of where you're standing. When the horror was over, more than two thousand bodies were floating in the debris. It was this shocking disaster that resulted in the erection of the dike named for Herbert Hoover, president when the enabling act was passed.

The erection of the Hoover Dike may have solved the flooding problem, but it gave rise to a new problem. Now that the lake was enclosed, how would you establish the water level? Naturalists and bass fishing interests wanted the lake kept low so eelgrass and bulrushes could thrive in the marshes and provide food for aquatic life. On the other hand, the townsfolk wanted it kept high as a secure source of drinking water, sugar interests likewise for irrigation purposes. The amount of water flowing through such dams as the one at Mayaca was so controversial that a council of representatives from each of the four counties bordering Lake Okeechobee was formed. Today this council constantly monitors the lake level to keep it from rising too high after the summer rains and falling too low during the winter drought.

The Port Mayaca Recreation Area is a favorite boat-launching point for fishermen. But there is less here to interest tourists. There is no walkway onto the dam, nor is there a good place to watch the lock in operation. The recreation area has some picnic tables with marvelous views of the lake, but there are no restrooms, which could hurry your viewing time.

Some people like to hike or bike on the trail that runs along the top of the Hoover Dike, but it is unpaved and the going is rough. Big plans are under way, however, to convert the dike into a true scenic trail with comfortable way stations at regular intervals, one at Port Mayaca.

Along Lake Okeechobee

Driving north on US 98/441, for the next twenty-two miles you'll be on the route blazed by Fingey Conners to the town of Okeechobee. Although this is a federal highway, most of the traffic is local, for truckers and auto speedsters are humming along on I-95 or the Florida Turnpike thirty miles to the east. There is very little development, even though much of the land is for sale in two-acre lots. When the homes come, they will probably be several stories high so the owners can view the lake over the Hoover Dike.

Long ago, the low ridge upon which you are traveling was mantled with dense stands of maples and water oaks mingled with rubber trees and palmettos. Where the ridge merged with the surrounding wetlands, magnificent cypress trees spread their limbs. In the swales grew such water-loving plants as saw grass and maiden cane. But during the mid-1920s, these trees were gobbled up by the voracious sawmill of the Osceola Cypress Company nearby. Today only the unwanted maiden cane remains along the damp roadsides as a rank grass that by autumn is more than head-high. As for the cypress, the name alone lingers at the Blue Cypress Golf Resort.

Not far beyond the Blue Cypress sign, watch for a front yard with a large prickly pear cactus. In such a rainy climate, cactus grow in very sandy soil that dries out quickly. What may catch your eye are the prickly pear cactus pads, half of which have been painted a variety of colors. They bear no advertising messages. Apparently they were painted just for the fun of it. Isn't that message enough?

Now that your eyes are on the roadside, you may wonder about other places on the way. Are the people who patronize the Happy Hour Tavern truly happy? Is there really a Butch who owns Butch's Fish Camp? Is he as tough as his name suggests? Do the rentals at the Awesome Rental Office honestly fill you with awe?

Then there is the village with the strange name of Upthegrove Beach. You may be interested to know the name came from the clan who settled here in the 1920s. There was Rob Upthegrove and his wife and his brothers, Ed and Jim (better known as Pomp). They were muscular chaps and helped fell the forest and deliver the logs to the Osceola Cypress Mill, three miles north. They enjoyed some good years, with money flowing in from logging and from the catfish they hauled from the blue waters of Lake Okeechobee. They and their neighbors even built a school for the young'uns. But when the cypress trees were gone, the mill closed. Then the catfish died out. And in 1926 the school was blown to oblivion by an errant hurricane. With that, the dreams died. Today Upthegrove consists merely of an unusual name, some fish camps, and a few homes strung out between the highway and the Hoover Dike. What happened to the three stalwart brothers and their wives? We don't know. But they made their own little mark on history. That's a deed few can accomplish.

Incidentally, there is another strange thing about Upthegrove Beach. That is, there is no beach—at least not for swimming. You'll undoubtedly find the reason simple and compelling: alligators.

The Fateful Decision at Taylor Creek

Three miles or so beyond Upthegrove you'll cross a little drawbridge over Taylor Creek, which has its own tale to tell. "Old Rough and Ready" Zachary Taylor conducted the biggest battle of the Second Seminole War in 1837 a short distance north of here. Taylor was not a good general, for he ignored the fervent urgings of his officers to encircle the Indians and instead rashly sent a thousand of his best men charging through a swamp directly into the withering fire of five hundred Seminoles protected by a barrier of trees. His losses were horrifying: more than ten percent of his force either dead or wounded before the Indians retreated. Despite the losses, the American public declared the Battle of Okeechobee a huge victory, for it virtually ended Indian resistance. Zachary Taylor became a popular hero and eleven years later was elected president of the United States.

Some Call It Paradise: The Town of Okeechobee

At Taylor Creek, US 98/441 follows the route of the old Conner's Highway as it made an abrupt turn north to reach the town of Okeechobee. Fingey Conners owned a small house near this corner, and it was here that his distinguished guests and undistinguished drinking buddies gathered on a hot summer evening in 1924 to celebrate the opening of the road that bore his name. As you head north you'll suddenly find yourself in franchiseville. Yes, the "burger gang" has found Okeechobee, and with a vengeance that will astound you for a town of fewer than six thousand. But for travelers coming down from the north, it's the only population center after leaving the environs of Orlando. And just how long can any civilized person go without a fast food fix!

In its early days Okeechobee had visions of being a major city—even proclaiming itself the future "Chicago of the South." For wasn't it on a great lake, like Chicago? And didn't it have a major railroad connection, like Chicago? And didn't its vast grasslands make it a natural for a cattle industry that would fill its stockyards, like Chicago? Officials of the

Florida East Coast Railroad had much the same vision. The company president, J. R. Parrott, even made sure his proud name was plastered on the main street. And when the town was platted, most of the streets were far broader than usual, for how else could they accommodate the horse carriages that would throng the avenues?

It didn't take long for Okeechobee to realize it would never challenge Chicago. Yet the wide streets remain as monuments to that impossible dream. Still, you can't help but be impressed by the dimensions of Parrott Avenue, which is also US 98/441. You will also be impressed by the town center at Parrott and Park Street. It is dominated by the park named for Henry Flagler, founder of the Florida East Coast Railroad. During the railroad's heyday its passenger cars were crowded with travelers, many of whom stayed at the Southland Hotel, the three-story landmark that once stood on the northeast corner of Parrott and Park. Some of Park Street's past glory remains in the form of a special parkway that must be forty yards wide. The town has recently joined Florida's Main Street Program and is sprucing up its downtown with lamppost banners, colorful sidewalk pavement blocks, and a general painting and fixup of store fronts. But there is still a long way to go.

Once Okeechobee had hoped it might become state capital. But this dream also disappeared, and the town had to settle for just being the seat of Okeechobee County. The town made the best of it, however, and the courthouse, which is a block north of Park off of NW Second Street, is the most imposing structure for miles around. Built during the 1920s, it has the facade of a Greek temple, with unique double-archway, exterior stairs leading to the second floor.

There is a plaque on the courthouse commemorating a meeting here in 1947 that began the campaign to induce Congress to adopt a vigorous flood control program. The precipitating factor was the flooding of the nearby Kissimmee River that drowned a lot of cattle. The agitation was so effective that by 1970 the river had been converted into a long drainage ditch thirty feet deep and several hundred feet wide called Canal 38.

Today the Kissimmee grasslands support large ranches that border the town to the north and west. The cattle and dairy industries have become the county's largest source of income, and Okeechobee County leads the entire state in beef production. This is no small achievement, for Florida is the fourth most important cattle state in the entire nation (following Texas, Montana, and Nebraska). For this reason you really can't get the flavor of the area without visiting the Okeechobee Livestock Market on US 98 a mile and half north of downtown. It is the nation's second largest such market. Cattle auctions are held every Monday and Tuesday after 12:30 P.M. The public is invited to watch from a comfortable grandstand. Admission is free and there is a restaurant for lunch. For those who chuckle at Okeechobee's boast of being the Chicago of the South, it is note-worthy that, at least in the matter of livestock, the town has far exceeded Chicago, whose once-famed stockyards have long since been relegated to old cowpokes' memories.

Rodeos are also extremely popular. They are held in the arena on US 441 on the north side of town twice yearly: first in March in conjunction with the speckled perch festival, then over Labor Day weekend. At these times you can watch bucking bronco riding, bull riding, calf roping, and steer wrestling. Admission is $10.

PAY TOLL AHEAD

While you're in Okeechobee, you should see the large mural on the exterior wall of the gymnasium at SW Sixth Street and SW Second Avenue. In one scene, artist John Gutcher—working with and supported financially in part by the Seminole tribe—depicts Seminoles in their native village. Another scene shows the arrival of the first white settlers, Peter and Louisiana Raulerson, in their covered wagon.

All in all, one gets a feeling that Okeechobee is on the go, although few Americans will be as effusive as a delegation of visiting Chinese in 1999. Part of a four-day cultural exchange program, they had gone to Disney World, of course. But they really wanted to see a typical American town. Down they went to Okeechobee, where cattle and cowboys are the style. Ah, that was more like it. Upon departing, they doffed the cowboy hats they had just purchased and called the town a "happy paradise." Rumor has it that on the plane back to China someone yelled "yippi ki oh!"

Lake Okeechobee's Prettiest Park

Drive south out of town on US 98/441 and head right at SR 78. Very quickly you'll come to a sign indicating the Jaycee Park. Turn on the entry road and drive over the Hoover Dike down to the extensive lakeside park, where there is a beautiful sandy beach that cries out for swimming. But once more you can keep your suit packed, for the water belongs to the alligators. Just because you may not see them, that does not mean they're not watching you. "There are a lot of gators in the lake," the director of tourism told me. "I'm talking about *big* ones—some up to fourteen feet! They're not usually aggressive except at mating season. But it's just better to stay away." The "usually" in her comment should be conclusive.

You can enjoy a pleasing water vista from the long pier, however, as well as participate in some of the state's premier bass fishing—if you have a license. Just be aware that you must release bass smaller than ten inches as well as breeders fourteen to seventeen inches.

Strangely, it was catfish, not bass, that originally supported an extensive fishing industry on Lake Okeechobee. Catfish camps were concentrated around the north end of the lake from Upthegrove to the mouth of the Kissimmee. The lake was so full of catfish that the fishing crews used seining nets up to one thousand yards long to haul them in. A net would be laid out in a vast circle, and, as it was hauled in, the water would churn with catfish packed as tightly as, well, sardines.

As early as 1900, Captain Ben Hall ran a forty-foot cargo steamer around this part of the lake, picking up from the catfish camps along the north shore. At first he had to transport them down the three-mile canal at Moore Haven and on along the Caloosahatchee River to the ice plant at Ft. Myers. However, when the Florida East Coast Railroad reached Okeechobee in 1915, that town became the catfish capital. At the height of the boom, one captain owned forty-five fishing boats and eight refrigerated railroad cars.

But hauls like these could not be maintained, and by 1925 the industry was in decline, the demise hurried by a law against seining as well as a pair of hurricanes that almost emptied the lake. After the commercial fishermen departed, the lake was left to sportsmen, who caught fish like gentlemen, with rod and reel, one at a time. In addition to fish, the park is frequented by many birds. A large group of sandpipers around a rain pool let me approach close enough to stare eye-to-eye with them. From the beach a road runs west along the water for a half mile—just long enough to make you wish it went a lot farther.

Back on 78, in five miles you'll come to the Okee-Tantie Recreation Area, where you should turn in.

An all-too-short road hugs the bank of Lake Okeechobee.

The Strange Saga of the Kissimmee River

Okee-Tantie is on the banks of Canal 38, known as the Kissimmee River in a former life. The Kissimmee was probably named by the Calusa Indians, who inconveniently disappeared before they could tell us what the word meant. Modern Floridians place the accent on the middle syllable, but it could just as well have been on the "kiss," which seems to please visitors. Whatever the name, the river was a humble entity, preferring to meander quietly for 103 miles among marshes and meadows until it lost itself in Lake Okeechobee. Once in a while it flooded, but it didn't mean any harm and settled back in its bed as quickly as possible. To control the flooding, the river was confined in a fifty-six-mile channel with reservoirs and other structures. Upon completion in 1971, much of the Kissimmee prairie dried out, enabling pasture to be extended into a third of the former wetlands.

But then the quality of Lake Okeechobee deteriorated because the floodplain no longer filtered out fertilizers and animal wastes. With that, the fish population plummeted. Simultaneously, the numbers of birds began diminishing as their wetland habitats were destroyed. Concerned citizens, environmentalists, and fish camp owners began calling for the restoration of the river. After years of agitation, in 1994 Congress decided to do the almost unthinkable: bring back the very river that it had recently spent $30 million to destroy.

Complete restoration was impossible, however, because during the intervening years farms and ranches had expanded into large parts of the former wetlands and it would be too expensive to buy them out. Also, because flooding was still a potential problem, some dams and reservoirs had to be kept. Thus it was decided to reestablish the river only along the center forty percent of its former route. Even so, this would cost the better part of a billion dollars and represent the most massive reconstruction of a river in the history of the world. The projected completion time was fifteen years.

Bass Heaven: Okee-Tantie Park

Unfortunately, the mouth of the Kissimmee at the Okee-Tantie Recreation Area is not included in the reconstructed portion, which begins twenty miles upriver. However, don't pass Okee-Tantie by. The park offers picnic locations along the water as well as campsites, a boat launch, a marina, and a fishing pier. There is also a restaurant open for lunches and dinners seven days a week. I am told that the food is superb—particularly the Lake Okeechobee catfish. And if you have a craving for gator tail, you can satisfy it here. Just don't order bass, for that is a no-no hereabouts. Bass have a place of honor among the Okeechobee anglers. Although it is legal for individuals to keep those ten to thirteen inches long and eighteen to twenty-nine inches long, a park notice strongly urges everyone to adopt a catch-and-release policy.

Catch-and-release is an important part of the bass tournaments that are held at Okee-Tantie almost every weekend. At these times pairs of fisherfolk (about ten percent are women) go out on the lake in up to 150 special "bass boats," constructed so as to hold what are called "livewells." These livewells extend down into the water and permit the storage of living bass. When the contestants reach shore, they put the bass in canvas bags, have them weighed, then release them into the lake. If a bass is dead, points are deducted. Spectators watch the tense bass weigh-ins at a small grandstand beside the river.

Some of the tournaments are big business run by national associations. Since they bring a bonanza of visitors, the associations are able to charge fees to the towns where they are held. "We have to pay as high as thirty thousand dollars to get a major tournament," an official of Okeechobee's Tourist Development Council told me. "If we don't offer enough, they'll go someplace else. Maybe even to Georgia.

But Clewiston, right across the lake, is our biggest competitor."

Before you leave Okee-Tantie, you'll undoubtedly have a burning question: from where did the "Tantie" in the park's name come? Well, give the honor to redheaded Tantie Huckaby, Okeechobee's first school-teacher. She made such an impression that the town itself was origi-nally named after her. Now the park has made her locally immortal.

A World of Long Vistas

Back on SR 78, you'll be traveling in a southwest direction as you follow Lake Okeechobee—although your only indication that the lake is really out there will be the everlasting Hoover Dike in the distance. You're now crossing a 230-mile north-south drainage flatland that includes the Kissimmee valley, the Lake Okeechobee basin, and the vast Everglades. But the fierce saw grass that makes the Everglades almost uninhabitable does not thrive here. The prairie grasses are more palatable to cattle, making possible the ranches that reach so far you can almost see the curvature of the earth. The road is arrow-straight, and a limit of sixty miles per hour may tempt you to speed.

Soon you'll come to the junction with CR 721, which leads to the

The cattle ranches along the north side of Lake Okeechobee seem to stretch almost to infinity.

Brighton Seminole Reservation a few miles north. Cattle ranching is important at Brighton, and rodeo spectators often fill their five-thou-sand-seat arena. However, it is the Wednesday through Saturday evening poker and high-stakes bingo that attract most non-Indians to Brighton.

At the same 78-721 crossroads is the Lakeport Lodge and Restaurant. If you're looking for an unusual picnic site, take the road beside the lodge south along the Harney Pond Canal. The road soon passes over the Hoover Dike and ends at a group of sheltered lunch tables accompanied by a restroom. Nearby are two narrow footbridges that lead over modest waterways to a marsh-land bordering Lake Okeechobee.

On SR 78 once more, you'll find yourself again traversing the grasslands. There is something exhilarating about a wide prairie, a gigantic cup of sky, and a country road that seems to lead to infinity. Yet the road does not lead to infinity—merely to Fisheating Creek five miles beyond.

Fisheating Creek

The Hoover Dike extends for some distance up both sides of Fisheating Creek. Here at its mouth, the creek is actually a three-mile-wide wetland called Cowbone Marsh. Other tributaries are Gopher Gully and Gator Slough. (Honestly, I'm not making up these names.) The picturesque wetland is home to black bears, panthers, wild turkeys, and swallowtail kites. A fifty-mile segment of Fisheating Creek, which is most of it, had been owned by the powerful Lykes Brothers Company, which raised cattle and kept the area closed for fear of modern-day cattle rustling. But the Florida Wildlife Federation and other organizations felt the public should not be prevented from enjoying such a primitive area. A lawsuit followed, resulting in the strange decision that this marshy maze of grass and weeds was actu-ally a navigable waterway and that, therefore, it belonged to the state. Naturally Lykes appealed. After much legal wrangling, the state agreed to pay Lykes $46 million for eighteen thousand acres along the creek and Lykes agreed not to develop the forty-two thousand surrounding acres. The state land is now being turned into a wildlife management area that may be open to the public by the time this book comes out.

Historically, Fisheating Creek goes back to the ancient Calusa Indians, who built a great mound a half dozen miles back from Lake

Okeechobee. Long after the Calusa vanished, the U.S. Army constructed Fort Center near the mound. The fort was used briefly as a base to track down the few Seminoles who remained after most had been shipped off to an area beyond the Mississippi.

As you travel the eight miles between Fisheating Creek and the town of Moore Haven, you'll notice the landscape change drastically. Gone are the cattle ranges. In their place are bountiful, densely planted stands of sugarcane. When the cane reaches its maximum winter growth, it stands twelve to fifteen feet high, forming a virtually impenetrable jungle. This change is due to the fact that the southern end of the lake had virtually no natural barrier to prevent Lake Okeechobee from overflowing as it merged with the Everglades. This damp, mucky land, so ideal for sugarcane, originally supported a dense growth of custard apples: smallish trees with crooked trunks and a maze of twisted branches. The custard-apple blossoms were huge and cream-colored. The fruit was shaped like four-inch bananas with soft pulp inside that looked like custard to some pioneers. It was palatable only if one were famished.

The pioneers hated the trees, which intertwined themselves in a two-mile-wide belt along the southern lake shore and made land transportation impossible. Furthermore, the wood was too soft to convert into boards and the fruit had no commercial value. The only thing good about them was that they were so easy to cut down. Yet when the last custard-apple tree had been felled, nostalgia set in. "I reckon it was near about the ugliest, most useless tree the good Lord ever made," recalled Lawrence Will, "and yet He made a heap of them, and I, for one, am right sorry they're gone."

The Feisty Lady of Moore Haven

Where SR 78 meets US 27 on the outskirts of Moore Haven, turn left on US 27. Although Moore Haven has a population of fewer than two thousand, it is the only significant town in Glades County—so, by default, it is the county seat. Most travelers see the little town as a few gas stations and a high-rise bridge and pass through it without a pause. But it is worth your time to pull off the road when you come to the courthouse on your right just before the bridge, for Moore Haven has a story to tell.

Since this story begins at the Caloosahatchee Canal, take Avenue J, which you'll find beside the courthouse, a few blocks east to the canal. This was once the heart of town, but the ramshackle buildings

The Caloosahatchee Canal at Moore Haven links Lake Okeechobee with the Gulf of Mexico.

that lined the waterfront burned beyond repair. In their place are a nice city park and the town library. Before the canal was constructed, this was a marshy area where the waters of Lake Okeechobee sometimes mingled with those of the Caloosahatchee River. Ancient Indians actually scraped out a canoe path with clamshells. But it was Hamilton Disston in the 1880s who used steam dredges to construct a three-mile canal to connect the two bodies of water.

This canal was only a minor part of Disston's bold plans for the Everglades basin, but he went bankrupt and mysteriously died before he could complete them. A couple of decades later a West Coast developer named James Moore decided to make a fortune selling Everglades land. The first thing Moore did was to name the townsite for himself. Then he put up a real estate office fronting the canal and opened for business. Moore knew how to run a speculation. He had a snazzy speedboat pick up prospective investors in Miami and shoot them through the Miami Canal and across Lake Okeechobee at thirty-five mph in time to reach Moore Haven for a sumptuous dinner and extravagant sales pitch. Moore's problem was not with spending money but with managing it.

So Moore sold out to John O'Brien and George Horwitz. They were doing well when Horwitz died. His place was taken by his widow, Marian, who was energetic and intelligent. More than that, when she duded up in her high-blown bonnet with the spume of colored feathers, she was a knockout—so much so that she soon became Mrs. O'Brien. Marian took to the frontier life and quickly became one of the area's largest landholders. And she did not just sit in her office relying on supervisors to tell her how things were going. She had her own horse, and many a time her farmworkers would find the boss scrutinizing them from astride her steed. The townsfolk respected Marian to the point that they elected her Moore Haven's mayor, reputedly the first woman in the nation to occupy such an office.

These were good times at Moore Haven. The town's location at the juncture of Lake Okeechobee and the Caloosahatchee Canal made it a natural commercial center, particularly when locks were built at the entrance to the canal in 1918. Then an increasing number of commercial and pleasure boaters stopped at Moore Haven's hotels and bars. That same year the Atlantic Coast Line provided a rail link with population centers to the north. Then an ice plant was built, enabling Moore Haven to compete with Okeechobee as a shipping point for the thriving catfish industry. As sugarcane began to thrive, a sugar mill was constructed. And when not one but two movie theaters went up, everyone believed there was no stopping Moore Haven.

Soon Marian was up in Tallahassee petitioning the legislature to make Moore Haven the seat of a new county, even though the town had a population of barely five hundred. Wanting to emphasize the richness of the soil, Marian at first called her new county Muck, which (if nothing else) would have been easy to remember. But somewhere in the process the name was cleaned up, and Glades County was born in 1921.

Marian was a dynamo. She became president of the First Bank of Moore Haven at the corner of Avenue J and First Street. At about the same time, she and her husband interested a Tampa banker, Alonzo Clewis, in helping them establish another settlement, named Clewiston, on a low, wooded ridge just down the lake from Moore Haven. Soon thereafter they built a railroad between the two towns. Although the rickety line ran just fifteen miles, its opening was highlighted by a fine barbecue and the driving of a golden spike, just like that of the two-thousand-mile Union Pacific.

But the end of the "Marian era" was fast approaching. It was not her fault, but that of her hot-tempered, Irish husband. The fact that he was Catholic and had brought in a Jesuit priest to hold church services didn't endear him to the townsfolk; the fact that he was also

During the violent flood of 1926, raging waters reached almost up to the second floor windows of the courthouse at Moore Haven.

bullheaded intensified the feeling against him. He further antagonized the locals when he hired blacks to work on his farms. One night someone sent a bullet through the O'Briens' window. A piece of the shattered glass cut Marian's scalp and could have put an eye out. When the couple did not take the hint, their home was torched. With that, the O'Briens departed—not only from the area, but also from history.

Although the loss of such an activist as Marian was bad enough, far worse was the 1926 hurricane. As the wind whipped up Lake Okeechobee, the citizens of Moore Haven felt secure behind the eight-foot-high mud levee they had recently constructed between their community and the lake. Thus no one was prepared when the flimsy levee gave way and a wall of water descended on the community. The rushing torrent crashed against the wooden buildings, carrying off walls, roofs, and occupants. That anyone at all survived was sheer luck. One Moore Haven citizen told me how her grandfather clung to the upper branches of a tree as the water roared beneath. With him were a boy and a huge water moccasin. The snake, ordinarily dangerous, ignored him as it hung on as frantically as he. But the boy weakened. A moment later he was swept away and never seen again. When the storm was over, nearly three hundred people were dead.

About the only building that withstood the terrible force of the flood was the courthouse. A county employee pointed out to me the faint waterline that still exists on the exterior wall, almost up to the second floor windowsill.

The Nation's Sweetest Town: Clewiston

Leaving Moore Haven on US 27, you'll pass more sugarcane fields, as well as a smattering of citrus groves and a few cattle pastures. Although today the roadway is smooth and broad, originally the only land transportation between Moore Haven and Clewiston was on the O'Briens' flimsy railroad. The right-of-way was so narrow that custard-apple trees snatched the hat of many a damsel who dared sit too close to a window. Because the rails had been laid on sand simply dumped over the wet muck, the passenger car swayed so violently that riders feared it would roll into the watery ditch. Indeed, the conductor prepared for that event by riding on the car step so he could leap off in time. The little engine puffed along at barely five miles an hour, prolonging the unnerving experience for three full hours.

As you approach Clewiston you'll see the smokestacks of the United States Sugar Corporation, the leviathan that controls the economy of this end of the lake. To get a closer look at the plant, turn south on Olympia Street after you enter Clewiston. The U.S. Sugar mill is directly ahead. When Olympia ends at Arroyo Avenue, in front of the cyclone fence that encloses the plant, drive east to W. C. Owen Avenue, where you'll find the plant gate. Here a guard will tell you that visitors are not allowed except on certain days, with advance reservations, and as part of a recognized group. Thus it's not strange that there are very few out-of-state visitors.

If you could have gotten into the plant, you'd have seen sugarcane stalks being unloaded from trucks or the freight cars of the company's 120-mile railroad. They would be placed on a conveyor that would transport them to a machine where they'd be cut into small pieces by revolving knives. Then, you'd have watched the mass crushed by a series of rollers and the juice collected. Next you'd have seen the juice boiled until the liquid was gone and only a mixture of sugar and molasses remained. This mixture would be put into high-speed, rotating cylinders, where the molasses would be spun off, leaving brown sugar crystals. Finally, you would have followed this raw sugar to the refinery, where it would have been turned into the familiar pure white crystals. All in all it's quite an operation and you would certainly have been impressed. Too bad you missed it.

U.S. Sugar has become very defensive over the past decades as environmentalists have zeroed in on its being one of the principal polluters of the Everglades. There can be no doubt that the runoffs of phosphorus used in fertilizers did contribute to the pollution of the Everglades. However, as U.S. Sugar spokespersons point out, the company was merely one of the six major cane growers. Furthermore, none of these companies was doing anything illegal at this time in permitting their waste to run down the canals that fed the Everglades. After all, it was the government itself that had dug these canals.

Nonetheless, many U.S. Sugar executives are apprehensive. For this reason, U.S. Sugar and the other sugar companies agreed in 1994 to pay $300 million to clean up the Everglades. Meanwhile, U.S. Sugar adopted such effective methods to control its phosphorus runoff that scientists found water leaving the sugar fields was cleaner than that of Lake Okeechobee.

In addition to U.S. Sugar's historic role in the pollution of the Everglades, its labor practices have been subjected to a great deal of past criticism. In 1989 Alec Wilkinson wrote a devastating book entitled *Big Sugar*, describing the horrible living conditions under which the company's West Indian cane-cutters lived. He found one labor camp

The Clewiston Inn still serves delicious meals and offers fine accommodations, just as when it was built as a guesthouse by the U.S. Sugar Corporation in 1938.

near Moore Haven consisting of three long, low dormitories that reminded him of poultry barns. With their corrugated metal roofs, the "coops" often became as hot as roasters. These conditions vanished, however, when cane harvesting became almost completely mechanized, reducing the need for seasonal workers from the Caribbean.

Sugar farming has long been as much a fixture around Clewiston as cattle ranching is at Okeechobee. U.S. Sugar's predecessor, Southern Sugar, was formed in the 1920s. When Southern declared bankruptcy in 1931, its assets were taken over by U.S. Sugar, which had been formed for that purpose by C. S. Mott, a wealthy official of General Motors. One of the first new buildings Mott had constructed was the luxurious guesthouse that has since become the Clewiston Inn.

Constructed in 1938, the inn was designed to make a good impression on visitors—and it still does. Herbert Hoover stayed at the inn when he dedicated his namesake dike. Another resident was artist J. Clinton Sheperd, who resided here in the 1940s while he sketched the lush Everglades scenes that he would later transfer onto the canvasses that adorn the walls of the cocktail lounge. During World War II, the inn was a favorite watering hole for high-strung Royal Air Force cadets training nearby. So pleasant were their memories that a dozen or so still return each year to relive their experiences, at least as best as seventy-plus-year-old bones will permit.

Today the Clewiston Inn is one of the finest restaurants for miles around. It also offers overnight accommodations at rates below $100, which include breakfast (800-749-4466). To get there from the plant, drive north on W. C. Owen Avenue to US 27 (which here is called the Sugarland Highway), then three blocks east to Royal Palm Avenue, where you'll have no trouble recognizing the building with its four trademark colonnades. U.S. Sugar's headquarters are directly across a park from the inn, but there is nothing to be gained by visiting it. There is no museum or any attempt by the company to attract visitors.

From the inn, you should continue north on Royal Palm Avenue. This beautiful street actually lives up to its name, with its magnificent border of towering royal palm trees. Many U.S. Sugar executives live along here. Continue north over a small bridge to Avenida del Rio, which you should follow east five blocks to Francisco Street. By turning left onto Francisco, you'll cross a campground, then climb the Hoover Dike, where a road runs along the top.

From the crest of the dike you get an idea of the tremendous work that went into this massive structure. You may feel that human efforts have tamed wild Okeechobee, but nature is patient, and the works of mankind are transitory. The lake was not designed to remain placidly in this artificial saucer. Its flow has always been over the southern shore and on down the gently sloping spillway into the Everglades. The Hoover Dike cannot stop that flow forever. Within the past few years, seepage in the dike has been discovered. In places, "boils" as large as four inches have to be plugged. These are particularly dangerous when lake levels are high after prolonged summer downpours or hurricane drenchings. Lowering the lake level by opening the floodgates at Mayaca or Moore Haven is not a good solution, for huge water discharges down the St. Lucie and Caloosahatchee canals not only put dangerous stress on the canal banks but also harm the plants and wildlife along their shores. On the other hand, keeping the lake level high while the water is discharged slowly tends to kill the eelgrass and other vegetation that form the basis of the food chain upon which the bass industry depends. It's all very complicated.

At the base of the dike is the Rim Canal, with picnic tables along its shore. The canal has become an important route for the smaller pleasure craft traveling the Okeechobee Waterway. Larger boats and commercial barges don't fear the sometimes-treacherous

The Rim Canal encircles Lake Okeechobee, seen in the far distance between the Australian pines.

waves and head directly across the lake.

Now go back on Francisco Street to Avenida del Rio. By driving a block farther east on Avenida, you'll arrive at Roland Martin's Lakeside Resort. Martin's offers premier fishing accommodations on Lake Okeechobee. You can rent a motorboat for $60 a day.

There is a great deal of old-time Florida about Martin's, some of which you can experience at the short-order restaurant overlooking the boat docks. The restaurant is open between 5 A.M. and 6 P.M. seven days a week. Tourists are also invited to stay at one of the motel units for $68 per night during the October 1 to May 31 season and $58 other times (800-473-6766).

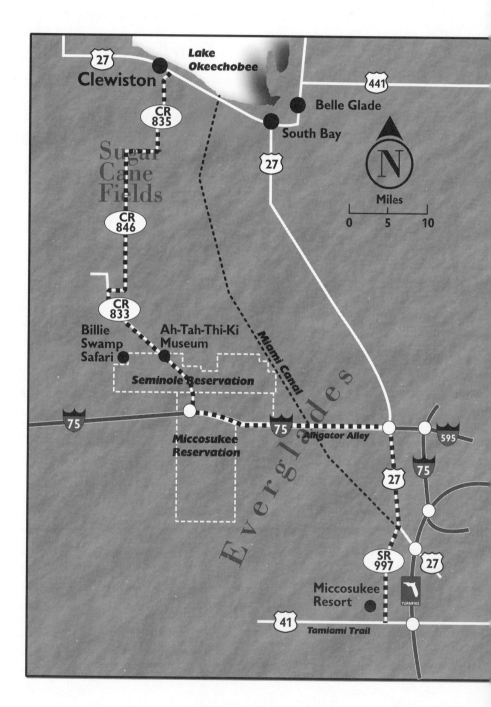

Sugar and Seminoles

Clewiston to the Miccosukee Resort • 107 Backroad Miles

The Song of the Road: Overview

The route south from Clewiston is through land where sugarcane grows in dense forests between late fall and early spring. Smoke from quick-burns usually drifts into the sky, and sometimes you may pass close by the flames. There is a sweet smell on the warm breezes that drift over flatlands that were once part of the Everglades. Harvest machines are active, as are trucks hauling cut cane to the U.S. Sugar refinery at Clewiston.

The sugarcane fields come to an abrupt halt as you approach the Big Cypress Reservation, largest of the five areas set aside for the Seminole tribe. Here you'll visit the Ah-Tah-Thi-Ki Museum, where excellent displays help you understand and appreciate the Seminole way of life. The tribe is further highlighted in a five-screen video show. You can also take a mile stroll along a forested boardwalk to a Seminole village.

Just down the side road from the museum is the Billie Swamp Safari. Here an airboat carries visitors deep into a silent swamp, where ghostly strands of Spanish moss sway from towering cypress trees, and Walter, the sullen alligator, leers from a mud island. Swamp buggies, also available, offer visitors close views of an environment unique to Florida. Those who desire an even more intimate experience can stay overnight in a Seminole chickee hut, close to raw nature.

The road south from the Big Cypress Reservation passes through cattle country to Alligator Alley, the descriptive name for the segment of I-75 through the Everglades. After spending a few moments on some of the turnouts overlooking the glades, you'll turn south on a road that edges through thick stands of melaleuca trees. This will give you a chance to see why this fast-spreading import from Australia has been called the "Everglades Terminator."

Finally you'll reach the Tamiami Trail, where the Miccosukee Resort and Convention Center rises out of the Everglades in a ten-story clash of yellow and orange. Misplaced though it may be, the newly built resort offers excellent rooms at favorable rates. It also gives you a chance to try your luck at one of the one thousand video pull-tab gaming machines—as well as at high-stakes bingo—in a setting accented by blue neon lights and weird music.

If you like gambling—er, gaming, as they call it—this is heaven. If you're not a gambler, then a stroll through the immense casino should confirm your wisdom.

On the Road Again

Setting out from Clewiston, drive south on US 27. Just out of town turn right onto CR 835 (832 on some maps). Soon you'll pass a sign denoting Old Highway 27. In the days before the interstate highways, this was the main road through central Florida to Miami. As you can see, it was a narrow and lonely road threading through clusters of scrubby trees—not a place motorists would care to have engine trouble. Continuing on CR 835, you'll find yourself amid vast fields of sugarcane, for this is the domain of the United States Sugar Corporation.

Mature sugarcane dwarfs a car.

The Sugar World

Long ago, when this was part of the Everglades, a sheet of fresh water flowed slowly from the southern shore of Lake Okeechobee to feed the great expanse of saw grass that grew tall and thick. But early twentieth-century Americans viewed the Everglades as wasted space that should be dried out and converted into farmland. The Hoover Dike (which cut off the overflow from Lake Okeechobee) helped do this, as did a network of canals and levees. The result was the creation of many miles of semi-dry land, on 180,000 acres of which U.S. Sugar raised cane—if you'll pardon the pun.

The road through sugar country is in good condition and virtually traffic-free, except for tractors, harvesters, and other field equipment of U.S. Sugar. Although most of the work is accomplished mechanically, not so long ago it was done by Jamaicans and other West Indian laborers. Alec Wilkinson in *Big Sugar* presents a distressful picture of the days when ten thousand black men did the harvesting for U.S. Sugar and the various other companies around Okeechobee's southern flank. It was difficult and dangerous work, for they wielded long, sharp knives to cut the tough cane stalks. Even though they wore metal guards on their shins and knees, one in three would eventually receive a severe cut, either from his own negligence or from the carelessness of a coworker. The temperatures were often stifling, and many workers suffered from heat exhaustion. Once in a while a worker would lose an eye when it was pierced by a sharp cane.

They worked from dawn to dusk, bent over at the waist. Each man was expected to cut eight tons of cane a day, the equivalent of a row the length of eight football fields. This was a ferocious pace that caused their arm and shoulder muscles to ache so badly that by evening some could hardly use their arms. But at dawn they were expected to be back in the fields. If they weren't, they were deported—sometimes without pay. Furthermore, their names were put on a blacklist that would prevent them from being hired again.

The Strange Saga of a Sugar Plant

Driving through cane country on CR 835, which eventually becomes CR 846, you'll see fields in various stages of growth. Some will have sprouts resembling corn, which is not strange since they are both from the same plant family. Many fields during the October through April harvest season will have cane up to fifteen feet high. Close by, you may see a just-cut field where the ground is littered with plant debris and the five-inch stubble that will grow to full-size cane in a year or so. A sugar plant can regenerate itself three or four times after it is first cut. Then it must be plowed under and a new plant started. These new plants come from stalk segments. Each cane is composed of distinct joints where there are small growths called "eyes." To sow a fresh crop, a plant is chopped into eighteen-inch segments, each with an eye, and dropped into eight-inch-deep furrows. The eyes will develop into new plants.

Fire in the Fields

One of the most interesting aspects of sugarcane culture involves burning the fields. This is a spectacular operation performed regularly during harvest time. The purpose is to dispose of the dead leaves so the harvesting machines can collect the cane more efficiently. These fires are fast moving and do not injure the cane. The sugar is affected, however, so the stalks must be delivered to the mill within a week. A good day for burning is one in which the wind is steady yet not so strong the fire cannot be controlled. Nonetheless the company has water wagons standing by at the edge of each burning field just in case.

Controlled flash fires eliminate dead growth while not injuring the sugarcane.

On burn days you'll see smoke rising from various fields. I've stood near a field as a farmhand came by with an apparatus that shot out a thin stream of flammable fluid. As the fluid was ignited by a spark, it exploded into a wall of dancing flame. I could feel the heat, and the air had a sweet odor akin to that of roasting corn. Almost immediately ashes began to cascade about me like dark, powdered sugar. I hunted out a good photo location and snapped a picture. By the time I lowered my camera, the flames were gone, the dead cane leaves were cinders, and the fire had moved on. I had never seen anything so large vanish so quickly.

Cane fires are important events, not only for humans but also for animals. Birds, in particular, seem to sense when conditions are right for a burn. Egrets, bald eagles, and even seagulls from the coast fifty miles away follow the water wagons into the fields. As the fires begin, they descend on the rats, lizards, snakes, and rabbits fleeing from the flames.

An Uncertain Future

U.S. Sugar has been harshly criticized for polluting the Everglades with fertilizer runoffs. These runoffs flow through the small canals and ditches that form an intricate latticework throughout the fields. But the Everglades Forever Act of 1994 required the reduction of runoff fertilizer by half. U.S. Sugar achieved this mainly by cleaning their ditches and depositing the sediment back in their fields. Most of the runoff now stays in the ditches until it is absorbed into the soil. The water that does flow southward does not end up in the Everglades until it has been cleansed in one of the government's six filter marshes.

But the cane fields may not be as permanent as they look. Despite the fact that U.S. Sugar and the other growers have at least partially satisfied the environmentalists, they are under attack from a far different and extremely well financed group of sugar users such as Coca-Cola and Hershey Candy. These corporations would dearly like American sugar to fall to the world price, which is often half as much. American growers say that foreign companies produce sugar so cheaply only by paying slave wages and ignoring environmental concerns. U.S. prices are maintained at their high level by the imposition of Congressional quotas that restrict foreign imports. Should these quotas be removed, many observers believe the U.S. companies would go out of business. If this happens, Clewiston and other communities hereabouts would become virtual ghost towns and the fields would revert to native grasses. The import quotas will be voted on again in 2003. The outcome is up for grabs.

Even if the sugar companies survive this challenge, there is another problem even more serious. That is wind and water. Every time thunderstorms or high winds pass over the cane fields, a thin film of topsoil is carried away. This soil is particularly susceptible to winds, for it is merely the powdery remains of what was muck from the lake bottom. When farming began, this muck was up to six feet in depth. Now there is just one foot left, and already white specks from the limestone bedrock are appearing. When the remaining soil is gone, the show will be over.

The Seminole Wars

After twenty miles, U.S. Sugar's vast domain suddenly gives way to pastures interspersed with occasional citrus groves. When CR 846 meets CR 833, turn left onto 833. In six miles you'll enter the Big Cypress Seminole Reservation. This is a remote part of the peninsula. When the first Seminoles migrated into the Florida territory, none ever dreamed they would end up here.

The Seminoles are not native to Florida. They were actually members of the Georgia-based Creek tribe, and their name means "wild men." They were requested to settle in north Florida by the Spanish after the original mission Indians either died of European diseases or were carted off as slaves by British raiders. After the Spanish sold Florida to the Americans, the new rulers demanded that the Indians move out of the northern territory. The Indians refused. This resulted in the First Seminole War, after which the Indians were forced to migrate to the unpopulated central part of the peninsula around what would become Ocala. The victors assured them they would be left undisturbed in their new homeland.

But the frontier was moving so quickly that in just a few years the government decided the land was too good to be "wasted" on the Indians. When negotiators failed to convince them that they would find the dry plains beyond the Mississippi more to their liking, the Second Seminole War broke out. The Americans thought victory would be as quick as in the first conflict, but they had not counted on such leaders as Osceola. The second war dragged on for seven bloody years. Although the Seminoles fought ferociously, they were driven ever southward. In 1837 the army broke Seminole resistance at the Battle of Okeechobee. Soon thereafter almost all the approximately four thousand Seminoles were packed off to Oklahoma, where most of the tribe remains to this day.

The army didn't bother pursuing the remnant into the Everglades. But a few years later the few remaining Seminoles were goaded into a desperate action called the Third Seminole War. Once more they were defeated, and all except around two hundred joined their unhappy brethren in Oklahoma. With that, the tribal organization in Florida virtually disintegrated.

The Tribe That Almost Wasn't

For the next hundred years, each family tried as best it could to eke out an existence in the inaccessible wetlands or as squatters on wasteland belonging to whites. Others became peddlers along southern Florida highways, selling alligator skins and bird plumes. The young men performed alligator wrestling, although that had never been a traditional Seminole sport. When hand-cranked sewing machines became available, the women used strips of discarded clothing to brighten up their drab wear. This distinctive patchwork garb enhanced the Seminoles' appeal as tourist curiosities.

In the early 1900s the government established three reservations: a small one at Hollywood, Florida, and larger ones at Big Cypress and Brighton. Although the Seminoles now had places in which to live without trespassing on land owned by whites, they were so distrustful of the federal government that for two generations they refused to settle on the reservations. Not until the 1950s did they finally move onto these lands. Now their tribal pride can be seen in their state-of-the-art museum, Ah-Tah-Thi-Ki.

"A Place to Remember"

Ah-Tah-Thi-Ki, which means "a place to learn, a place to remember," is located immediately off CR 833 and is open Tuesdays through Sundays from 9 A.M. to 5 P.M. Admission is $6 for adults and $4 for students.

Before visiting the main area, stop at the five-screen theater for the short orientation film. Then enter the exhibition hall, which is partitioned into three large, though intimate, rooms. The exhibits depict Seminole life as it was a hundred years ago. Aerial photos of long-vanished Seminole camps show thatch-roof chickee huts surrounded

The old life and the new mingle for this young Seminole, who holds a deadly rattlesnake he has just caught at the Big Cypress Reservation.

by banana trees and vegetable plots, with dugout canoes lined up along the encompassing swamp.

Each room emphasizes certain aspects of traditional Seminole life: hunting and gardening in one, camp life in another, and the sacred Green Corn Ceremony in the third. The lights are dim and the ceiling high, and the sounds of wild animals and the calls of exotic birds create the sensation of being outdoors. Life-size manikins make you think a real person is hunting or grinding corn inside a hollowed log. Other manikins are engaged in the Catfish Dance. In this ceremony, a group of chanting men and women waved their arms like fins as they moved slowly forward and backward in a circle to the rhythm of rattles.

Many people are surprised to find such a fine museum so far from the usual traffic lanes. The Seminoles too had many doubts. It took thirty years of planning, pleading, and cajoling by Seminole activists until the museum was finally opened in 1997. It could not have been completed without profits from the tribe's four casinos. For this reason the Seminoles are quick to defend their gaming activities, pointing out that tribal income was scrimping along at just $600,000 a year before gaming revenues shot it up to $3 million!

After leaving the building, take the 1.2-mile boardwalk that leads through a cypress dome. Part way along you'll come to a replica of a Seminole village.

Walter's Watery World: The Billie Swamp Safari

From the museum most visitors continue west a few miles on the side road to the Billie Swamp Safari. This was the dream of James Billie, who as a youth had been taken on many canoeing trips in this sawgrass and cypress wilderness by his grandfather and uncle. After Billie was elected tribal chairman, he decided, as he put it, "to share this place with the world." Under his leadership the forbidding wetland was transformed into a stylized Seminole village.

There are the usual events that appeal to tourists, such as alligator wrestling. Sometimes they don't go as scripted, however. Recently Chief Billie himself, at the age of fifty-five, spontaneously climbed into the ring to wrestle a seven-foot-long alligator. Because he had not indulged in such an activity for ten years, he failed to grab the gator's jaws properly. The alligator clamped down on Billie's right hand and spun him around. Although Billie was able to extricate his hand, he lost one finger in the process. "It didn't hurt that bad," Billie said from the hospital. "The only thing I hurt was my pride." As for

This genial Seminole guide takes visitors on fast-moving adventures in his airboat at the Billie Swamp Safari.

Walter the alligator turns a malicious eye on strangers aboard the Billie Swamp Safari airboat.

his finger, he retrieved it and plans to wear it on a necklace. Will he continue wrestling gators? Of course. So will his four-year-old son.

 The most popular rides at the park are the hour-long swamp safaris in "buggies" specially raised to permit the best viewing. Also popular are the half-hour airboat rides that speed over the saw grass, then glide quietly through the placid water inside a cypress dome. Such a swamp is like no place you've ever seen. The trees grow tall and the water is calm as twilight. Spanish moss drips from the limbs. An eerie silence envelops the area, broken only by birdcalls echoing through the shady corridors. Alligators are at home here, and you'll probably stop a few feet from old Walter, who will regard you malevolently from his mud island. Smaller gators usually swim uncomfortably close to the boat as they snap tidbits the Seminole guide tosses their way. Then the guide will restart the engine, the airplane propeller will whirl to life, and you'll be back in the saw grass that surrounds the dome. It's an experience you'll not forget. (The buggy ride costs $20 for adults and $10 for kids six through twelve. The airboat is $10 for anyone six and up). For food, the Swamp Water Cafe is open between 7:00 A.M. and 8:00 P.M. daily. It serves gator tail nuggets, catfish, and other dishes, both Seminole and American.

Those who crave more are invited to spend the night in a chickee.

Chickee guests can enjoy a sunset canoe paddle or an evening safari in the swamp buggy driving by spotlight, or hear Seminole stories told around a campfire. The chickee costs only $35, so don't expect a private bath or shower. Also, the chickee has no walls, only screening. But that permits guests to fall asleep to the mystical sounds of the swamp. Oh, be sure to bring mosquito repellent. For reservations, call 800-949-6101.

A People Reborn

By heading back to CR 833 and turning south you'll drive through the heart of the reservation. So here's more background information.

In the 1950s the Seminoles were fragmented and leaderless. In fact the tribe was so disorganized that Washington decided to terminate it as a recognized entity. This shocked the Seminoles into setting up a governing body. This council, based at the Hollywood Reservation, consisted of one representative elected from each of the three reservations and a chairman elected by the tribe as a whole.

Although the tribe was thus saved, the conditions at its reservations were harsh. Unemployment was endemic, for local jobs were virtually nonexistent. Many residents survived at a bare subsistence level. Initially everyone lived in chickees—one for sleeping and one for cooking. These chickees consisted merely of a palm-frond roof, dirt floors, and no walls. Thus they afforded little protection during cold snaps or the lashing thunderstorms so common in Florida. The inhabitants slept on mats, which left them exposed to mosquitoes, spiders, and snakes. There was no plumbing and no electricity. The Seminole council could offer no help, for even into the 1960s, when Betty Mae Jumper became the first woman chairman, the treasury had barely $38.

An epochal event occurred when the federal government began building the cement block homes that are so common today. This meant that electricity, plumbing, and running water could be installed. These modern facilities brought a radical change to life on the reservations. Soon radios then televisions made their appearance, bringing an onslaught of white culture that caused a severe strain on the traditional way of life. The new homes also had another unforeseen downside, for the once-gregarious families turned inward, absorbed in their own interests. Betty Mae Jumper recalled that in the years before the block homes "everyone worked together. . . . We would all visit one another, spend time together. Life was hard, but we didn't know the difference. All in all, I really miss those times."

The Modern Osceola: Chief Billie

Another important change came in 1979, when James Billie was elected tribal chairman. Billie was an unusual person. Born from the union of a Seminole woman and a white man, he had the ability to understand both worlds. As a young man he served with the Army in Vietnam. Then he went to college, which was quite rare for a Seminole at that time. With this education, Billie became a respected speaker in the tribal councils and was elected chairman at the age of thirty-five. Almost immediately he took the unheard-of action of transforming the tribe's mild parlor bingo into a high-stakes game designed to bring funds into the rattling Seminole coffers. This was the first such large-scale Indian gaming enterprise. It proved so lucrative that by the end of the century the Seminole casinos at Hollywood, Brighton, Immokalee (forty miles west of Big Cypress), and near Tampa were grossing $100 million yearly. The actual management of the gaming was done largely by professional non-Seminoles operating under supervision of the tribal council.

The Seminoles want to open a huge new casino in Hollywood, Florida, to the tune of a third of a billion dollars. Realizing that it's necessary to have strong political support, the Seminoles have become the sixth-largest soft-money campaign donor in the state. Among all tribes nationally, the Seminole tribe is the top donor.

Not content with his gaming success, Chief Billie moved the tribe into other fields. Two of Billie's most successful enterprises are the Ah-Tah-Thi-Ki Museum and the Swamp Safari. More income is collected from rent on reservation land leased to non-Indian citrus companies. The tribe has also become an important factor in the cattle industry. Billie is even dipping the tribal toe into high tech with the purchase of a small aircraft manufacturing company in Ft. Pierce.

Profits from the various enterprises have enabled the council to give $2,000 a month to every man, woman, and child in the tribe. However, what these enterprises have not done is to provide more than a minimal number of tribal members with employment. The jobs are there, but for a variety of reasons—among them transportation, education, and lack of experience—relatively few Indians have taken them.

The New Seminole War

The tribe has now grown to around twenty-six hundred. The Big Cypress Reservation is "in many ways the spiritual and cultural core of the Seminole tribe," writes Brent Richards Weisman, who did the latest study of the tribe in his book *Unconquered People*. These reservations are virtually independent little entities that in many ways are outside of American life. Tribal ways sometimes even flaunt state law, as in the case of feeding alligators. The council reigns over the reservations largely free from federal controls. The tribe pays no federal or state taxes, although individual Seminoles do pay federal income taxes. The tribe maintains order with its own police force. The school at Big Cypress goes from kindergarten through high school. It is probably the most powerful tool in the preservation of the Seminole culture.

Yet there is a new Seminole War brewing. This does not involve bullets and blood but something even deeper. White civilization may slowly be killing the tribe's culture. Many Indian youths, finding the reservations boring, seek the thrills of Miami and other cities. Ironically, a main factor in holding the tribe together is the lack of higher education, particularly in the field of technology. Thus Seminole youth usually find employment at the entry-level pay scale, which keeps them from being absorbed into the corporate world. The best jobs are furnished by the tribal government itself, and this, in some ways, is for the better, since it promotes a unity that might otherwise be lacking. Such a spirit is very much needed, for the ancient Seminole tongue is rarely used today and the old religion, as typified by the traditional Green Corn Dance, has now largely given way to Christianity.

The Deer Girl

As you head south from Big Cypress on CR 833, a story told by Betty Mae Jumper in *Legends of the Seminoles* may aid in your understanding of the tribe. "The Deer Girl" recalls the times long ago when the tribe held four-day dances in the Big Forest. One evening, as the campfire roared and the turtle shells rattled, a beautiful girl mysteriously emerged from the shadows. All the young braves wanted to dance with her, for she had the loveliest eyes anyone had ever seen. But just before dawn she disappeared into the forest. The next three evenings, however, she returned to join the festivities. On the last night one brave was so in love with her he asked her to marry him. She said, "I can't. I'm different from you." Still, the brave was determined and when she darted into the woods at the evening's end, he followed her. But she was too fast and when daylight came the brave found himself alone in the woods. Then he saw a fawn staring directly at him. And those eyes, such eyes. They were wide as the sky and deep as forest pools. But in their depths there flashed embers like the council fire. As quickly as it came, the fawn disappeared into the forest. The brave stood transfixed. Suddenly he understood the oneness of humans and nature.

Betty Mae Jumper's tales are alive with the spirits that the Seminoles once believed comprised the world around them. There was the Deer Girl, of course, as well as the spirits of the alligator, bobcat, turtle, raccoon, and rabbit, who was the perennial trickster. Jumper tells these stories to the young whenever she can. And they are fascinated by them. While she lives, the stories of the Deer Girl and the others will haunt the forest. But she is old, and soon her voice will be stilled. Will the spirits die with her?

The Strange Cypress Domes

County Road 833 south from the Big Cypress Reservation traverses Seminole cattle country. The grasses are specially planted nutritious varieties that have replaced their tough wild

Cypress domes mingle with fine grazing land on the Seminoles'
Big Cypress Reservation.

cousins, which would have eliminated profitable beef production. The land is very flat, for it was once part of the Everglades. The surface water has been largely drained by canals like the one that parallels the road. You'll notice periodic cypress domes. They were formed in the watery pockets that resulted when segments of the underlying limestone dissolved. The largest cypress trees grow in the deeper water in the center of the near-circular depressions. As the depressions become shallower toward the edges, the trees become smaller. The interiors of these domes are shady, watery worlds.

Gateway to the Everglades: Alligator Alley

In fourteen miles you'll reach Interstate 75, also called Alligator Alley. This strange nickname dates to the days when the Florida legislature was debating the feasibility of constructing an expressway through the Everglades. The opposition derided the proposed road as nothing but an alley for alligators. Oddly enough, the derogatory name Alligator Alley had a strange appeal that provided the roadway with a personality all its own, so proponents adopted it. It's even possible that the nickname helped inspire planners to include the scenic turnouts and boat ramps that are so unusual for an expressway.

These turnouts allow travelers to enjoy views of the boundless sawgrass wetland. Each turnout provides informative leaflets pointing out that, although the expanse looks barren of life, it is filled with animals. Alligators are there, of course. They often appear around the boat ramps built for people who want to fish or hunt. Because these ramps are also popular with snails and crawfish, they are favorite pantries for wood storks, great blue  herons, white ibis, and other wading birds. River otters, raccoons, snakes, and an occasional deer also make their appearance here.

The water is not stagnant but part of the immense drainage system that extends from the Kissimmee wetlands and through Lake Okeechobee to Florida Bay. This water flows in a wide sheet usually less than a foot deep. Although it averages a mere hundred feet a day, this is enough to justify the Everglades being called the River of Grass.

Burning the Glades

Looking out toward the horizon, you may see smoke. This is probably a fire set by rangers. Many people are surprised to learn that the glades can actually burn. During the periodic droughts, the glades dry out. At this time fires are essential, for they not only consume dead debris that would otherwise clog the water flow, they also provide the ashes that furnish nutrients for proper plant growth. Don't worry that the fires will injure the saw grass, for their buds are buried deep in the soil, well protected by overlapping leaf insulation. The animals also survive: the mammals find safety in the forested hammock islands, the alligators in the remaining spaces of open water, and the fish in the hollowed recesses of the underlying limestone.

 Soon you'll come to the Miami Canal, which connects Lake Okeechobee with the Miami River. There is a good-size recreation area and other facilities here. Not far beyond, take the US 27 exit going south.

The Terminators

US 27 pushes through a dense wall of low trees with silver-gray trunks and shaggy bark. When planted singly, these trees present a pleasing appearance. But *en masse* they have a sinister aspect. These are the dreaded melaleuca, also known as the "Everglades Terminators."

The melaleuca arrived from Australia, where their rapid growth provided a quick source of lumber. In Florida they were welcomed for their prodigious thirst, which made them perfect candidates to dry up the Everglades and thus enable it to be turned into productive farm-land. Such was their absorption rate that a single acre of melaleuca could consume twenty-two hundred gallons in a single hour. With no enemies in America, melaleuca could be killed only by severe and prolonged freezes, by which southern Florida was rarely bothered.

So the melaleuca were planted along the edges of the Everglades, where they proceeded to work diligently at their assigned task. At first the going was slow, for the Everglades was so very wide and they were so few. People tended to forget about them. Yet they multiplied . . . and multiplied. By the time the environmental movement took root in the 1970s and naturalists began to appreciate the uniqueness of the Everglades, the melaleuca had gained strength. Soon it was clear that they were gaining momentum at a frightening pace.

Unfortunately the melaleuca are probably in the Everglades to stay. The trees cannot be flooded out. And fires only cause their seeds to open more quickly. Poisons will kill individual trees, but the seeds remain. Frantically seeking to control the melaleuca, scientists examined the snout beetle from Australia. After spending five years in tests and observation, the U.S. Department of Agriculture concluded that these insects thrived on melaleuca and no other plants. They were released into the Everglades in 1997, so now we hope they're chowing down on savory melaleuca. But they have an awful lot of eating to do. And if they should consume all the melaleuca, will the beetles be content to meekly die out? Or will we have unleashed a new monster?

There's no need to worry yet. You'll probably look in vain for signs that the snouts are banqueting along US 27. But remember, it took a while for the melaleuca itself to get started.

Merlin's Castle

Fourteen miles from I-75, the road splits, with US 27 going left and SR 997 going right. Take the state route and continue south. You'll be paralleling one of the many levees that guide the water through the Everglades. Since this is a protected area where development is prohibited, you'll undoubtedly enjoy its wild aspect. That is, until you come to the garish, ten-story hotel and gambling casino at the corner of US 41, the famed Tamiami Trail. You may mumble unkind words about the avaricious white developers who are wrecking the grassy paradise so treasured by the Indians. But if you do, your unkind thoughts will be misguided, for this is Indian land and the building is the pride of the Miccosukee tribe.

The Miccosukee Gaming Resort seems out of place in the Everglades.

The Forgotten Miccosukees

The Miccosukee tribe was closely associated with the Seminoles during the three wars that pushed them successively southward. By the time American troops had completed their mission, the Miccosukees were reduced to fifty destitute individuals existing in the most hostile portion of the Everglades. Although they thought they were safe in their extreme isolation, they did not take into account the relentless spread of civilization, culminating in the construction of the Tamiami Trail directly through their watery realm in 1928. As white travelers began appearing, the Miccosukee turned to selling handicrafts, bird plumes, alligator skins, and other exotic goods along the highway. Soon they became known as Trail Indians.

The Miccosukee became formally recognized as a tribe in the 1960s by the federal government, which classified it as something called a "sovereign, domestic dependent nation." No one really knew how a group that was "sovereign" could also be "dependent." This is a special concern of the State of Florida, which is engaged in a lengthy court battle to determine whether the Miccosukees are a dependency subject to state jurisdiction or whether, as the tribe contends, it is a sovereign nation subject only to the international agreements it makes directly with Washington. If that sounds very highfalutin, you can boil it down to whether the tribe's lucrative gambling operation violates Florida law.

Elusive Riches

Whatever the outcome, the Miccosukee Resort and Convention Center is an impressive place. Rising like a magician's apparition, it is of mountainous size, especially given the flatlands that surround it. As you enter the lobby, one of the first things you'll notice will be the Miccosukee logo in the floor. It is a round design with four concentric rings of yellow, red, black, and white. In the center is a chickee. On the outer ring are the words "Miccosukee Tribe of Indians of Florida." Interestingly, they refer to themselves as Indians, not Native Americans.

 You'll enjoy spending the night in this brand new building, where everything sparkles. The room rates are between $105 and $175 (depending on the season) and include a full breakfast. All guests are provided with a message from Billy Cypress, chairman of the tribe, which now numbers six hundred. Billy expresses the hope that your stay will be a "fantastic entertainment experience" and that you "will return again and again to share our warm hospitality." But if you look for Miccosukees to thank for their "warm hospitality," you'll be hard put to find any, for the tribe has wisely hired professionals to manage and run the operations. Perhaps it is the tribe who should thank the patrons for *their* warm hospitality, since Miccosukee coffers ring with the profits from the gaming as well as from the 8.75% tax it adds on to the room rates. This take runs into the millions and enables the tribe to build new homes and provide a health clinic, a school, and its own police force.

Even if you do not consider losing money to be entertainment, you should at least make a slow circuit through the huge gaming hall that takes up nearly the entire ground-floor lobby. It's a masterpiece of what some might call the "art-decadent" style. Supporting the ceiling are massive pillars accented by amber lights with glowing neon strips of lavender. One section of carpeting is bright green with red, black, and yellow designs. Another is a violent red with blue accents. The air vibrates with loud sounds that could be music. Whatever, it's a mind-numbing dissonance apparently intended to imbue gamblers with a sense of unreality in which their money loses substance and flows as easily as quicksilver.

There is row after row of gaming machines—one thousand of them. They may look like slots—and many people call them that—but they are not, for slots are against the law. Instead they are officially known as "video pull-tabs," and the games are called a variety of lotto, which is legal. There are also poker tables—fifty-eight of them.

Because the gambling goes on twenty-four hours a day, the same bizarre lights and insane music that were flashing and blaring when you went to bed will welcome you when you enter the lobby in the morning. Some gamblers were probably there all night, for the delicatessen serves food and the Cypress Lounge presents entertainment all day and night.

It will probably be with relief that you'll drive out of the parking lot and turn west on the Tamiami Trail (US 41), where the colors are muted and the music is from birds, not machines.

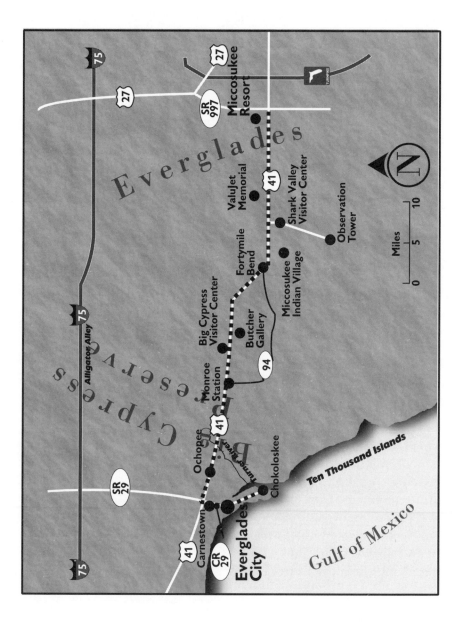

Across Glades and Swamps
Miccosukee Resort to Everglades City • 78 Backroad Miles

The Song of the Road: Overview

Slow travel through the Everglades and the adjoining Big Cypress Swamp on the Tamiami Trail (US 41) can be a memorable experience. The Everglades saw grass is an awesome sight, stretching from horizon to horizon like a shag carpet. There is a fearsome aspect to such a grassland, as you'll see when you stand before the memorial to the 110 passengers who died on the ValuJet plane swallowed by the saw grass several years ago. Farther down the Tamiami Trail, at the Shark Valley station of Everglades National Park, you'll be able to ride an open-air tram out into the saw grass past alligators to a fifty-foot-high observation tower. For an additional experience you can board a Miccosukee airboat that almost flies through the Glades.

Continuing westward, you'll enter the Big Cypress Swamp. Here you can visit the gallery of Clyde Butcher, whose huge black-and-white photographic landscapes are renowned. Farther down the Tamiami Trail, the Big Cypress Visitor Center will introduce you to the unusual array of plants and animals that inhabit the swamp. The museum also provides a wide variety of hiking and educational programs.

The Everglades and Big Cypress are virtually uninhabited, except for scattered Miccosukee villages. The only town is Everglades City, which, despite its high-sounding name, has a population of considerably fewer than a thousand. The town's broad streets and rehabbed buildings date back to when it was the headquarters of Barron Collier, whose money and persistence were major factors in the completion of this part of the Tamiami Trail. Everglades City is also the location of the Gulf Coast Visitor Center, part of the Everglades National Park. From here you can take boat trips into the extensive mangrove islands that make up the Ten Thousand Islands. Everglades City also has fine restaurants and highly rated overnight accommodations.

On the Road Again

This exploration begins at the junction of Florida's Turnpike and US 41. By driving west on US 41, you'll pass through thick growths of the melaleuca trees that are rapidly encroaching on the Everglades. In six miles you'll reach the Miccosukee Resort, where, if you took the previous exploration, you may have spent the night— and possibly some dollars. Ahead lies the famed Everglades. Today the road is broad and well traveled, but when it was constructed as the Tamiami Trail, it was a lonely path formed from limestone blasted out of the bedrock.

Determination and Dynamite: Building the Tamiami Trail

The idea of a road between Tampa and Miami through the Everglades was scoffed at when it was first proposed. Even the name "Tamiami" was ridiculed as bumping along like a string of tin cans attached to a dog's tail. Not only would the engineering present tremendous problems, but the financing would be almost as difficult. The goal was to have each community pay for the portion traversing its area. Tampa and Miami were able to meet their quotas, and initial steps for construction were taken in 1915.

Once the supplies, equipment, and workers were assembled, work began. The road-building crews operated with the efficiency of a Ford assembly line. First came the rod men, who cut their way through the vegetation with machetes, then drove stakes into the ground every hundred yards to mark the center of the road. Behind them a crew laid rails for the drilling machine. This machine had three pneumatic drills spaced six feet apart that penetrated twelve feet into the limestone bedrock. It would move ahead only six feet before stopping to dig new holes. The drills made so much noise that it's said the men operating them nearly went deaf.

After the holes were dug, blasting crews inserted narrow pipes into them, pumped out the water, and inserted up to forty sticks of dynamite. More than two and a half million sticks were used on just a single thirty-one-mile section. Each blast sent rocks spewing high into the air and opened the way for the dredges. These dredges ran on rails and were wide enough to straddle the twenty-foot blasting area. They scooped out the debris and piled it up to form the roadbed. The excavation, which quickly filled with water, became a canal that was then used by supply barges. The supplies needed were considerable, for the machines at the "front" required ten thousand gallons of gasoline each week, to say nothing of oil and spare parts.

Once the rocks had been piled, grading crews flattened the rocky roadbed using motorized "skimmers," forerunners of bulldozers.

When the bed was level and smooth, it was asphalted. Despite the coordination and efficiency, the operation moved ahead barely a mile and a half per month. Thus thirteen grueling years passed before the Tamiami Trail was completed.

The Everglades Forever?

The Everglades today is far different from what it was when the Tamiami Trail first penetrated this wild and beautiful wilderness. It is far different, even, from when Marjory Stoneman Douglas published her epochal book, *The Everglades: River of Grass*, in 1947. In it she wrote eloquently about the unobstructed, windswept hinterland she had grown to love, respect, and hold in wonder: "The saw grass, pale green to deep-brown ripeness, stands rigid. It is moved only in sluggish rollings by the vast push of the winds across it. . . . The bristling, blossoming tops do not bend easily . . . but stand in edged clumps . . . all the massed curving blades making millions of fine arching lines that at a little distance merge into a huge expanse of brown wires."

Today, as you drive along this part of the Tamiami Trail, the view Douglas described is gone, for a long levee will block your view to the north and a mishmash of scrubby trees and bushes will obscure it to the south. This is the result of a policy adopted by the Army Corps of

Control dams regulate the flow of water through the Everglades. Many will be removed under the restoration plan.

Engineers in the 1950s and '60s, when it constructed 1,000 miles of such levees, another 1,000 miles of canals, 150 control dams, and 16 major pump stations. The object was to prevent flooding, but the disruption of the sheet-flow water, upon which the saw grass thrived, led to the invasion of intrusive plants such as melaleuca, groves of which are visible to the south. Invasive plants are active in a third of the Everglades—and spreading fast.

Marjory Douglas complained vigorously against the policies of the Army Corps in an addendum to her book twenty-five years later. As she saw it, the Corps' focus seemed to be "getting the water off the land as quickly as possible to meet the demands for immediate speculative development." She voiced her displeasure over the expansion of the highly fertilized sugar farms around Lake Okeechobee, over the continued blocking of water flow by the Tamiami Trail, over the deepening of major canals such as the St. Lucie and Caloosahatchee (which diverted even more water from the Everglades), and particularly over the conversion of the pollutant-filtering Kissimmee River into the pollutant-carrying Canal 38.

Despite Douglas' highly publicized warnings, it wasn't until 1994 that Florida passed the Everglades Forever Act. This law envisioned the cleanup to cost around $685 million, to be shared equally by the state and the sugar growers. The restoration effort was to be spread over twenty years. But it was quickly apparent that the money allotted under Florida's program was pitifully insufficient. The job was so huge that aid from the federal government was needed. Thus in the fall of 1994 the revamped Army Corps of Engineers conducted a series of public meetings in south Florida to get feedback from the general public as well as from experts in all fields. Five years later the Corps came up with a new twenty-year cleanup program that would cost a jaw-dropping $8 billion! The federal government would pay half, and the state and the South Florida Water Management district would share the other half.

This plan involves projects on many fronts. In order to obtain more liquid for the Everglades, water that formerly emptied into the ocean will be stored in reserves to be constructed in the Kissimmee basin, around the St. Lucie and Caloosahatchee Canals, and within the Everglades itself. Additional water will be routed into great underground "bubbles" of the Florida aquifer. During droughts, this "new water" will be used to replenish the Everglades.

In order to improve the flow of water across the Everglades, more than 240 miles of canals and levees will be removed. One of the waterways to be filled will be a major portion of the Miami Canal, constructed in the early twentieth century to help dry out the Everglades and turn it into farmland. Another part of the project will eliminate the twenty-mile levee along the Tamiami Trail, elevate the highway, and install a series of low bridges to allow unrestricted flow of water southward. In order to facilitate this sheet flow, the overgrown canal along the southern side of the Tamiami will be eliminated.

Even with all its research and extensive consultation with the South Florida Water Management District and other state and federal agencies, the Corps warns that "this plan does not provide all the answers." It is a huge project—"the greatest environmental restoration effort ever undertaken in the world," said the president of the Florida Audubon Society. Many unforeseen factors will emerge as the environment is altered. It will be slow, but there will certainly be improvement if funds continue to be made available. These funds will depend on Congress, the Florida legislature, and, ultimately, continued public support. For south Floridians, who will benefit the most, the cost will figure out around $19 per person per year. For other Floridians the cost will be around $7 yearly. For Americans outside of Florida it will be about 77 cents. Can you afford it?

The Spirits Are Angry: The ValuJet Crash

A dozen or so miles into the Everglades you'll see a series of low block columns on the north across the old construction canal. This is the memorial to the victims of a crash in 1996 that killed the entire crew and all the passengers of ValuJet Flight 592. To reach the memorial, cross over a control dam and take the short road beside the levee. While the memorial is not particularly impressive from US 41, once you stand beside it, it takes on an entirely different aspect. There are 110 columns, each about the width of a human body, arranged in aisles—just as on a plane. They are set on a triangular foundation whose apex points northward into the Everglades, toward the place where the plane crashed about eight miles distant. The columns are tallest at the center and become shorter as they reach the apex—just as the angle of a diving plane. The shadows cast by the columns are long, bleak, and sad.

There was no premonition of tragedy when Flight 592 roared down the runway at Miami International Airport. No one knew that in the cargo hold were more than a hundred unauthorized oxygen

The ValuJet Memorial presents a simple yet evocative tribute to the 110 passengers aboard Flight 592 who died in a 1996 crash.

canisters, many of which did not have the safety caps that prevent accidental ignition. Just six minutes into the air some of the canisters caught fire, fueled by the tires stowed next to them. Heavy smoke began seeping into the passenger cabin. The pilot, "Candi" Kubeck, desperately tried to turn back, but her effort was too late. Passengers screamed as flames shot into the cabin. Quickly the heat became so intense that the aluminum supports for at least one of the passenger seats turned molten. But by then most of the passengers had died. Five minutes after the fire broke out the plane crashed into the saw grass.

The search for remains began immediately. The crash site was accessible only by a one-lane road along a levee. The land around the memorial site became a virtual city of tents, trailers, command posts, and canteens. There was a jumble of hastily assembled fire and police vehicles, telephone cars, power trucks, fuel tankers, backhoes, and, most ominous of all, morgue vans. Communication antennas rose like a forest. Reporters scrambled about, trying to glean information they could relay to listeners tuned in on every network.

Meanwhile, out in the saw grass, the crews started the gruesome search for bodies and parts of bodies. The saw grass rose head high, each blade serrated and sharp as a butcher's knife. Alligators hovered about, ugly reminders that others besides humans were looking for the remains. Lightning often flashed dangerously from dark, passing thunderstorms. Meanwhile the temperature rose into the nineties, and the glaring sun almost broiled the polyethylene-suited men moving in weary search lines through the muck. "There is nothing fragile about the endangered Everglades," one worker complained. "It is an indomitable, unyielding enemy." To those who knew Indian lore, it was not surprising. The spirits who dwell in the Everglades were angry. They had shown their power.

Although much of the metallic wreckage was found, the warm soupy water quickly dissolved human flesh until the workers could barely stand the odor of putrefaction. When it was all over several weeks later, not one intact body was recovered and the remains of only thirty-six people could even be identified. The rest had become part of the Everglades for eternity.

The memorial is usually quiet, for few remember yesterday's tragedies. But the husbands and wives and children of the victims remember—they will forever. The memorial is all they have. One hundred fifty of them gathered here at the dedication in 1999, some from as far away as Italy. You probably won't see any of them, but you may find evidence that they have been here—a bouquet of faded flowers, a note taped to a column, a stuffed teddy bear. Yes, they've been here.

A Voyage on the Sea of Saw Grass

Because the dike ends at the ValuJet Memorial, from there the vista opens up all the way to the Everglades National Park's Shark Valley Information Center six miles farther down the Tamiami Trail. The entry fee is $8 per car, which entitles you to hike along a paved road into the Glades or to pedal a rental bike for $4.25 per hour. If neither of these appeals to you, however, and you don't wish to take the tram ride described below, there's not much reason to pay the entry fee. The park has no museum and no restaurant.

The park's two-hour, fifteen-mile, open-air tram ride will probably be the highlight of your passage through the Glades. During the ride a park ranger will give you information you probably could not learn on your own. For example, did you know that a common scum called *periphyton* is actually a complex association of numerous types of algae, which provide nutrients for snails, small fish, and many other tiny creatures that are themselves essential components of the

Everglades' complex food chain? Try mentioning *periphyton* among your friends and see how learned you'll seem.

The ride costs $10 for adults and $5.50 for kids twelve and under and usually leaves at 9:30 and 11:00 A.M. and 1:00 and 3:00 P.M. (Call 305-221-8455 for exact times.) Although mosquitoes can be an uncomfortable distraction, you'll be happy to know they have their own problems, for their larvae make juicy meals for a host of creatures delighted to find them wiggling in the water.

The tram will take you down a roadway originally built in the 1940s by an oil company to one of its drilling sites. You'll probably come across alligators sunning themselves on the pavement. When you do, the tram usually stops for photograph taking. But don't get too close, or the gators will slide into the saw grass and vanish. They live and breed in the Glades. Here they construct two-foot-high nesting sites where they lay between twenty and fifty eggs. The temperature in the nest determines the sex of the newborn gators. It may not surprise you to discover that the eggs at the top, being hotter, become males.

In the Everglades a few inches of elevation make a world of difference. Although saw grass is the dominant plant, a very slight depression will result in a clump of small trees called a willow-head. On the other hand, a slight rise will allow a hardwood hammock to thrive.

The tram's main destination is a fifty-foot tower with a spiral ramp to the summit. The view from the top, or from almost any portion of the ramp, is, well, inspiring. Saw grass reaches from horizon to horizon in a variegated mosaic of olives, tans, and browns. Speckled here and there are bright green hammocks composed mostly of cabbage palms. The landscape seems to shimmer in the sunshine as air currents flicker across it. Here you can appreciate Marjory Stoneman Douglas' description of the Everglades: "Nothing anywhere else is like them: their vast glittering openness, wider than the enormous visible round of the horizon, the racing free saltiness and sweetness of their massive winds under the dazzling blue heights of space."

But the Everglades of today is a pitiful emptiness compared with what Douglas described more than five decades ago. Then, birds by the thousands whitened the cobalt skies. Today few remain. Will the Glades under its new management policy be able to bring them back? Stay tuned.

*The Miccosukee Tribe offers airboat rides into the Everglades
as well as a visit to one of their traditional villages.*

Another Way of Life: The Miccosukee Village

A half-mile farther west of Shark Valley on the Tamiami you'll
come to the Miccosukee Indian Village. During the disastrous
wars with the United States in the first half of the 1800s, the tribe was
closely allied with the more numerous Seminoles. For many years
after their defeat, the Miccosukee remnant managed to exist by
peddling bird feathers, animal skins, and native handicrafts along the
Tamiami Trail, where they were known as "Trail Indians." Today the
tribe, which numbers around six hundred, is thriving, due mainly to
their lucrative casino nineteen miles east of here.

The village may seem to be a tourist trap, but because the
Miccosukees are justly wary of white people as they recall the
empty promises of yore, this is probably the closest you'll get to
seeing their way of life. Some Indians do really live here and the
village itself is said to pre-date the Tamiami Trail. So pay your $5 fee
($3.50 for kids five through twelve) and try to be satisfied. A guide
will tell you about the Indian way of life, and craftsmen and
craftswomen will demonstrate wood carving, basket weaving, and
other arts. There are some alligator wrestling shows, which the

tribesmen have been doing for tourists ever since the Tamiami Trail opened. There is also a gift shop where you can purchase Miccosukee

patchwork as well as items made by Cherokees and Navajos. In the restaurant you can surprise your taste buds with alligator tail.

Incidentally, don't call the Miccosukees Seminoles. They are a completely separate tribe and resent being lumped together with their more numerous rivals.

The Miccosukees also offer exciting airboat rides into the saw grass at speeds high enough to make your eyes water. It costs $10 for a half-hour ride, but the experience will be something you'll recall with pleasure for a long time.

Introduction to the Big Cypress Swamp

The landscape changes radically after you pass what is known as Fortymile Bend, not far beyond the Miccosukee tribal headquarters, for suddenly you've entered the Big Cypress Preserve. The water here differs from the Everglades in that it lacks the steady flow in which saw grass thrives. Instead, it rests quietly in this large basin thirty miles wide by forty miles long. This permits cypress seedlings to germinate.

These dwarf cypress may be more than a hundred years old. The rocks in the foreground were probably dynamited from the bedrock during construction of the Tamiami Trail.

The Big Cypress Swamp is far different from the Everglades, which it adjoins.

Few environments can match the beauty and diversity of the Big Cypress, which is technically known as a swamp. There are several distinct plant communities in the preserve. Predominant are the prairies, where cattails, various reeds, and some saw grass extend for miles. Scattered throughout these prairies are pond cypress—not the towering forms, but a dwarf variety. Pine forests make up a second community. They thrive where the land is somewhat higher—sometimes only a foot or even less makes all the difference.

A third group of plants exists in the strands that you'll pass soon. These strands are shallow channels several miles wide through which surplus water drains during the heavy summer rains. Most of the time, however, the strands remain swampy, allowing the growth of imposing bald cypress, lofty royal palms, and lacy ferns, some ten feet tall. There are colors aplenty in the strands, from soft grays to pale buffs, as well as crimson splashes from bromeliad air plants. Orchids, too—some found no place else on earth—add to the palette.

The Wet and Wonderful World of Clyde Butcher

But sometimes color can detract from the essence of a scene. This is the philosophy of black-and-white photographer Clyde Butcher, whose gallery in a lovely swamp setting beside the Tamiami Trail is

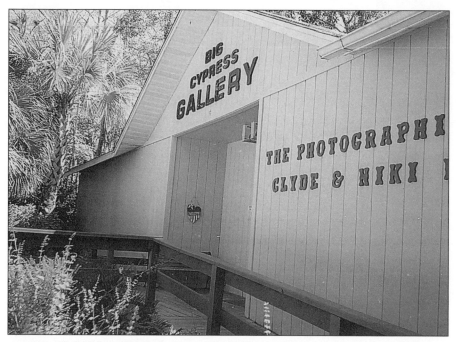

A stop at Clyde Butcher's gallery to view his black-and-white photographs is a highlight of the drive along the Tamiami Trail.

open Wednesdays through Saturdays between 10:00 A.M. and 5:00 P.M. Each Butcher photo is so vivid and precise, it feels as if one could walk right into it. Most are scenes from the Big Cypress Swamp and the Everglades. Butcher captures the interplay of light and shadows in stark contrasts and subtle nuances. Each photograph has a mood of its own: some are placid, some threatening, some almost quiver with the unexpected. You see an endless array of forms that are the essence of each subject. He likes to produce his photos on a grand scale. "Large images," he says, "necessitate that people experience the place depicted, and see it with new and clearer eyes." If you have never realized the simple beauty of tree limbs, trunks, grass spikes, and still water, you will after viewing Butcher's photos. And there are clouds that seem so substantial you could squeeze them as if they were wet sponges. He does not take pictures. He creates encounters with nature.

Butcher delights in seeking out subjects in unusual places. Sometimes he'll tramp through a steamy, sun-seared prairie. Other times he'll paddle deep into a swamp, don hip boots, and set up his tripod in the water itself. He rarely gets birds in his photos, for by the time he has selected his subject and assembled his paraphernalia, the birds have long since flown to a less thrashing locale. Once such a picture is taken, Butcher then has to free himself from the mud. He tells of the time he reached down to loosen his boots and his wedding ring slipped off. He never recovered it. But to make the best of it, he captioned the photo: "Thar's gold in that thar swamp."

Although admission to the gallery is free, Butcher's work commands high prices. To take home a sixteen-by-twenty-inch photo, be prepared to shell out more than $400. If you want something larger, a five-foot-by-nine-foot, framed masterpiece may cost well over $5,000. But just in case you find these eye-popping prices intimidating, you can settle for an oversized postcard reproduction for $2.50.

Clyde Butcher has not always been this successful. He has had a long and rocky life. Born in 1953, the only child of an itinerant metal worker, he grew up in trailer camps around the Midwest. Although he went to California Polytechnic University, where he concentrated on architecture, he was basically a loner—more at home on his motorcycle than with crowds of fellow students. Nonetheless he attracted the attention of Niki Vogel, whose parents were put off by his unconventional lifestyle and unkempt appearance. But Niki was intrigued by a man in whom she saw romance and adventure. Quitting college, she married him at the age of eighteen. Clyde himself was barely twenty.

Life together in the San Francisco area was hardly a romantic adventure. Niki took such jobs as telephone operator and bank teller to help support them while Clyde tried to find his niche. The birth of two babies, Jackie and Ted, did not help their financial situation.

The Butcher family moved to Ft. Myers, Florida, in 1980. Here Clyde began peddling his photos at art and craft shows. Sometimes he drove a small, borrowed motor home. When Niki and the kids came along, the family's meals often consisted of bread and peanut butter. They managed to survive, barely.

But the worst was to come when their seventeen-year-old son, Ted, was killed by a drunken driver. Just days later, Clyde's father, who had doted on Ted, suddenly took ill and died. At about the same time, Niki's father told them he had cancer.

This series of tragedies affected Butcher deeply, causing him to reexamine his life. His epiphany came in a whirl of dizziness, then "in its place was a vision, a web of infinitely subtle form and variety," wrote his biographers in *Seeing the Light*. "In a stroke, he knew exactly how to capture it all, exactly what to do for the rest of his life."

Dumping all his color photos, he vowed to do his work in black and white from then on and to concentrate on the swamp and the Glades. He felt that he had been given a mission by a force beyond understanding, a force that some might call God.

He was warned that black and white photos wouldn't sell. But at the next art show, people flocked to his booth. And when it was over he received the blue ribbon award. As his popularity grew, he decided to set up his own gallery. Niki was instrumental in getting an irascible old hermit to sell them his dilapidated roadside stand beside the Tamiami Trail in the Big Cypress Swamp. Again the Butchers felt as if they were being guided by some mysterious destiny, for an old surveyor's stake designated the site as T11786. To the Butchers the T1 was for Ted; 17 was his age when he died; and 86 was the year of his death.

The gallery opened in 1993, and today the Butchers are at last able to pursue their life's mission: to capture the beauty, majesty, and, yes, spirituality, of the south Florida wilderness. Clyde uses a special, wide-angle lens camera with a bent bellows to photograph scenes twice as wide as an average camera, with no distortions toward the edges. He has closed his lens to pinhole size in order to have long exposures that record the most minute details.

So when you enter his modest gallery, take the time to scrutinize each of the almost life-size photographs. When you do, you're likely to find yourself in the swamp, or amid the saw grass, or on a cypress knoll with a rack of clouds rising above you like another continent. Then, for a moment, you'll know what Clyde Butcher is all about.

An Environment under Stress

For many years few people realized this swamp was just as threatened as the Everglades. Thus there was almost no opposition when, during the late 1940s and early 1950s, loggers began cutting down the great bald cypress trees, whose six-hundred-year-old trunks were ideal for everything from home siding to coffins. The logging companies ran roads and railroad spurs far out into the hinterland. As the felled trees were dragged to loading areas, smaller trees in the path were destroyed. Then, with the protective shade gone, the ground became parched during the winter dry season, and much of the remaining vegetation died from either lack of water or the wildfires that now began to rage.

Even worse times were apparently on the way when, in 1966, the Gulf American Corporation began promoting Big Cypress land for residential development. In order to increase the area available for housing, the company was planning a system of drainage canals to lower the water table. One canal was actually built, causing several wildfires to sweep over the dried-out area. Another danger came from a government agency, which announced plans for the construction of a jetport at the swamp's eastern edge. Under these threats the Big Cypress National Preserve was formed in 1974. Today all plants and animals within this preserve are protected by federal law—although fishing and hunting are permitted under state and federal regulations.

The Big Cypress Visitor Center

The Big Cypress Visitor Center is a mile or so beyond Butcher's gallery. It is located at what was once a landmark: the midway point between Naples and Miami. While not large, the Visitor Center will help orient you to the swamp world. Certainly the most eye-catching display is the mounted panther that was killed by a car not long ago. This was a young animal and its death was a real loss, for there are only a dozen or so Florida panthers left in Big Cypress—and only four or five dozen more in the entire state. The local panthers are not as healthy as the others, for deer hunting has reduced their food supply. Inbreeding is also a problem. Wildlife officials had hoped to alleviate this problem by breeding the panthers with eight female Texas cougars introduced into the territory in 1995.

The Texas cougar episode has become a comedy of errors. Although the program was so successful that within a few years there were three dozen hybrid offspring, suddenly state and federal officials realized that such a massive hybridization would eventually eliminate the pure Florida panther. To that end they implanted birth control devices in the cougars and their hybrids and then asked Texas to take back the original cougars. But Texas didn't want them! So most of the cougars have been removed from Florida and placed in zoos around the country.

The Visitor Center has a menu of programs including free one-hour walks on the Florida Scenic Trail. There are end-of-the-week evening campfire talks (often illustrated with slides) and for those who want to meet the swamp more personally, there is a rugged two-and-a-half-hour hike. For this activity be sure to wear tough pants to blunt the rasping saw grass and shoes that can take mud. Accept the possibility that you might have to slosh through water waist high. After all, this *is* a swamp. Plenty of bug repellent is also a necessity. If you're interested, call 813-695-4111—you'll need to make reservations a couple of weeks in advance.

As you leave the Visitor Center, take a moment to examine the stones that form the building's outdoor walls. You'll see in them thousands of fossil shells from creatures that lived here when this was a shallow sea.

The Florida Mounted Police

Back on US 41, you'll soon pass Gannet Strand, outlined by a thick row of trees that stands out starkly from the grassy prairie and the dwarf cypress dotting it. Swamp water oozing through this elongated depression during the rainy season allowed organic materials to form a mucky pudding that once enabled large bald cypress to thrive in it. But most of these cypress trees are gone now, having fallen to the loggers' saws.

In a few miles you'll come to the Monroe Strand, where you'll be greeted by a dilapidated building dating back to the era when it was occupied by Florida's mounted police. But the mounts these men rode consumed gasoline, not hay, for they were motorcycles. In the days when the Tamiami Trail was just a lonely gash in the wilderness, similar stations were built every ten or so miles in Collier County. Here grateful motorists could purchase fuel, food, and drink. From each station, a Mountie patrolled his section of the highway on the lookout for stranded motorists rather than crooks.

Swampy Landscapes

As you continue along the Tamiami, notice mangroves growing densely beside the canal. These plants are only bush-size, for mangroves prefer a more salty environment. Their prop roots stand out as thick, grayish tubular fingers extending into the water to grasp the muck beneath. They provide shelter for an entire universe of tiny creatures that live their lives unseen by humans.

Soon you'll pass the Turner River Canal, head of a canoe trail that leads down the river to Chokoloskee Bay. The Seminoles once had an encampment here. Preserve rangers often conduct two-hour hikes along the Turner River Road. Call the Big Cypress Visitor Center for times and days.

Three miles farther west you'll come to Ochopee, which consists of a spot on the map and a post office that isn't much larger. In fact it's the smallest post office in the entire U.S.A. Yet Ochopee didn't start out that way. The name means "big field," recalling plans to turn the surrounding area into a major agricultural district. The mammoth tomato farm that was started here upon the completion of the Tamiami Trail was thought to be the harbinger of future greatness. Ochopee reached its peak in 1935, when it contained several workers' barracks, stables for plow horses, two packinghouses, and three commissaries. But the soil would not support agriculture and eventually about all that remained was the lonesome, capsule-size post office.

Just beyond Ochopee is Seagrape Drive, a short road that ends at the Halfway Creek Canoe Trail. To enjoy the trail, you must have your own canoe. A mile west you will come to Carnestown, where there is a typical Chamber of Commerce Visitor Center, meaning it is loaded with leaflets from every purveyor of lodging, meals, and recreational activities within a radius of one light-year. Despite the overwhelming amount of bright and useless literature, a few actually contain valuable information about Everglades City. Your assignment, should you choose to accept it, is to find them.

The 1923 Trailblazers

Pause for a few moments at Carnestown and look down the paved road over which you have just come. Now consider the view that presented itself to a motorcade of nine autos carrying twenty businessmen and adventurers who arrived at this point in 1923. They had just traveled seventy bumpy miles over a mostly shell road from Ft. Myers. But that had been the easiest part of their journey. For the road ended here and before them stretched a row of surveyors' stakes marking what might become the highway to Miami—if anyone could prove that the Big Cypress Swamp (with its massive trees) and the Everglades (with its devilish saw grass) could be conquered. This was their goal, and for that reason they called themselves the "Trailblazers."

"The first car drove off the end of the grade into the muck," wrote young Russell Kay, one of the participants. "It traveled about one hundred yards or so, and then mired down to its running boards. The second car followed with exactly the same result, and it appeared that the project was doomed. . . ." But a tractor from nearby Everglades City dragged the cars to higher ground. From there the caravan sloshed slowly and carefully into the great unknown. The men had vastly underestimated the difficulty of the trip to Miami and had taken only a three-day supply of food. So they ran out when they were still many miles from their destination and had to live off cattail roots and swamp cabbage. This was augmented by deer meat brought to them occasionally by Miccosukees, amazed at the inability of white men to support themselves. After eleven grueling days, they got to within five miles of their goal. Here they had to abandon the last of their broken-down autos and stumble the rest of the way to Miami on foot.

The Tamiami's Toughest Section

Building the Tamiami Trail through the Big Cypress Swamp proved to be the most difficult job of the entire Tampa-to-Miami road project. Before any major construction could be done, sawyers had to cut down cypress trees that were sometimes seven feet thick. To do so, they used two-man handsaws and worked in waist-deep swamp water. Yet obtaining financing proved to be an even greater problem. Each township was expected to finance the portion going through its territory. But there were not enough wallets below Ft. Myers to pay for an alligator path, to say nothing of a paved road. Work was at a virtual standstill until 1923, when a Yankee business tycoon named Barron Collier promised to complete the seventy-six remaining miles.

Barron Collier: The Forgotten Hero

Collier was an amazing individual. Photos show a handsome man with pleasant features and a velvet expression. Yet there was steel behind the gentle facade, for he had gained his fortune through business skills and indomitable willpower. He began his remarkable career in Memphis, Tennessee, when he bought into a small print shop. Then, as electric streetcar lines began replacing the old horse-drawn vehicles, Collier talked the new companies into letting him install advertising signs on their cars. He was so successful that he expanded to other cities and within a few decades owned practically every streetcar advertising franchise across America. With considerable resources now available, he turned to other fields.

Eventually Collier became interested in Florida and began buying land in the undeveloped southwest portion of the state. Ultimately he accumulated ninety percent of what became essentially his own private domain when Collier County was created in 1923. Yet to own this vast acreage served no purpose until it could be developed. And for that it was essential that the Tamiami Trail be completed. Indeed, the state had granted Collier his county mainly on his promise to ensure the Trail's completion.

In order to fulfill his obligation, Collier required a local base for supplies, equipment, repairs, and housing. For this he selected the tiny, waterlogged community of Everglades City, slouching beside a shallow stream once named the Allen's River after the first permanent settler but now rechristened the Barron. Here he dredged up river muck sufficient to raise the town high enough to avoid the inconvenience of being flooded by each storm. Next, he constructed along the river an industrial area called Port DuPont, where he installed docks to handle the oceangoing ships upon which he was to depend for his supplies. Then he erected a boatyard large enough for his eleven dredges. These were followed by workers' barracks and a mess hall. Then he installed a sawmill, warehouses, and machine and repair shops. And, of course, he built a railroad yard where logging trains could unload. The railroad also carried laborers and their equipment to the warehouse and assembly center at Carnestown, from which they departed for work on the Tamiami Trail.

The Village That Was a City

From Carnestown take CR 29 into Everglades City. In the days when the town was the headquarters of Barron Collier, this road was thronged with vehicles transporting supplies and workers to the construction site. On the railroad alongside the road, freight trains carried massive trees cut in the Big Cypress Swamp to Collier's buzzing sawmill.

Watch for DuPont Road. Turning right, you'll enter what's left of Collier's old port. The street is only a few blocks long, and you'll probably pass large piles of traps used by commercial fishermen to catch lobsters and crabs in fishing grounds six miles downriver.

Now return to CR 29, which is known in these parts as—what else?—Collier Avenue. Collier Avenue is four lanes, befitting its original function as the entry to the seat of Collier County. The Atlantic Coast Railroad terminal, standing where Collier Avenue ends at Broadway, is now the Everglades Seafood Depot Restaurant.

Turn right onto Broadway, which is as wide as its name implies. Down two blocks is a rotary with the town's signature building: the two-story, Greek Revival structure that was once the county seat but is now merely the administrative center of this small town of around six hundred people.

Everglades City was Collier's town. Virtually all of its residents owed their livelihoods to him. He owned all the homes. The company whistle woke everyone up each morning and blew again when it was time to go to work or to school. Work continued, with an hour for lunch, until 6:00 P.M., when the whistle sounded again. Sunday was the whistle's day of rest. But the townsfolk found there wasn't much to do on their free day. The cheapest recreation was riding the electric streetcar that ran from Broadway and the river to Port DuPont. The streetcar, the only one in Collier County, was free since it served mainly as a gimmick to promote Everglades City. Collier even loaded it with his advertising placards—not that most of the working class families could afford the goods so offered.

Aside from the streetcar, the most excitement came from a good rattlesnake fight. On these occasions crowds would sit on the court-house steps cheering their favorite snake as it fought its adversary to the death. No one was sorry to see the snakes kill each other—rattlers were all too common. One blasé resident even used rattlesnake fangs as toothpicks.

Far worse than rattlers were the mosquitoes. In those days the only effective skeeter killer was a kerosene-based compound called Flit sprayed from a hand-pumped vaporizer. Although the penetrating smell was distasteful to humans, a squirt or two did the job on mosquitoes. But flies only seemed to chuckle until they were drenched.

The greatest event in Everglades City's history occurred on April 26, 1928: the day the Tamiami Trail opened. To celebrate this momentous accomplishment, Barron Collier led a motorcade of nearly five hundred autos—all gaily decorated and almost honking their hoods off—all the way down from Tampa, where the Trail began. Among the throng were members of the original Trailblazer party. After an overnight stay in Ft. Myers, the festive motorcade arrived in Everglades City in time for a sumptuous lunch. Afterwards there were speeches, then a gala parade down Broadway by most of the town's four hundred citizens—so many, in fact, that there was almost no one left to watch. But who cared! Today was for fun. Tomorrow they might all be rich.

However, the Tamiami Trail did not bring the expected bonanza either to Barron Collier or to the citizens of Everglades City. By the time the Trail opened, Florida was suffering from a severe real estate panic. Then the Great Depression hit and during the 1930s traffic on the Trail was almost nonexistent. Barron Collier's advertising business fell off, and, when he died suddenly of a stroke in 1939, much of his estate was gobbled up by taxes. Although Everglades City continued

The Rod and Gun Club has been a fixture in Everglades City for more than a century.

as the seat of Collier County for many years, it was so isolated from the rest of the county that in 1962 the seat was moved to the burgeoning city of Naples.

During the long, bleak years that followed, about all that kept Everglades City from sinking back into the swamp was the Rod and Gun Club at the foot of Broadway. The club had been the modest home of first settler William Allen but was enlarged by George Storter, who bought the entire site of Everglades City from Allen for $800. Because it was on the river with direct communication to the rich fishing grounds in Chokoloskee Bay and the Gulf of Mexico, so many sportsmen began dropping in on Storter that he turned his home into the Rod and Gun Club. Barron Collier, who bought out Storter, upgraded it into a private club reserved for his most special guests. Later it became public, as it is today.

Dwight Eisenhower, one of the famous people to stay there, posed proudly (with his famous Ike smile) in front of a row of fish he caught during a charter trip. Richard Nixon took a charter cruise before he was president. When the boat made a sudden turn, he tumbled into the water. He returned wet but not humbled, for, as the nation was to learn, humility was not a trait that he found to his liking.

If you hanker for the thrill of landing a tarpon, redfish, or snook, you can hire a boat and a guide at the Rod and Gun Club for $400 a day. Or, if you like to eat (not catch) fish, the Club's restaurant serves excellent lunches and dinners. Staying overnight at the club costs $95 between November and May. For reservations call 941-695-2101.

Today Everglades City is undergoing something of a revival. It is working diligently at resurrecting itself as it was during the happy, Barron Collier days. In 1998 it won an award as Florida's Outstanding Rural Community of the Year. Now the real estate market is picking up—particularly for waterfront property. "We've had three or four new houses built in the last few years," a proud realtor told a Naples reporter, "and that's a lot for us." The Museum of the Everglades at 105 West Broadway, the former company laundry, presents an impressive display of photographs and artifacts Tuesdays through Saturdays between 11:00 A.M. and 4:00 P.M.

Everglades City is a good place to spend time because it is centrally located for several day trips. On its southern outskirts is the Gulf Coast segment of the Everglades National Park, with fascinating boat tours of the mangrove coastal islands. Three miles farther south at the end of a causeway is Chokoloskee Island, where the vintage Ted Smallwood store tells a story of frontier life salted with gunplay and murder.

There are several other historic lodgings in town. On Broadway, close to the Rod and Gun Club, is the 1923 bank, which has been converted into a bed and breakfast called On the Banks of the Everglades. The rooms have intriguing names like Trust Department and Checking Department. The President's Suite occupies the offices of Barron Collier. If you're daring, try Foreclosures. You'll enjoy the Vault, which is a breakfast nook. Room rates vary. If you don't mind sharing a bathroom, you can stay for $70–$80 per night. Rooms with private baths and kitchens go for $125. All rates include breakfast as well as the use of a bike. For reservations call 888-431-1977.

The Ivey House Bed and Breakfast is another vintage conversion from the Collier era. It was originally in Port DuPont, where it served as a recreation hall for workers on the Tamiami Trail. Today it has been relocated to 107 Camellia Street, which is five blocks north of the former courthouse. Rooms are $85 per night with a two-night minimum. For reservations call 941-695-3299.

This boat takes sightseers into the extensive mangrove islands along the Gulf of Mexico.

The Mangrove Tidelands

Now take Copeland Avenue (CR 29) from in front of the old courthouse south a mile to the Gulf Coast Visitor Center. It's open seven days a week between 7:30 A.M. and 5:00 P.M. Within are displays and videos showing the unusual forms of life that frequent the area. But the real highlight is the $16 boat ride ($8 for kids), which leaves regularly throughout the day. For exact times or other information, call 800-445-7724.

The boat glides through a maze of tiny keys covered by dense growths of mangroves. As it edges through narrow waterways, mangroves crowd in and even brush the hull. There is an almost eerie stillness that may cause you to imagine nothing else exists in the entire world except these trees, the muggy air, and the smell of salt and growing things.

Many who take the ninety-minute boat tour are surprised, and some are disappointed, that they are not out in the sawgrass prairie. They don't realize that, although they are technically within the Everglades National Park, they are actually in the Ten Thousand Islands, which extend along Florida's extreme southwestern coast for more than 140 trackless miles. Far from being disappointed, they should relish the opportunity to experience close up this unusual,

Mangroves form a dense matting over the maze of small keys in the Ten Thousand Islands.

even weird, rarely visited part of Florida.

Until recently these islands were the haunts of drug runners, who found the many secluded coves ideal for their nefarious dealings. Although not many people in this twilight profession care to divulge their activities, such was not the case with Loren "Totch" Brown, who highlighted his career in a book entitled *Totch: A Life in the Everglades*.

Totch grew up in Everglades City and on Chokoloskee Island, which is just down the CR 29 causeway from the Visitor Center. Making a living was tough, but it became even tougher in 1947, when the National Park was formed. The problem, according to Totch, was that now the do-gooders said it was illegal to kill the no-account gators for their hides. So Totch had little choice except to turn to the drug business. The decision was easy: "I found out from Sonny," he wrote, "that the pot-haulers in the Glades were plain people just like myself; in fact most of 'em were my own friends." However, running drugs from Colombia to Florida was not as easy as it sounded. The sleazy characters, the threat of gunplay, the harassment of the Coast Guard—it was enough to cause any god-fearing citizen great concern. "The fright that came with pot-hauling," Totch admitted, "would scare a full-grown tomcat out of all its nine lives." Thus he may have been relieved in 1983 when lawmen allowed him to rethink his chosen career during fifteen months in prison.

Browsing through Yesterday: Chokoloskee

With this introduction, take the CR 29 causeway to Chokoloskee Island. The drive should be scenic, but the view is largely obscured by mangroves.

Chokoloskee goes back beyond even the Seminoles, who named it the "old house" because of the Calusa ruins they found here. The Calusa were a sea-oriented tribe who came to the island for its shellfish. After feasting, they would toss the shells onto ever-growing heaps behind their camp. Over countless centuries these heaps grew into the mound that today is topped by modest homes of those Floridians who have grown to love the "old house," pungent with the scent of the bay and the Gulf of Mexico just beyond.

One of the earliest American settlers was Ted Smallwood, who first came to Chokoloskee at the turn of the last century. In 1906 he constructed a general store that served every fishing crew, farm family, and Seminole trader within miles.

The boat landing at Ted Smallwood's store in Chokoloskee was the site of gunplay and murder during the early 1900s.

Smallwood was trusted by the Seminoles as no other white man in the vicinity. He liked them too and even went to the trouble of learning their language. The Indians would regularly paddle down the Turner River in their dugout canoes, loaded with fresh venison and wild turkeys as well as alligator and deer hides. In return they would receive calico, hand-sewing machines, thread, and needles. Smallwood also provided them with an ample supply of firewater, for the Indians demanded it. The Seminoles' drinking bouts could be dangerous, since sometimes a hundred or more would be camping along the shore. For this reason, they willingly gave their lethal assortment of guns and knives to Smallwood for safekeeping until hangovers announced the riotous times to be over.

Ted Smallwood was a quiet man who went out of his way to avoid trouble. Yet his store was on the frontier, where desperadoes drifted in like tidal flotsam. There were, for example, four bank robbers who hid out in the mangroves east of Chokoloskee. But they needed supplies, and one of them (on his way to Smallwood's) was shot dead by two alert locals. When a second robber rumbled toward Chokoloskee the next day looking for his companion, locals plugged him too. After a third robber drowned mysteriously, the last man frantically hired a couple of fellows to escort him to the safety of the Ft. Myers slammer.

Gunplay came even closer to Smallwood with the arrival of a hothead named Ed Watson. Although Ed had teamed up out West with the Belle Starr gang, Belle was not his type of gal, and he had to kill her—or so he bragged. After this incident, Ed drifted to Arcadia, Florida's wildest cow town. While there he was obliged to do in Quin Bass. Next Watson popped up near Chokoloskee, where folks had learned not to question a man's past. Here he began raising sugar-cane, which he converted into syrup and carried down to Key West in his own little schooner. In Key West he got into another fracas and was obliged to cut Adolphus Santini's throat.

Watson was a frequent visitor to Smallwood's store. "He used to trade with me for years," Ted recalled in his brief memoirs. "I never had any trouble with him." Smallwood even stocked some of Watson's syrup. At least once Watson spent the night with Ted and his wife, a round and jolly lady named Mamie.

One day Smallwood could see that Watson was particularly angry. He claimed that Lesley Cox had just killed some of his cronies and he was going to get Cox—which he did. Evidently Cox had friends in the area, for a group of them gathered at the dock in front of Smallwood's store when the sound of Watson's motorboat announced he was headed there. Watson always had a gun handy, so Smallwood knew something disagreeable was going to happen. Grabbing Mamie, he made a quick exit to their house, a hundred yards back. From here he heard shouting, then the sound of gunshots. When he returned, he found Watson lying in a pool of blood.

Smallwood ran his store in Chokoloskee for more than four decades, surviving the outlaws and the heat and the mosquitoes and even the constant storms, which caused him to put his store on stilts just before the arrival of a ferocious hurricane that might have escorted it off to the Yucatan. Although Smallwood died in 1951, his store stayed open for another three decades, during which time it was placed on the National Register of Historic Places. It was closed for several years until recently reopened by Ted's granddaughter. Located at the foot of Mamie Street, the store has become a popular attraction in this otherwise somnolent village. Nearly ninety percent of the original goods are still on the shelves. For $2.50 admission (free for kids under twelve), you can wander down the aisles, where you'll find everything an early settler needed, from boat propellers and cigar boxes to medicine bottles, milk churns, and a fruit press.

The store is open seven days a week between 10:00 A.M. and 5:00 P.M. (fewer hours April through November). The gift shop sells Seminole handicrafts as well as the usual T-shirts and lots of "et ceteras." You can also purchase Charlton Tebeau's paperback, *The Story of Chokoloskee Bay Country*, which contains Smallwood's too-brief reminiscences.

The interior of the store is divided into three long sections. Bare, over-head light bulbs create stark contrasts between illuminated areas and the shadowy recesses, where you'd almost expect a dozen, steely-eyed Seminoles to be watching you. Sitting on a stool composed of two Clorox cartons is Smallwood himself—compliments of a life-size manikin that is almost identical to a nearby photo. His benign expression reflects the relaxed nature of this genial man. Nearby is the wooden chest where Smallwood kept the silver and weaponry the Seminoles gave him for safekeeping while they enjoyed their evening carousals.

The exterior is also interesting. The store still rests on stilts, for hurricanes do not always honor historic buildings. Chokoloskee Bay continues to lap the sand where Seminole families once camped and where, during the daytime, they carved miniature wooden canoes that Smallwood sold for twenty-five cents. Mangroves crowd close to the shore, much as they did on the outlying islands where outlaws hid. The landing where Ed Watson was shot is gone, for the building was not on stilts at that time. But it is easy to imagine his boat heading toward the shore, where angry men cocked their guns.

Aside from the Smallwood store, there is not much to see in Chokoloskee, so take the road back to Everglades City, where this exploration ends.

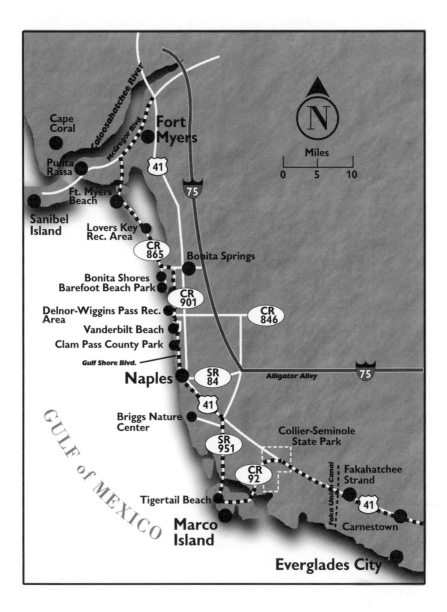

The Platinum Coast

Everglades City to Ft. Myers • 98 Backroad Miles

The Song of the Road: Overview

Seldom does a relatively short trip have such diversity as this. It begins at the offbeat little town of Everglades City, twenty miles south of the Interstate 75 exit via SR 29. Having delved into Everglades City on the last trip, you'll head northwest on US 41. The first stop is at the Fakahatchee Strand for a stroll down the long boardwalk through a dense subtropical jungle displaying some of the most magnificent cypress trees remaining in Florida. Just beyond the Strand is Collier-Seminole Park, where you can view one of the giant dredges that helped carve the Tamiami Trail through Big Cypress Swamp and the Everglades. The park also offers sightseeing excursions into the outlying mangrove islands as well as rental canoes for the more intrepid explorers.

You'll find a new world when you enter Marco Island. Much of the island was originally a mangrove salt marsh but is now a highly desirable community interlaced with boating canals and fronted by Marco's famed Crescent Beach, available for swimming and some of the best shelling for miles. Northward is Naples, which boasts one of the highest average income levels in America. Shopping here is an enjoyable experience, as is dining at one of the many waterfront restaurants, some offering sightseeing cruises around Naples Bay. Or you can be content to merely watch the parade of expensive pleasure craft. Next the route continues north along Gulf Shore Boulevard, glittering with expensive condos and posh marinas. There are several fine public beaches along the way, such as the world-famous Delnor-Wiggins Park.

Beyond Naples you'll have access to more wonderful Gulf beaches. At Bonita Shores you'll discover Barefoot Beach State Preserve, with its fine sand, nature trails, and a palm-thatched little museum. Northward is Lovers Key, where a tram will carry you across protected dunes. You can swim here, or rent a canoe or bicycle, or go on narrated nature paddles. Finally, you'll enter Ft. Myers along one of the nation's longest and most impressive aisles of royal palms.

On the Road Again

We begin at Carnestown, an important depot for men and supplies arriving from the port at nearby Everglades City during construction of this section of the Tamiami Trail (US 41). Since this chapter is more or less a continuation of the previous one, I'll assume that you're familiar with Everglades City and the Tamiami Trail.

Hundred-Year-Old Dwarves

Heading northwest on the Tamiami Trail, you'll encounter grand prairie vistas where saw grass mixes with cattails. There are also cypress of the dwarf variety. Because the limestone bedrock is so close to the surface, there is a lack of nutrients necessary for proper growth. Thus a cypress that is barely ten feet tall may be almost a hundred years old. During the winter the scattered trees are ghostly skeletons. But when the needles come out in the spring, they seem to be transformed into beach umbrellas waiting for laughing children.

The highway is accompanied by the canal, where dredges once brought up rocks and small boulders—blasted from the limestone below—to build the roadbed.

The River of Vines

After traveling seven miles, you'll become aware of a line of tall vegetation approaching from the east. This is the Fakahatchee Strand, famed for its luxuriant growth of tropical and subtropical plants, including some of the rarest and most sought-after orchids on earth. Fakahatchee means "the hunting river" or "the river of vines" in the Seminole tongue. The Strand is actually a long, shallow river channel through which water from the Big Cypress Swamp drains ever so slowly into the Gulf of Mexico. This channel has accumulated a rich layer of muck, which is ideal for plant growth. The muck also provided habitats for the animals once hunted by the Seminoles.

The Jungle Boardwalk

Turn onto the roadside parking strip at Big Cypress Bend, then take the five-minute stroll down a sand path to the elevated boardwalk that wends its way through the Strand for two thousand feet. This is a fascinating walk that you'll want to enjoy at a leisurely pace. Certainly the most impressive trees will be the great bald cypress, whose massive trunks rise up like pillars supporting the sky. This is one of the last extensive stands of these splendid, old-

A strangler fig along the Fakahatchee boardwalk grasps this cypress in a death vise.

growth trees. That they escaped the timber companies' saws is truly a miracle. As with other cypress, they lose their needles in the fall, but by late winter they begin to sport a fresh growth of delicate green. Strangler figs have latched onto a few of the cypress, and their iron grasp will eventually cut off the cypress' circulation. Then the cypress trees will die, their trunks will rot, and they will eventually crash into the swamp, carrying the stranglers with them.

Royal palms also thrive in the swamp, their trunks as straight and dignified as Athenian columns. This is the largest group of such trees in the world. Mixed with them are sabal palms, Florida's state tree, which are also known as cabbage palms. Their fronds give the appearance of human hands, from which the name "palm" was derived. The third dominant plants in the Strand are ferns, the likes of which you've probably never seen. Particularly impressive are the leather ferns, reaching up to ten feet in height. The undersides of ferns are thick with spores which, when ripe, float away on the wind to begin new plants.

As you wander down the boardwalk, watch for bromeliads (often called "air plants") clinging to the tree limbs. Most obvious will be the bright red bracts of the wild pine, blooming from January through the summer. They are large plants, related to the pineapple, with stiff leaves that may reach three feet in length.

The walkway ends at a platform overlooking the central slough, which is the deepest part of the Strand. Water remains here many months after the rainy season ends, providing a wet retreat for alligators. Many of the trees around the slough are low-growing pond apples and pop ash. Both of these trees provide friendly environments for orchids, forty types of which thrive amid the heat and humidity of Fakahatchee. This is the largest concentration and greatest variety in North America. Perhaps you'll be lucky enough to see the extremely rare ghost orchid in bloom.

The Orchid-nappers

Because the Strand is a state preserve and, furthermore, the orchids are classified as endangered, their removal is strictly prohibited. Yet the potential for flowery profits has lured many poachers to the Strand. Perhaps the boldest were four orchid-nappers who were apprehended a few years back. Here's the story gleaned from Susan Orlean's book *The Orchid Thief.*

One day in the winter of 1994, as the head ranger was patrolling along one of the old timber roads, he spotted a car parked at an unusual place. When he investigated, he came upon four hauling bags filled with more than two hundred rare orchids and bromeliads, some of which would fetch $100 on the open market. Although this was an obvious violation of the law prohibiting the removal of endangered species, the situation was complicated. Three of the men were Seminoles, whose tribe had a treaty exempting it from the Endangered Species Act. The fourth man was not a Seminole but was employed by the tribe to manage their plant nursery and orchid-propagation laboratory. This man was a strange individual named John Laroche.

Laroche was out of fiction. Tall and slim and still in his thirties, he was strikingly handsome. Yet he was so eccentric that the Seminoles nicknamed him the Crazy White Man. Laroche had an overwhelming fascination with rare orchids. As he viewed it, he was not stealing the orchids; he was helping preserve the species by taking them to his laboratory to reproduce so they would become available in greater numbers for other orchid lovers. How dare state laws interfere with him! He knew better than politicians—or rangers or court judges—what was best for his beloved flowers. He had an infatuation with them that bordered on outright lunacy, says Susan Orlean in her book, subtitled *A True Story of Beauty and Obsession.*

It took four years to resolve the orchid theft case. The government contended that all four men were guilty since they had taken the branches, which included the orchids; the branches were not "endangered," and therefore the Seminole tribe had no exception. Realizing that the ruling would be against them in the long run, Laroche and the three Seminoles finally pleaded no contest. Thereupon Laroche was fined $500 and the Indians $100 each.

The state was disappointed with the outcome. Because the fine was so low, due to the no-contest plea, other poachers would not be deterred. The Seminoles were angered that their rights had been ignored. "Just like any other treaty you guys sign," a tribal spokesman grumbled, "it isn't worth the paper it's written on." Even Susan Orlean, who got a best-selling book out of it, was disappointed. She had had expectations that the story would be made into a movie pretty much the way she had told it. Yet when the scriptwriters could not adapt the book to the screen, they turned the movie into a story about themselves and their problems. But that's Hollywood, and the author admitted that she was gratified the movie was being filmed at all.

Icky and Spooky

During her research, Orlean talked Laroche into taking her on a hike through the Fakahatchee wilderness. It was a horrible ordeal she'd never forget. "The water we stepped into was as black as coffee," she wrote. "It was hard to tell how far down we would go, and when our feet touched the bottom it yielded like pudding." As they sloshed along, she was constantly battered by branches and snared by underwater vines. She feared one of the deadly water moccasins might attack her, but fortunately none did. When they came to open areas, the sun smote her. The humidity made her hair curl like a corkscrew. "You smell the tang of mud and the sourness of rotting leaves and the cool musk of new leaves and the perfumes of a million different flowers floating by, each distinct but transparent, like soap bubbles." It was an unreal mélange of heaven and hell. But there was more hell. "No offense to Fakahatchee," she later told a reporter, "but the hours I spent there were about the most miserable I have ever spent." In the end she decried Fakahatchee as "icky and spooky."

But the Strand need not be icky or spooky to those who stay on the boardwalk, where civilized humans belong. Neither will the humidity or the insects bother you if you come during the winter months when the trek amid the bald cypress, royal palms, ferns, and bromeliads is a pleasure long remembered.

Back on the Tamiami Trail, you'll soon pass over the broad Faka Union Canal. On the far side is a recent, upscale housing development. When the canal was constructed three decades ago, the Gulf American Company developers viewed it as just the first of an extensive network that would dry out large portions of the swamp to make them suitable for housing and commercial centers. In the process these drainage canals have probably destroyed the Fakahatchee Strand. The formation of the Big Cypress Preserve ended this menace, but just seeing this splashy outreach of civilized sprawl is chilling enough.

Memorial to a Dredge: Collier-Seminole State Park

 Seven miles farther west on the Tamiami Trail is the entrance to the Collier-Seminole State Park, once the site of the Royal Palm Hammock unit of Florida's mounted police—officers on motorcycles who aided stranded motorists during the long years when the Tamiami Trail was distressingly distant from civilization.

 After paying the admission ($3.50 per car), drive a short way down the entry road to the "walking" dredge, one of those that helped build this portion of the Tamiami Trail. The dredge scooped up the rocky debris left by the dynamite crew and formed it

This dredge in Collier-Seminole State Park helped dig the roadbed for the Tamiami Trail.

into a rough roadbed twenty-four feet wide. The dredge's legs were attached to wheels that ran along steel rails laid over brush mats piled four feet thick on the soggy jungle soil. When the bucket moved and the weight shifted, the twenty-ton dredge often tipped perilously to one side as the mats sank into the spongy muck. It was a dangerous operation and as the road-builders became more experienced, they abandoned this type of machine in favor of dredges that floated on the canal that emerged as the rocks were removed.

Continuing down the entry road, on the right fork is a replica of a blockhouse used during the Seminole Wars. Within are displays depicting the history of the Seminoles and the earlier Calusas as well as of the plants and animals found in the park. There is also information regarding Barron Collier, whose vital role in the construction of this portion of the Tamiami Trail was highlighted in the previous chapter.

Taking the other fork of the entry road, you'll pass a memorial to Collier consisting of six Greek columns. This fork ends at a waterfront docking area, where sightseeing boats leave on one-hour, narrated tours among the mangrove islands. They set sail seven days a week and cost $10 for adults and $7.50 for children six through twelve. If instead you prefer the whisper of water to an amplified narration, you can rent a canoe. Hikers enjoy the trail through a salt marsh to an observation platform presenting a many-mile vista across an eerie expanse of reeds and grasses.

Marco Magic

Immediately beyond Collier-Seminole State Park you'll come to the CR 92 junction. Turn left on CR 92 for the eleven-mile jaunt to Marco Island. The road is two lanes through a wetland dominated by mangroves. It is flat and uninhabited and will leave you completely unprepared for the sight that greets you from the high arch of the Goodland Bridge. There in the distance is the Gulf of Mexico fringed with a long necklace of high-rise buildings as out of place as a duck in a desert.

Not long ago Marco was an undistinguished mangrove island. But in 1964 the Deltona Company began an operation whereby it dug nearly a hundred miles of canals, using the dredgings to create new land. Next they laid water and sewer lines in a core area, brought in electricity, and built roads. After ridding the site of mosquitoes, they constructed several dozen model homes and began selling lots.

Deltona was something rare for that time: a conscientious land

Marco is a former mangrove island converted into prime properties.

developer. But in the early 1970s it ran afoul of environmental laws that had not existed when they began developing Marco. As a result, permits were denied to create buildable lots on wetland property already sold for future delivery. This necessitated huge refunds that forced the company to dispose of their extensive holdings at pitifully cheap prices. In researching the story of Marco for my book *The Last Paradise*, I interviewed Deltona's co-founder and inspiration, Frank Mackle. Once he had been a vigorous, cheerful, and optimistic person. But in 1986 he was bent, reflective, and bitter. "One thing people have always said about Florida developers," he told me, "was that they wanted to sell you worthless land underwater. But in my case I wanted to sell a good piece of land that was developed. But they wouldn't let me! I don't know what was in their damned minds! . . . I tried the best I could. But they beat me."

The developed portion of the island is honeycombed with canals, most lined with piers where pleasure craft wait to serve their masters. Homes and lot sites on the canals, or one of Marco's several bays, are highly desirable. The most expensive are south on Barfield Drive, which is the first stoplight. Once you get on Barfield continue all the way to the end, for the farther you go, the more scenic the locales and the pricier the mansions.

 Return to CR 92, here known as San Marco Drive, and continue west. Watch for the firehouse at the corner of Bald

Eagle Drive. This was the location of Deltona's sales office, which was the only structure for several miles when it was built. During the island's grand opening on January 31, 1965, more than twenty-five thousand people flocked to this isolated island to see the wonders that Mackle's company was working here. Among them were commissioners from Collier County, who had welcomed Deltona as "a breath of fresh air," as one of the commissioners told me. But today Deltona is almost forgotten and there is not even a plaque to indicate what once was here.

Continue on San Marco until it terminates at Collier Boulevard on the Gulf. It was from here that Frank Mackle and his two brothers walked out to inspect the beach prior to becoming involved with Marco. "We had made a special trip over from Miami in sixty-two," Frank told me. "We stood on Crescent Beach where the State Road ended and it was fantastic. Just fantastic. I decided right on the spot to turn Marco into a paradise everyone could enjoy."

Now drive south on Collier to the Marriott Hotel. When Deltona built it, it was known as the Marco Beach Hotel and was the finest resort hotel on the Gulf Coast. The hotel's gala opening ceremonies in December 1971 were attended by dignitaries from all around the country, including the governor of Florida. "It was my pride," Mackle said. "I felt good every time I entered it." But Mackle had to sell the hotel to Marriott in order to obtain money to refund to buyers of properties Deltona owned but was not permitted to develop. The hotel is still a showplace. Quinn's Restaurant (directly on the beach) serves everything from sandwiches to full dinners.

Mackle had intended to keep the magnificent southern portion of Crescent Beach from the hotel down to where the island ends at Cape Marco as a grassy golf course free from buildings. But Deltona had to sell the land now worth millions for a pittance. Today it is occupied by a virtual wall of buildings. Among them are the Hilton and the Radisson Hotels—each with lunch and dinner facilities with good views of the Gulf.

Heading back north on Collier, you'll pass a glittering array of Deltona-built, high-rise condos fringing the Gulf. The tallest is the Summit, where Frank Mackle owned a unit. It was here that he spent much time during the years after he was forced out of Deltona. Looking down the fabulous beach, he recalled the dreams he had had.

The general public swims at Tigertail Beach, which you can reach

There are always interesting marine specimens in the low-tide flatlands at Marco Island's Tigertail Beach.

 by driving a half mile north from the Summit to Tigertail Court, then four blocks west to Hernando Drive, and left a few blocks to the beach. Admission is free but there is a $3 fee for parking. Tigertail has changing rooms, a concession, and expansive frontage on the sandy arc that has made Marco so popular with vacationers. At low tide the beach is one of Florida's choice locations for finding beautiful seashells.

 From Tigertail Court, Collier Boulevard continues past Marco's quaint business section, where most of the buildings were constructed by Deltona. Then you'll leave the island over the soaring SR 951 bridge. The exit highway is four lanes through a mangrove wetland that is fast being replaced by golf courses and housing developments.

 Watch for the side road to the Conservancy's Briggs Nature Center on Rookery Bay. Here there is an interpretive museum and a half-mile boardwalk through various plant communities. The center is open every day except Sunday. Admission is $3 for adults and $1 for kids three to twelve. The Conservancy also offers canoe trips, lectures, hikes, and many other opportunities to learn about nature along this unusual portion of the Gulf Coast. The Conservancy was the chief opponent of Deltona, whose long-term plans included development of the land between SR 951 and the Gulf as far as the edge of the Briggs Center. It brought a series of court cases that delayed Deltona long enough for the federal government to pass the Clean Water and Environmental Protection Acts in the early 1970s. These laws, and those that followed, made it illegal to destroy mangrove wetlands unless other sensitive areas were set aside under a doctrine called "mitigation." To learn more about the Briggs Center call 941-775-8569.

Eight miles after leaving Marco you're back on US 41, where you should turn left toward Naples.

On the Road to Naples

Although you're still on the Tamiami Trail (US 41), you may find it difficult to believe that this multilane artery ablaze with fast food and fast roadsters was ever a primeval forest. But when the Tamiami Trail was cut through here, the workmen encountered "a mass of trees of all kinds and sizes . . . woven together with bamboo, rattan, and vines," complained K. B. Harvey, who was in charge of the operation. Attacking the vines with saws and machetes, the sweating workers found that "perhaps several hundred would be chopped off at the ground before the mass would fall. . . . " When Harvey ordered a dredge brought in, the sand and muck over which it ran quivered so violently that he feared the forty-thousand-pound machine would topple over and be wrecked.

That era is long gone now. Today Naples is an active city of twenty-one thousand and the seat of Collier County. Collier is one of the fastest-growing counties in the entire nation. You'll pass the extensive county complex at US 41 and Airport Road. The entire atmosphere of Naples is so different from that of the former county seat, Everglades City, you may need a moment to adjust.

Fabulous Fifth: Naples

Anyone visiting Naples must at least drive down its vaunted Fifth Avenue South, which branches off US 41 as it turns sharply north in the center of town. Glamorous today, Fifth Avenue is a case study in the revitalization of a depressed downtown.

Not many years ago, Fifth Avenue was drab and unkempt, with fully half the storefronts vacant. Depressing during the daytime, Fifth Avenue was downright ghostly at night. Then concerned landlords, civic leaders, and citizens got together and worked out a revitalization plan. They received expert help from the state when the city was brought into the Main Street Program. Soon the slogan "Everything old is new again" rang through the downtown. Landlords began fixing up their buildings, most accepting the newly adopted Mediterranean-style architectural code that promoted clay tile roofs, stucco walls, vintage shutters, and wrought-iron balconies and terraces. Ultimately Fifth Avenue's extensive facelift would cost a whopping $30 million.

But it was worth it. As Fifth Avenue became more desirable, merchants began to return. Their stylish shops and chic restaurants attracted shoppers from the Gulf Shore areas, who were transforming Naples into one of the wealthiest cities in America. Today there are few Florida downtowns that can compare with Fifth Avenue South.

New Olde Naples

With this accolade, it may seem incredible that any place nearby can challenge Fifth Avenue. But the fact is that Naples, with all its affluence, has more shopping space per lady's purse than almost any other American city. Thus if you turn left off Fifth Avenue at Third Street South, in a few blocks you'll come to a completely different commercial area. Third Street is more homespun, more relaxed, more, if you will, new-Olde Naples. This is not surprising, for Naples' first

Naples' Third Street South combines fashionable shopping with glimpses of the past. The three-story structure is the historic Mercantile Building, still in use.

commercial building was constructed here in 1919. In those days, if you needed any item that had not sprouted from a local farm or been bagged by a local hunter, the Mercantile Building at 1186 Third Street was where you went.

The Mercantile Building, which is still in use, was just about everything to early Naples. Its importance was even recognized by bootleggers, who furnished the citizens with so much refreshment during Prohibition that the town was called "Naples on the Gulp." Earl L. Baum, who wintered here, tells how he sent a friend over to the store to ask for a smuggler known simply as Mr. W. Someone identified himself as Mr. W., but when Baum's friend told him what he wanted, the man flashed a marshal's badge and grunted that he'd be arrested if he pursued the matter. Baum's friend hurried off, thoroughly shaken and muttering about Baum's inability to find reputable bootleggers. Yet not more than a half hour later, a second man appeared at his door with three choice bottles of Bimini's finest redeye. Turns out he was the marshal's brother. And that's the way things went during the Noble Experiment that failed.

If you want to understand Naples, it's worth your time to wander among Third Street's quaint buildings redecorated in delicious pastels. The shops contain everything from clothing and jewelry to groceries and sandwiches. If you want to stay overnight to capture more of the spirit, consider the Olde Naples Inn at 801 Third (941-262-5194).

Finding a place to park on Third (or the contiguous streets) is not easy, but there is a parking lot one street west on Second Avenue at Thirteenth Avenue. It's large and centrally located. This was the spot where the venerable Naples Hotel stood until time and termites pillaged its prestigious planks.

The city got its start here in 1888, when the Naples Town Improvement Company constructed a modest structure to house prospective purchasers who came here to inspect the company's land. Although people were attracted by ads that promoted the site as America's own bit of Mediterranean sunshine, the fact that it could be reached only after a rocking voyage on the Gulf caused sales to be slow until the 1920s. At this time, the arrival of two railroads and the completion of the Tamiami Trail finally provided dependable land access.

The Naples Hotel expanded with the community. The guiding force was Ed Crayton, who could be charming to his guests but was as tough as overcooked clams with his business associates. He owned the hotel as well as a goodly portion of what is now Naples. His office was next to the Mercantile Building on Third Street, but he head-quartered in the hotel. Earl Baum was a friend of Crayton's and a frequent visitor to the hotel. "When I first came here in 1922," Baum wrote in his entertaining booklet, *Early Naples and Collier County,* "the social activity was centered entirely around the Old Naples Hotel. In fact, there was no other place in Naples where we could all get together." To add to its grandeur, Crayton graced the hotel grounds with an honest-to-goodness sidewalk—the only one for miles around!

The Historic Pier

The hotel was two blocks from the Gulf, connected by a long veranda to an impressive wooden pier reaching six hundred feet into the water. On one side of the veranda was a pair of wooden rails, over which wagons transported supplies as well as guests to and from the ships that linked Naples with the rest of America. The pier was a social center. Cooled by Gulf breezes, it was often used for dances. Many a romance blossomed during evenings on the pier when silver-crested waves murmured moonlight serenades.

During the daytime, many folks gathered on the pier simply to watch the large freighters disgorge their cargoes. "I can still see the ice in huge bales of sawdust," recalled one young visitor, "being unloaded at the pier into trolleys with iron wheels, waiting to be pushed to the hotel." And there were the colorful yachts from Ft.

The Naples city pier has been a popular gathering spot ever since the town was founded.

Myers, Punta Gorda, and other Gulf ports. Then too the pier was a wonderful place for anglers. "Huge schools of fish were common sights," recalled Earl Baum. "I have movies of a catch of fifty-four thousand pounds of mullet taken between Gordon Pass and the pier." The professionals used linked seines that reached for a quarter of a mile. Fish were so plentiful that sometimes a thousand pounds was left on the beach to rot.

But when darkness fell on moonless nights, the pier sometimes attracted a less desirable clientele. "I remember sitting on the pier one night," Baum wrote, "just after sundown. . . . All at once, coming up the shoreline, was an old skiff with two men in it. . . . [Then] here comes a truck down 12th Avenue, backed right onto the sand. I never saw whiskey unloaded so fast. . . ." Their haste was caused by a rapidly approaching revenue cutter. But by the time it got there, the truck was gone and the two bootleggers indignantly demanded to know how the Coast Guardsmen could possibly suspect them of anything illegal.

The pier is still a popular gathering place. It's open day and night with no admission fee. There is a concession offering snack food, and restrooms are available. Fishing from the pier is fair-to-middlin', with catches of snapper, grouper, and many other species including small blacktip sharks. If you don't have a pole, you can purchase a cheap one on the pier. There are even cleaning boards and fresh water.

Because the pier protrudes boldly into the Gulf with no protective coves, it is not a place to be in stormy weather. The first pier fell victim to a hurricane in 1910, and its successor was battered beyond repair by another hurricane in 1960. The current pier was built just a few years ago and has cement pillars. But cement has never thwarted a determined hurricane, and someday this structure will join its ancestors. When it goes, you can be sure that another pier will quickly take its place, for Naples without its pier would be like the Gulf without its sunset.

The Homes of Olde Naples

Many of the town's most picturesque historical homes are near the pier. Although they are modest compared to the more princely dwellings built later, inhabitants of Olde Naples adore their comfortable enclave. Many of their homes are relished hand-me-downs. "We shared a lot of happiness here in the days when Naples was like one family," noted one longtime resident. "This was my grandmother's house. The phone number was twenty-seven."

Why not just roam the area and savor the quiet days of long ago? One of your stops should be the Palm Cottage on Twelfth Avenue, a block east of the pier. If you don't mind the $6 entry fee, a curator from the historical society will take you back to 1895, when the foot-thick tabby walls—made of seashells, sand, and lime mortar—were put up. From Twelfth, walk a block north to Broad Avenue, which is lined with early homes, such as the one at 107, in which Earl Baum lived for three decades. As well as the author of *Early Naples and Collier County,* Baum was one of the town's first doctors. Sometimes he would find eight people waiting on his porch to be treated. One street farther north, at 287 Eleventh Avenue, is the Inn by the Sea, a 1937 home that claims to be Naples' only bed and breakfast (800-584-1268). If you like the flavor of the past, including pine floors and brass beds, you'll find the rates (between $149 and $189) to be acceptable.

Naples Bay

When you are through exploring the west side of Olde Naples, take Twelfth Avenue a few blocks east to where it ends at the City Dock beside Naples Bay. Prehistoric Indians found the future Twelfth Avenue an ideal route between the Gulf and the bay, for they constructed a great canal along here. This canal was as much as fifty feet wide and twenty-five feet deep, and remains of it impressed the first white settlers.

   The Indians built their canal because thick oyster beds across the bay's mouth made it too shallow for boats to cross over to the Gulf. The pass was eventually deepened, however, so that today there is a large marina in what is known as Crayton Cove. This is also the location of one of Naples' voguish restaurants, The Dock, open for lunches and dinners (941-263-994).

Another waterfront destination is nearby at Tin City, which is a group of restaurants, gift shops, and assorted bric-a-brac vendors occupying a rustic makeover of some clam and oyster warehouses. To reach Tin City from the City Dock, go north a few blocks on Eighth Street to Sixth Avenue, then a few blocks east to Tin City. Nearly everyone has something to eat at either the Riverwalk Fish & Ale House (941-263-2734) or Charley's Crab (941-430-1357). To get closer to the water, there are sightseeing boats that go on ninety-

Naples' Tin City has restaurants directly on the Gordon River.

minute narrated trips around the bay. A cruise costs $20 for adults and $10 for kids under thirteen. Boats leave every two hours. For exact times and reservations call 941-263-4949. But you don't have to buy, chew, or float to enjoy Tin City. Just to wander through this jigsaw jangle is an experience in itself.

Now go back to Eighth Street. Drive a block farther north to Fifth Avenue, then west along the dazzling downtown strip where you started this ramble. When you reach Gulf Shore Boulevard, turn north. Here begins a thirty-nine-mile backroads jaunt along the coast to Ft. Myers.

Driving along Easy Street

Before I hear disgruntled comments about the upcoming boulevards hardly being backroads, I'll retort that nowhere have I said a backroad has to be through an unpopulated area. I'm taking this route for two reasons. First, it leads past commodious homes, stylish high-rises, and chic shopping plazas, the likes of which most of us don't ordinarily frequent. And second, there is no other way to Ft. Myers except on US 41—and *that* motorized cacophony is to be avoided at all costs.

Naples beaches are tranquil at daybreak.

Gulf Shore Boulevard is shaded by the tall palms with which Naples has a love affair. The cross streets end at beaches where public swimming is allowed—all you have to do is find a parking place, and that can be challenging. But don't be concerned; there are many nice beaches with accessible parking farther on.

Soon you'll pass the exclusive Naples Beach Hotel and Golf Club. When it was built in the late 1930s, it displaced the Naples Hotel as the place for the young set to "hubba hubba." Earl Baum tells of the couple who slipped away from a party early for a moonlight skinny-dip in the Gulf. Some snoopy teenage girls followed them and, when they were otherwise occupied, ran off with their clothes. "I leave it to your imagination," Baum wrote with his usual twinkle, "how they returned to their respective homes," adding that the pair looked very mosquito-bitten the next day.

Just beyond the hotel is Lowdermilk Park, named after a progressive city manager. You can park in the metered area at the north end, unless you care to purchase a seven-day permit for $10, which will give you access to any space in the entire lot. Lowdermilk has restrooms, changing areas, and a concession stand. And, oh, did I forget to mention the wide beach with its caressingly soft sand? The park is particularly appealing in the morning, when El Greco shadows make sinuous patterns across the sand. Just take care not to get hooked and forget the song of the road.

Gulf Shore Boulevard does seem to sing of people who have made it—at least before their creditors found them. For them this *is* Easy Street. The buildings glisten in Naples' nearly perpetual sunshine. The grounds are landscaped with shrubs that have no dead leaves. The flowers are always in bloom. People drive Mercedes and Lamborghinis, and when they stroll down the sidewalks, they sport the latest, most expensive fashions.

Soon you'll begin seeing yachts on your right, where Hurricane Harbor forms an ideal mooring cove. At this point the road turns west. As it crosses over the harbor, it becomes Mooring Line Drive. On the other side is Crayton Road, where you will turn north. All this land once belonged to Ed Crayton and his wife, Lindsey, who outlived him by many years. Lindsey sold the Moorings area in the 1950s for $3 million. Thereupon the frugal old lady commented, "Now I can afford to have my house painted."

You'll pass the Moorings Country Club and Golf Course. Golf is a common playtime activity here, and Naples has more country clubs than any other city in the entire world! Just because they are so common does not mean they are cheap. Initiation fees can run up to

The Naples area waterfront has many marinas and luxury condos.

$200,000! If this doesn't faze you, maybe you'd like to purchase a home in Naples. They average around $650,000—although you might prefer one for $18 million, which was what an uncompleted beachfront estate recently went for. Not surprisingly, Naples real estate is the most expensive in the entire state.

Turn west on Harbor Drive to reach Gulf Shore Boulevard again. Once more you'll be among ritzy, high-rise condos and apartments. This is a newer section, for Naples is expanding along the Gulf—as well as in almost every other direction. Nearly all of Collier County "is in over-drive," noted the business-oriented *Florida Trend* magazine. Collier's population sprouted thirty-five percent in the past eight years, compared with twelve percent for Florida as a whole. It was such a staggering spurt that the governor ordered county officials to come up with a stricter plan for environmental protection or risk losing millions in state funds.

When you reach Park Shore Drive, you'll find a mall called The Village on Venetian Bay. Someone with imagination and style planned this group of apparel stores, art galleries, gift shops, and restaurants that straddles both sides of Park Shore. The buildings are reminiscent of the real Venice without the smells and grungy water. Be sure to stroll the fine promenade along Venetian Bay.

A broad boardwalk through thick mangroves leads to the beach at Clam Pass County Park.

Why Pass Clam Pass?

Follow Park Shore Drive east over Venetian Bay to Crayton Road, which will lead you north through an area of homes to Seagate Drive. If you're beginning to wonder if you'll ever view anything natural (read: not man-made) again, turn left here to Clam Pass County Park. It costs $3 per car to park in the lot, which is adjacent to the classy Registry Resort, with its five restaurants, three swimming pools, fifteen tennis courts, and prime-time room rates between $255 and $530. But you'll feel far from civilization as you take the twenty-minute hike (or six-minute tram ride) through a mangrove bayou to the beach. Once there, you'll enjoy the swimming. There are restrooms and a concession where you can get snacks and soft drinks.

Leaving Clam Pass, go east on Seagate Drive one long block beyond Crayton Road to West Boulevard. Turn left here and in a few blocks you'll come to Pelican Bay Boulevard, location of Naples' highly rated Philharmonic Center for the Arts. Culture lovers come here to enjoy the theater, ballet, opera, symphony, and even jazz and children's shows.

Now follow Pelican Bay Boulevard as it leads west, then arches north. Pelican Bay is an exclusive enclave where the condos and residences are set amid wide, grassy areas. This quiet boulevard presents a marked contrast to the hustle along Gulf Shore. There is plenty of money at Pelican Bay, but it murmurs a more subdued melody. The prices are not subdued, however. It will cost you more than $500,000 to move into the Coronado condominium. Nearby, the Marbella commands over $600,000. But this is pigeon crumbs compared to the Montenero, where you'd need a cool $1 million to set up house-keeping. Yet astonishingly, the dwellers here are relatively poor compared to the really rich who live in the Bay Colony at the northern end of Pelican Bay Boulevard. Here condo prices at the Gulf-front Windsor have lofted above $3 million. If you consider this too much, you can stay overnight at the nearby Ritz-Carlton Hotel. It was voted the top resort hotel in the continental U.S. and Canada by the discerning readers of *Travel & Leisure* magazine. During the prime winter season, for just $449 nightly you can get a room with no particular view. But, as long as you're there, why not stay in a Gulf-front suite? It will only cost $300 more. For reservations call 800-241-3333.

A Fishing Hole for Scammers

With all this wealth, you'd think the residents of Naples (a good percentage of whom are self-made men from the Midwest) would be content just to run their yachts and count their gold. Yet despite their tough exterior, many are surprisingly susceptible to guile. In an article for *Florida Trend* magazine entitled "Ready, Aim . . . Scam," John Finotti tells how rich Neapolitans lost $100 million in one confidence game and just eight months later were taken by another for $59 million!

The larger scam involved what the article called a "classic boiler-room operation." Glib salesmen working for a certain investment company telephoned wealthy people, touting young companies whose stocks were certain to spiral upwards. This was especially appealing to the Midwesterners, who felt a kinship with such entrepreneurs. As they began investing, the stock dutifully rose. So they invested more . . . and more. And still the stock climbed. What they didn't realize was that most of these companies were owned by the investment company itself. By the time the stock peaked, the company had dumped its holdings and the Naples investors were left with virtually worthless stock.

Have the wealthy learned from these experiences? "It'll happen again," the article concluded. "There are simply too many with too much money who are too eager to believe a good story."

The Pleasures of Vanderbilt Beach

The boulevard continues for slightly more than two miles before turning east. At this point, watch for either North Pointe Drive or Hammock Oak Drive on your left. These streets take you out of Pelican Bay to Vanderbilt Beach Road, where you should turn left. The road will quickly end at Gulf Shore Drive North and the Gulf of Mexico, where there is a public beach. The parking lot has been landscaped so well that it is difficult to see, so watch for it on the left side of Vanderbilt.

Although the lot costs $3 for non-county visitors, it's worth it to park here and walk south on Vanderbilt Beach. Almost immediately you'll come to the Ritz-Carlton, where a sign invites the public to the Gumbo Limbo and Beach Pavilion Restaurants. They are, in essence, wide places in a tree-shaded boardwalk that runs along the crest of a low dune just above the sea grapes and other vegetation. If you order a Coke or even a cookie, you can say you dined at the Ritz and spent less than $4! Of course, you can't have them both at that price.

Continuing down the beach, you'll pass a row of magnificent high-rises, including the Windsor, where the rich and famous have the same vista from their $3-million suites as we humble shell-pickers on the sand. You'll also find Vanderbilt Beach ideal for swim- ming. But you'd better be wearing your bathing suit when you arrive. Although there are restrooms, there is no changing area.

Gulf Shore Drive runs north from Vanderbilt Beach. The road is only two lanes, and, although it is lined with fashionable condos, they are not as tall or showy as those farther south. There is even a quaint, single-story motel called the Vanderbilt Beach Resort, with units on the Gulf for around $140 per night (800-243-9076). The motel's highly regarded Turtle Restaurant serves food directly on the beach. Across the street, the moderately priced Lighthouse Restaurant features a deck overlooking the Vanderbilt Lagoon.

With all these references to Vanderbilt, you may be wondering where the name came from. It goes back to the 1930s, when Barron Collier, the dominant landowner in the county, was negotiating with General Vanderbilt for property along the beach. Collier was so sure the deal would go through that he wrote "Vanderbilt" on the plat. However, the general inconveniently died, and soon thereafter so did Collier. The name remained on the plat even though Vanderbilt never purchased the land—at least that's the way the story was related to me by a curator of the county historical museum. If true, it was an unusual way to achieve a modicum of immortality.

Naples' Best Beach? Delnor-Wiggins Pass

Gulf Shore ends at Bluebill Avenue, entry to Delnor-Wiggins Pass State Recreation Area. Delnor-Wiggins is included on almost any list of top world beaches. Admission is $4 per car, but the five parking lots are often full by mid-morning. Originally the only person enjoying this beautiful spot was Joe Wiggins, who lived here in a ramshackle trading post during the late 1800s. Later, Lester and Dellora Norris were instrumental in turning it into a public park. The beach, of course, is superb, and the park offers changing rooms and an outdoor shower. There are some short hiking trails with picnic tables and grills. At the far north end of the park is an observation tower that gives an encompassing view of *leaves* and needs another story added before it lives up to its name. Fishing is good at Wiggins Pass at the park's northern extremity. Shelling is also a popular recreation.

Now head east on Bluebill for a half mile to Vanderbilt Drive (CR 901), where you should turn north once more. This is wetland where the march of humanity has paused. You'll pass over Wiggins Bay, with the Pelican Isle Yacht Club and a good-size marina in the distance. Then comes more marsh. When the land gets slightly higher, some housing developments appear. But they are set back from the road and don't intrude excessively. In a few miles Vanderbilt terminates at CR 865, Bonita Beach Road.

Barefoot Beach

Follow CR 865 west. When it approaches the Gulf, watch for a sign on your left indicating the way to the Barefoot Beach State Preserve. The name alone should entice you. Follow Lely Beach Boulevard to Barefoot. On its way, Lely meanders through Bonita Shores, one of the prettiest little communities in these parts. Its homes and condos are artfully spaced along the boulevard, which edges between the Gulf and a bay lined with pleasure craft. When Lely ends at the park entrance, sea grapes and other sand vegetation take the place of the manicured lawns and ornamental trees.

Admission to Barefoot Beach is $3 per car. The beach is ideal for swimming, and there are changing rooms and a concession. A boardwalk leads along the dune shore. Shade would be welcome here on certain days, but the tall Australian pines that used to provide it have been destroyed as unwanted exotic trees. Nearby is the open-air Learning Center, with displays of native plants and animals. It also features a massive Calusa battle-ax with a stone head almost a foot wide. The Center, in the form of a tribal chickee, features a roof composed of more than five thousand palm fronds laboriously installed by Seminole craftsmen.

Yes, There Really Is a Lovers Key

Back on CR 865 and driving north you'll soon ascend the lofty bridge over New Pass. Strung out before you will be a seascape of pastel blue and green studded with many islands ringed with golden-white sand. Four of these islands have been grouped together as the Lovers Key State Recreation Area. The entry is off of CR 865 and costs $4 per car.

Lovers Key has about all you can want (except you'll have to bring

A tram takes visitors to the Lovers Key beach.

along your own lover): swimming on a beach two and a half miles long; canoes and kayaks for exploring the many tantalizing back bays; and bicycles for pedaling down three miles of off-road trails. The canoes and kayaks rent for $20 for half a day; bikes are $5 for half a day. If you want to probe the island complex more deeply, a naturalist conducts two-hour narrated paddles for $25 per person. For more information, call 941-463-4588.

With all this build-up, you may be curious as to where the name came from. When I asked officials on the spot, they didn't know. I had to go to the park manager. He wasn't entirely sure, but he had heard that when the islands were accessible only by boat, they were popular with couples (newlyweds and otherwise) who wished to pursue certain private matters without interruption. If that was the case, the island should change its name, for today you can hardly go anywhere without an onlooker popping up unannounced on a bike or in a silent kayak.

Beyond Lovers Key, the fun is over for a while as you travel along commercially active Estero Island. But there's only one through-road along the coast, so grit your teeth, ignore the honky-tonk, and plod on to Ft. Myers Beach.

Getting to Know Ft. Myers Beach

 Although I've driven through Ft. Myers Beach only three times, I believe I know almost every sandblasted house and beer-basted tavern along CR 865, at least from the outside. You too may get to know them, for not only is the town of around fourteen thousand people strung out interminably, its congestion would put Los Angeles into the hayseed category. The highlight of your visit will probably be sighting the bridge to Ft. Myers.

The Cattle Trail to Punta Rassa

Once in Ft. Myers, you'll be on San Carlos Boulevard. Stay on it until you reach McGregor Boulevard, where you should turn right. McGregor was an army trail during the Second Seminole War. It led to the supply depot at Punta Rassa, near the modern bridge to Sanibel Island. After most of the Seminoles had been shuttled off to Oklahoma in 1842, the trail became a passageway for herds of half-wild cattle driven by cowboys almost as rambunctious as the cows themselves. They were headed for the pens at Punta Rassa, from which the cattle would be shipped to Cuba and other destinations. On payday, the cowpokes would hole up for a few days at Jake Summerlin's bunkhouse. Here they'd spend their time in proper frontier fun: gambling, drinking, and fighting. They all packed revolvers, and it's reported that the bunkhouse was peppered with bullet holes, from rafters to rat holes. A chapter in Patrick Smith's historical novel of early Florida, *A Land Remembered*, offers a wonderful description of a cattle drive into Punta Rassa.

The Road of Palms

The railroads brought an end to the raucous revelries at Punta Rassa. But the road lived on. Thomas Edison chose a spot along it for his winter quarters. In order to beautify the dingy path, he planted hundreds of royal palms from Cuba. Then, in 1912, a grande dame whom everyone knew as Tootie offered to pave much of the road with shells if the city would name it after her deceased husband, Ambrose McGregor. Over the years the forested portion of McGregor has expanded. So when you first get on the boulevard, you'll be among the newest and smallest palms. But as you continue, they get progressively taller until you find yourself driving down a pillared roadway. It's an exhilarating experience.

Eventually you'll come to the Thomas Edison estate, which is

Ft. Myers' McGregor Boulevard presents miles of magnificent palms.

open to the public. When Edison decided to make his winter home in Ft. Myers in 1885, it was a sleepy cattle town of fewer than four hundred people. One persistent (though unconfirmed) story goes that when Edison offered to install electric streetlights, the townsfolk objected, saying the lights would disturb the cows. The Edison compound brings out the human side of this genius, who helped begin the modern age when he perfected the first commercially practical incandescent lamp, as well as the movie projector, the phonograph, and more than a thousand other inventions. His laboratory, with all its mysterious scientific gadgetry, is just the way he left it when he died in 1931. There is the swimming pool where his children frolicked. In the home itself is the piano played by his wife, Mina—although Thomas was oblivious to the melodies, being almost entirely deaf. The Edisons' warmest friends were Henry and Clara Ford, who owned the home next door (also open to the public). Henry loved to square dance and would move the furnishings from his living room onto the porch so they could do-si-do.

Tours of the Edison and Ford homes are offered from 9 A.M. to 5:30 P.M. Mondays through Saturdays and 12 noon to 5:30 P.M. on Sundays. Admission is $12 for adults and $5.50 for kids six through twelve.

Not far beyond the Edison/Ford complex, McGregor Boulevard enters the downtown area, where it becomes Main Street. At this point turn a block north on Monroe Street to First Street. First Street is the heart of the historic district. It was originally right on the Caloosahatchee River, named for the ancient Calusa tribe who lived along its banks. In 1850 the U.S. Army constructed a large fort here to overawe the Seminoles. There were fifty-seven buildings and a wharf that extended nearly a thousand feet into the water. After the Seminoles were gone, American settlers began building their town. During the first half of the twentieth century, it became an important shopping and business center. But with the advent of outlying shopping malls, the downtown suffered a devastating decline. Current programs are promoting downtown Ft. Myers as a recreational center.

Drive east on First Street through the heart of downtown to Lee Street. Go north on Lee two blocks to the yacht basin, where the Riverwalk affords a pleasant stroll along the water. J. C. Cruises runs boat tours from here, some upriver and some down. They vary from two hours for $15 (kids $7.50) to five hours for $24 (kids $12.) The upriver cruises usually include sumptuous buffet meals. For the departure schedule, call 941-334-7474.

The high-rise Ramada Inn anchors the eastern end of the riverfront. Here you can enjoy breakfast, lunch, or dinner in the second-floor restaurant offering a fine view of the Caloosahatchee. Spending the night here costs $90 to $120 (941-337-0300).

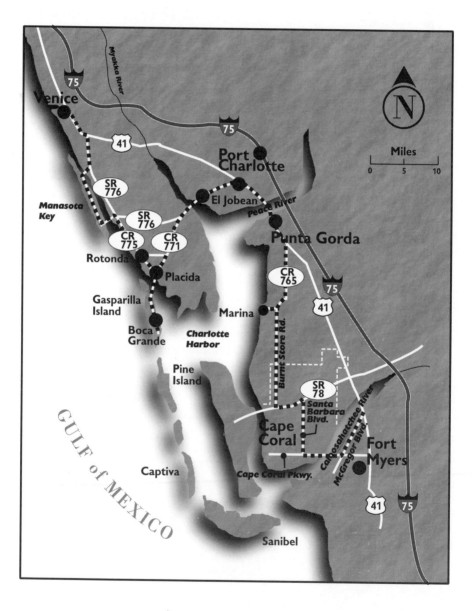

The Leeward Coast
Ft. Myers to Venice • 109 Backroad Miles

The Song of the Road: Overview

From Ft. Myers the road leads across the Caloosahatchee River to Cape Coral, a new city brought to a life by the Rosen brothers in the 1960s. Although it can be a beautiful place, Cape Coral has inherited a heavy burden from the Rosens' defunct real estate giant, Gulf American. Driving north on Burnt Store Road you'll see vacant homesites, unused boulevards, and canals that go nowhere.

It's different in Punta Gorda, a long-established, largely residential town that features the shops and restaurants of Fishermen's Village. Continuing north, you'll pass through a disquietingly deserted community called Rotonda, so named because of its layout as a huge wheel. Beyond Rotonda, the road heads across Gasparilla Sound, named for a fierce pirate who supposedly hid out along here. Boca Grande, on Gasparilla Island, is famous for its picturesque lighthouse, fine beaches, and excellent seafood restaurants. In addition, the thrill of its summer tarpon fishing is almost legendary.

The road from Boca Grande to Venice includes a section along Manasota Key, along which are several palm-fringed, Gulf-front public beaches. Venice's downtown is a work of art. You can also drive to the long jetties at the harbor mouth, where the fishing is nearly as good as the yacht-watching. But what makes the town truly unique are prehistoric sharks' teeth deposited by waves onto the sand in great numbers. The fossilized teeth are beautiful keepsakes, although most are less than half an inch long. Diligent searchers sometimes find teeth several inches long, however, which can bring several hundred dollars on the open market.

On the Road Again

From downtown Ft. Myers, head southwest on McGregor Boulevard (CR 867), lined on both sides with a stately row of seemingly endless royal palms. Continue past the estates of Thomas Edison and Henry Ford, which were described in the last chapter. After six tree-lined miles, and after passing the Midpoint Bridge, you'll come

169

to the Cape Coral Bridge, where you should turn right.

The Colonel in Nightclothes

The Cape Coral bridge spans the Caloosahatchee River, which extends halfway across the state to Moore Haven. Here a canal and lock link it to Lake Okeechobee and the St. Lucie Canal, enabling it to be part of the cross-state waterway between the Gulf of Mexico and the Atlantic Ocean. The bridge ends at Harney Point, where a plaque marks the site of a small army post during the Seminole War. The twenty-six troopers were commanded by Colonel William Harney, a muscular, six-foot-three-inch giant. Harney failed to post guards during the night of June 23, 1839. A surprise attack by the Seminoles cut him off from his men, and he had no choice except to beat a humiliating retreat clad only in his nightshirt and underdrawers.

The Chamber of Commerce has a welcome center at Harney Point on Cape Coral Parkway, where you can pick up many pieces of free literature. Oddly, you're not allowed to use the restroom. Perhaps it is not so odd after all, for Cape Coral itself is a somewhat odd place.

The City Built by Showmen: Cape Coral

On the surface, Cape Coral seems quite normal. There is a feeling of pride and fulfillment in the air. Its population has burgeoned to one hundred thousand, making it more than twice as large Ft. Myers, its more vocal neighbor. Yet even with this tremendous influx of people, Cape Coral is the safest city in Florida (according to official FBI figures). It is expanding its business base by becoming a Foreign Trade Zone. It has joined Florida's Main Street Program, and its many refurbished storefronts and landscaped center parkway recently won an Honor Award from the Florida Redevelopment Association. These good tidings are amplified by the fact that the price of a three-bedroom home in Cape Coral is fifteen percent below the national metropolitan average. The city has many miles of beautiful canal and riverfront properties.

Yet there are also many miles of bleak, treeless wasteland where the boulevards have enticing names but no houses. There are deserted canals with their water becoming stagnant and their sides in danger of caving in. It is not only a depressing scene, it's also a severe financial drain on the city, which had its beginning back in 1957, when the Rosen brothers, Leonard and Jack, bought a relatively small piece of land at Redfish Point, just downriver from Harney Point.

The Rosens were unlikely city founders. After their father, a Russian-Jewish immigrant, was killed by a streetcar, the brothers had to quit school (Leonard not yet in his teens) and support their mother and themselves. The two boys hawked various products at New Jersey county fairs and on the streets of Baltimore. This was their main education, and from it they developed into expert, fast-pitch salesmen. Carefully saving most of their earnings, they eventually bought a small shampoo company. Showmen from the beginning, Leonard's first TV appearance involved having an egg smashed on his head as an advertising gimmick. Understandably, this created considerable stir and caused sales to soar. Other provocative stunts enabled the Rosens to sell the company for a pleasing profit of $2 million.

With this money the brothers decided to try their hands at real estate development. They purchased the marshy land on the banks of the Caloosahatchee (mainly because it was cheap) and named it Cape Coral—not because it was a cape (which it wasn't) nor because there was coral (which there wasn't). It just sounded good.

The Rosens realized they would need large sums of money to turn this waterlogged area into saleable land, so they formed the Gulf American Corporation. Investing just $125,000 of their own money, they ultimately elevated Gulf American into the largest land sales company in the United States, potentially worth $115 million—an almost unbelievable achievement meticulously documented by David Dodrill in *Selling the Dream*.

The Incredible Twelve-year Rosen Saga

Now drive eight blocks west from the Welcome Center on Cape Coral Parkway to Coronado Parkway. In the beginning, the Rosens' sales office was on the southwest corner. At that time it was the only building in town. Cape Coral Parkway, now the heart of the business section, was so quiet it was often used as a landing strip for the company's single aircraft, piloted by a hotshot who savored flying *under* the telephone wires as he landed.

At first it was a shoestring operation, for few bankers cared to gamble on what they regarded as an off-the-wall project with little chance of success. Thus the Rosens forced their suppliers to help with the financing by waiting three or more months for their money. The only way the struggling company could obtain the station wagon it urgently needed was by bartering a choice homesite for it.

Expenses soared, for not only was it necessary to bring in the machinery to dig the canals and to spread the fill to raise the land, but roads, sewers, electricity, and water had to be made available. Another financial drain was the construction of the yacht club and golf course. When Leonard Rosen received criticism from Gulf American investors for diverting funds for the golf club, he shot back: "You know what you guys' problem is? . . . You're looking at it as a capital investment. That's not what it is. It's the biggest goddam bulletin board in the United States." Despite continued objections, the golf course was completed in 1961. A year later the yacht club opened. It boasted a picturesque basin with a two-hundred-boat capacity, an array of tennis and shuffleboard courts, a swimming pool of Olympic size, and a fine bathing beach on the river. Now the Rosens were ready to bring in prospective buyers.

With Gulf American's treasury perilously low, the Rosens began a do-or-die advertising campaign in selected Northern cities. All you needed to get a slice of paradise was $120 down and payments of just $20 a month. Buy now, the ads shrieked, for sales were rocketing and prices were spiraling upward. If you weren't prepared to move to paradise right away, buy for retirement. Or buy simply for speculation: hold it a year or two and sell for a juicy profit.

Gulf American sponsored free chicken dinners, where the only obligation was to listen to a so-called "brief" sales talk. People were encouraged to make down payments without seeing their property, then accept the "fly and buy" program where the company flew them to Cape Coral for three carefree days as pampered guests. It didn't seem to matter to most prospective buyers that they could not really inspect their property, for most of the roads were just sandy ruts suitable for bulldozers, not private cars. They were treated to an excursion in the company plane, where the pilot roared in low and tossed out a flour sack to mark their particular lot—although his accuracy was not of the highest order.

As sales soared, a strange thing happened: the company took on an existence beyond the control of the Rosens themselves. It became a voracious monster. The flood of buyers brought the need for more property to sell, and the new property required the digging of canals. This meant more expenses. So advertising had to be increased. This brought more buyers, who required more land, and so a chain reaction was created. Eventually Gulf American purchased tracts a dozen lonely miles from the town center. Cape Coral's city limits soon were more extensive than any city in all of Florida save for Jacksonville!

Eventually even the salesmen had no idea where the property they were selling was. But it didn't matter, for now the vast majority of buyers were buying on pure speculation, with resale profits as their goal. By 1967 an estimated ninety-two thousand homesites had been sold, yet only thirty-one hundred families had moved to Cape Coral.

To see the Cape Coral that was shown to buyers, drive south on the boulevard that is first called Coronado Parkway, then, as it makes a graceful left turn, becomes Lucerne, which becomes Driftwood as it bends right. The road, bordered by tall palms, is four lanes with a grassy center strip. It ends at a sandy beach on the Caloosahatchee River, here wider than most Florida lakes. Across a parking area from the beach is the yacht club, impressive with its sandstone façade and high-pitched, two-and-a-half-story roof. Nearby is the swimming pool and, just beyond, the basin where pleasure craft sway slowly in the calm water. A spacious canal borders the club on the east. Across it are the company's showplace homes, each with its own dock. It is not difficult to understand how Gulf American salesmen could beguile their Northern guests with such an idyllic setting.

Indeed, the setting is beguiling even today. The beach is available to the public, and there is a bathhouse for changing. Nearby, reaching far into the river, is the city pier, where everyone is invited to fish or enjoy the beautiful sunsets. A sandwich shop serves lunch on a raised deck overlooking the pier, beach, and river. The yacht club, which still graces the waterfront, is no longer private. It's open to the public for weddings, dances, and other social functions.

The Other Cape Coral

Now it's time to meet the Cape Coral that few buyers ever knew. Return to Cape Coral Parkway and drive west a mile to Santa Barbara Boulevard. The town originally ended near here, but Gulf American gobbled up the Matlacha Cattle Ranch, a large stretch of land that reached westward all the way to Pine Island. Driving north on Santa Barbara through former ranch land, you'll soon be out in the country. Yet this is still Cape Coral. Despite its current growth, the town is still two-thirds undeveloped. The land is scored with canals that go nowhere. Indeed, there are more canals in Cape Coral than in Venice, Italy!

When you reach Pine Island Road (SR 78), head west four miles to Burnt Store Road (CR 765). All the land hereabouts once supported a

Most Cape Coral buyers got unimproved sites like this one on the town's
vast and lonely northern expanse.

fine growth of tall pines, but timber companies in the 1920s and
1930s turned them into siding and sawdust. It seems incredible that
during the Gulf American era people would have bought home lots
in an area so desolate and so far from town. One would have thought
that just the name, Burnt Store Road (commemorating a Seminole
escapade), would have been warning enough. Yet you'll pass broad
streets (called parkways) with ironically grandiose titles like
Tropicana, Diplomat, and Gulf Stream. And you'll pass over canals,
some so wide that a fleet of gondolas could easily have navigated
them. But the canals were dug merely to obtain landfill, and most
end at dead ponds. There are no homes, no stores, no people, and no
realtors' offices—how hopeless can you get? But Cape Coral taxpayers
are dutifully supporting a small firehouse that sits by itself in this
weary wilderness.

The Law and the "Scoundrels"

The land out here was sold during the last years of Gulf American,
when the company was virtually out of control. One of the
salesmen's worst tactics was to make glib assertions that, if the
purchaser could not make a sizable profit, the company would gladly
buy the property back. But the company had no intention of buying

anything back, gladly or otherwise.

Eventually Gulf American's immoral sales tactics became so blatant that Florida Governor Claude Kirk declared the Rosens and their associates "scoundrels." Accordingly, he ordered the Florida Land Sales Board (FLSB) to investigate.

At first the Rosens scoffed at the investigation. Leonard, in particular, became arrogant and sometimes didn't even return the governor's phone calls. But it soon became apparent that the FLSB was amassing a mountainous volume of complaints from irate purchasers. The Rosens felt the noose tightening and at last, fearing that these matters would be aired in the national press, admitted that Gulf American was guilty on five counts. Thereupon the FLSB not only suspended sales for an entire month but also forced the company to accept five monitors to oversee its operations for 150 days.

With Gulf American now thoroughly discredited, sales plunged. So the Rosens decided it was now time to bail out. Thus in 1969 they unloaded Gulf American on a company called GAC, which struggled with Cape Coral for ten years before going bankrupt.

The Rosens came out far better than expected, for both brothers ended up with estates worth upwards of $10 million. However, despite their fortunes, the future turned out grim. Jack Rosen died of a heart attack the same year the company was sold. Len too was plagued with heart problems, not helped by the federal government's investigation of income tax evasion. Eventually he pleaded no contest to the charges but was inexplicably pardoned several years later. He died in 1987 a sick and unhappy man.

Even though it's been more than three decades since the Rosens departed from Cape Coral, the city is still harassed with the problems they left. The many interior canals have no outlet to the vaunted fishing in the Caloosahatchee and the Gulf beyond. And those who purchase lots on these canals must put in seawalls to prevent erosion, for Gulf American didn't bother with them. Taxpayers must fund mosquito spraying of the almost-endless canals in the deserted areas. Eventually sewers and water will have to be brought in if this land is to be made suitable for residences.

But that's the concern of the citizens of Cape Coral. You and I are just passing wayfarers. We have other places to visit, other backroads to wander, other stories to discover.

"Cruisin' the Good Life": The Burnt Store Marina

On the extreme northern border of Lee County you'll come across Burnt Store Marina signs offering the chance to enjoy "Cruisin' the Good Life." It's worth the time to take a brief jaunt down the entry road past the crisp new homes to the marina.

Here you can pause beside the 425-slip harbor, which claims to be the largest privately owned such facility on Florida's west coast. Salty's Harborside Restaurant, overlooking the boat basin, serves lunches and dinners Tuesdays through Saturdays, as well as brunch on Sundays (941-639-3650). Real estate at Burnt Store is surprisingly reasonable, at least compared to other waterfront communities. If you would like to reside at the Harbor Towers II, prices begin around $100,000. But, of course, you can induce the sales staff to sell you a unit for five times that figure if you try.

A Most Livable Town: Punta Gorda

Continuing on CR 765, in a few miles you'll reach US 41, which you should follow north the short distance to Punta Gorda. When you get to Marion Avenue, turn left. This is the town's main street and has been the object of an extensive renovation. Given the fact that Punta Gorda's population is only around

Fishing boats frequent Fishermen's Wharf at Punta Gorda.

fifteen thousand, it's surprising what hard work and creativity can do. The downtown streetscape resulted in the installation of pavement bricks, benches, planters, streetlights, and shade trees. In addition, the Historic Mural Society has promoted the painting of more than thirty colorful pictures on downtown buildings. The civic spirit extended in so many directions that *Money* magazine recently named Punta Gorda one of the nation's most livable small towns.

Continue west on Marion, down an aisle of palms, four miles to Fishermen's Village, where you can enjoy shopping or feasting with views of the Peace River in the background. If you have time, continue west on Marion to Ponce de Leon City Park. The park, which offers beautiful sunsets over the Gulf of Mexico, helps recall that Punta Gorda's roots extend all the way back to Ponce's landing in 1513. It was during the Spanish era that the site acquired its name, which means "Fat Point," or, as the Chamber of Commerce prefers, "Broad Point."

Driving back on Marion, take a short detour north when you reach McGregor Street, which was lovingly bricked by volunteers in the 1980s. McGregor ends at Retta Esplanade, the town's premier historic, residential street. The homes, built by families wealthy from cattle or shipping, look out on the spacious Peace River—a view enhanced today by Gilchrist Park. Immediately east of the park is the Best Western Motel, with rooms as well as a restaurant offering scenic views of the river and the graceful US 41 bridges (941-639-8116).

Charlotte's Mystery: Port Charlotte

Leaving Punta Gorda by way of US 41, you'll cross the river to Port Charlotte. In some ways this town is analogous to Cape Coral, for both were built by developers in the 1950s and '60s. But Port Charlotte is not nearly as interesting as Cape Coral, for the Mackle Brothers and General Development did it right. It has 165 miles of canals and is growing fast too. But its population is only about half of Cape Coral's.

Possibly the town's most interesting footnote concerns the derivation of its name. The founders called it after Charlotte County. The county, established in 1921, was named after Charlotte Bay. The bay, in turn, had been named by the British (when they owned Florida) in honor of Charlotte Sophia, the wife of King George III. This was a natural adaptation of what the Spanish before them had called Carlos

Bay, a corruption of the Indian tribe inhabiting the region: the Calusa. And from where did the Calusa receive their name? That's for conjecture. Sorry to leave you hanging.

Success Is More Than a Name: El Jobean

Upon reaching SR 776, turn left. Although the road goes through land that is mostly pines and marsh, it is four lanes, a forecast of coming dredge and fill developments. Already there is the newish, six-thousand-seat Charlotte County Stadium, home of the Texas Rangers baseball team during spring training and of the mighty Charlotte Rangers for the rest of the season. The road becomes two lanes when it reaches El Jobean, which consists mainly of a gas station or two, a bait store, and a few assorted edifices along the Myakka River. Don't try to look up its meaning in a Spanish dictionary, because you won't find it there. It's an anagram made from the name of a developer, Joel Bean. Mr. Bean came here in 1924 for a building fling. He was disappointed because, although the name had a zing, the place did not.

SR 776 crosses the Myakka River, where you'll probably see fishermen casting their lines, then leads through land that is mostly unoccupied now but is destined to sprout houses in the near future. In a mile there is a fork, where you should head south on CR 771. After traveling two miles, watch for Rotonda Boulevard East and turn right. Soon you'll pass over what is designated as the Rotonda River but is actually a rather unassuming canal. You are now in a thriving community of nearly 190,000 happy people living the good life amid golf courses and a system of lovely waterways with a direct link to the tarpon-rich Gulf of Mexico. At least that's what you would have been told was Rotonda's future if you were an unfortunate buyer three decades ago.

The Broken Circle: Rotonda

Rotonda was a breathtaking concept. It was laid out in the form of a huge wheel covering forty square miles and encircled by the Rotonda River. Entry was by way of a pair of landscaped boulevards—one from the east and one from the west. Both ended at Parade Circle, which formed the center of the wheel. Radiating from Parade Circle were four other major boulevards that defined water-enclosed golfing and boating communities with inviting streets like Par View Place and Sportsman Way.

Rotonda was designed to be a major town, but the heart of the development is an overgrown wasteland.

But the developers quickly found that it required more than a unique design to make an investment thrive. They overlooked the fact that Rotonda was too far from anything to give it much appeal. The salesmen did their best—more than their best, for their pressure tactics and unkept promises resulted in a deluge of lawsuits that prompted an investigation by the Federal Trade Commission in 1975. That same year the company went bankrupt, leaving the buyers crying in the wilderness and much of the property in the unwilling hands of the lender, Citicorp.

Today the street names seem brazenly out of place as you drive among the overgrown wax myrtles, scrubby pines, and bristling saw palmetto. Perhaps you will come across the same sign I saw along Rotonda Boulevard East: "Lots for sale. Association owned foreclosures." But change is in the air. Although the eastern portion of Rotonda never had the appeal of the western, the Long Marsh Golf Club has recently been established off of White Marsh Road at the eastern end of Parade Circle. The public is welcome, so if you happen to have a bag of clubs handy call 941-698-0918 for tee times. Otherwise you can settle for a snack and conversation at the club grill.

The main activity at Rotonda is in the western portion, where two of the seven communities have caught on. They are behind the scrub on both sides of Rotonda Boulevard West. Realtors' signs have even begun appearing—a sure indication that the old wheel is starting to turn at last.

It's No Longer Placid at Placida

The wheel is turning for more than Rotonda. This entire isolated corner of Charlotte County is apparently in the beginning stage of what may be explosive growth. One harbinger is the Lemon Bay Golf Club, where Rotonda Boulevard ends at CR 775. Turning south on CR 775, you'll pass more golf courses as well as a lot of building activity at Cape Haze. If you need more evidence of growth, notice the just-built Publix supermarket.

This area was long known to Cuban fishermen for its calm waters, which they called "placido." The word must have seemed apropos to the later Americans, although they didn't get the Spanish quite right when they translated it to Placida. Things were not so tranquil, however, during the Second World War, when German submarines sank scores of freighters in the nearby Gulf of Mexico. Thereupon tiny Placida was mustered into wartime service as an assembly point for electronic mines. These deadly devices were loaded on Navy mine-layers and deployed around U-boat–infested localities.

The Pirates' Causeway

When you see the sign for Boca Grande and Gasparilla Island, turn right onto the private causeway. You'll cross the Intracoastal Waterway on a small toll bridge where pelicans often sweep around the pylons. As the causeway traverses the shallow bay, the water on both sides becomes soft blue-green. Paralleling the road is a second causeway once used by the Charlotte Harbor and Northern Railroad. The line was once a vital link between Gasparilla Island and the mainland, but now the tracks have been taken up and parts of the causeway are choice fishing sites.

Around you are many coves where an outlaw ship could hide—a ship such as the one once captained by José Gaspar, who has come to be known to us as the feared pirate Gasparilla. Although José was born to a noble Spanish family, he lost all morals when he sailed from his secret harbor on Gasparilla Island in the 1790s and early 1800s. Many were the richly laden ships that he captured, murdering the crew and distributing the ladies to his lusty band, saving the most lovely for himself. He buried much of his treasure on Gasparilla

Island, but the exact location was lost when he and his cutthroats were surprised and killed by the crew of an American man-o-war.

The story is fun to tell, but unfortunately there is no hard evidence that anyone called José Gaspar ever bloodied the seas hereabouts. Nonetheless the tale will not die, and most of the Indian mounds that once abounded around here have been assaulted by frustrated treasure-seekers.

A World Apart: Gasparilla Island

Upon reaching Gasparilla Island, the road makes a southward turn near a small shopping strip called the Courtyard, where you can pick up an armful of good information at the Chamber of Commerce. Continuing down what has now become Gasparilla Road, you will notice a bike path on your left, built on the bed of the abandoned railroad.

You will soon enter the village of Boca Grande. At Fifth Street, jog right and continue south on Gulf Boulevard. You'll pass old homes that exude charm and hint at strange stories to be told. Then you'll emerge onto a sandy arm of land where modern developments are challenging future hurricanes. On your right is the recklessly informal South Beach Restaurant facing the windy Gulf of Mexico. Swimming here is especially appealing in the late afternoon, when the lowering sun sparkles on the waves.

The Beacon Burns Again: The Boca Grande Lighthouse

After a gentle bend, the road ends at the Gasparilla State Recreation Area, where honest visitors deposit $2 per car in the untended cash box. The most obvious attraction here is the 1890 lighthouse. It's built in an unusual design with the tower rising directly from the keeper's living quarters. During the early years this beacon was essential for ships navigating into Charlotte Harbor. But by 1966, improved navigation, as well as the installation of other coastal lights, had decreased the need for this lighthouse, so the Coast Guard shut it down. It stood dark, deserted, and deteriorating for two decades until a local association restored the light. Today it is once more a component of the coastal navigational system. The keeper's house has been converted into a maritime museum featuring displays that range from the history of the lighthouse to the development of Boca Grande. It's open Wednesday through Sunday between 10 A.M. and 4 P.M. A donation of $1 per person is requested for entry.

The Boca Grande Lighthouse is now a museum.

From the lighthouse, walk to the beach facing Charlotte Harbor. The harbor is a huge pocket of water fed by the Peace and Myakka Rivers. The southern shore is delineated by a low wall of greenery spiked with Australian pines. Down the beach to your left is a long pier where tankers unload fuel oil, which is stored in giant, unsightly cylinders nearby. Later, barges transport this oil to the power plant at Ft. Myers. It's said that this operation will be phased out soon, so by the time you're here the scene may be far different.

As a matter of fact, Gasparilla itself may be "phased out" within sixty or seventy years, if we are to believe certain scientists' long-range forecast of higher seas. The island—essentially a long, low sand mound—is not designed to be one of nature's more enduring creations.

Riptides in the Boca Grande Pass

Now walk west along the channel, which the Spanish called "boca grande," meaning wide mouth. Notice the sign that warns "Dangerous Current – No Swimming," as well as a second sign pointing out that tidal forces impel great amounts of water very swiftly through this deep, narrow pass. Boats anchored here have actually been sucked beneath the water during particularly strong tidal flows.

The passage through the Boca Grande Pass is so treacherous that oceangoing ships have long been required to take on a local pilot. For seven decades the piloting duties were assumed by members of the

Johnson family. Carey Johnson wrote of those days in a series of newspaper columns that have since been collected into a booklet entitled *Boca Grande—the Early Days: Memoirs of an Island Son*. One of Carey's most vivid experiences happened in 1927, when he was not quite fifteen.

A Stormy Tale

The night was wild and wet as young Carey Johnson walked from the lighthouse toward town. Although a fierce wind was kicking rain into his eyes, he saw a small light out in the churning Gulf. Realizing that it was probably a tar barrel ignited as a distress signal, Carey rousted out the Coast Guard. The cutter was hastily made ready, and Carey, as spotter, joined the crew. The ship sped from its berth on the Charlotte Harbor side of the island, through the turbulent channel, and out into the Gulf. Breakers crashed over the deck. One nearly carried a seaman over the side. Then Carey spotted the stricken vessel, which had been battered so hard that only its masts and bowsprit were above the waves. The cutter tried to approach, but the boat was in such dangerous water that it was impossible to do so. There was nothing to do except return to shore and await calmer weather in the morning. If there were men amid the wreckage, they'd have to simply brave it out until then.

When morning came, the seas were still so rough that it was obvious the cutter would have no chance to reach the distressed boat. The only choice was to take the *Comet*, the shallow-draft pilot boat. Carey remained on shore, watching through a spyglass as his older brothers guided the *Comet* through the dangerous seas. When the *Comet* got close enough to the wreck, the brothers were astonished to find nine half-frozen men clinging to the rigging. One was clutching a scared little dog. Because the water was so rough, the *Comet* could not tie up to the wreck, so one of the brothers tossed the men a line. Then each man was pulled singly through the water to the pilot boat. The seas were still dangerous, and twice Carey saw the *Comet* hit broadside by a breaker that completely submerged it. When the last man had been hauled aboard, it was suddenly realized that they had forgotten the little dog. It was impossible to get close enough to induce the frightened animal to swim to the rescue boat. Finally they had to give up and head for shore. Soon thereafter a huge wave crashed over the wreck. When it subsided, the masts, rigging, and little dog had vanished.

Hooking the Fabulous Silver King

Between late April and mid-July, massive numbers of tarpon funnel through the channel. They have attracted so many fishing enthusiasts that Boca Grande has proclaimed itself the "tarpon capital of the world." The average tarpon weighs around eighty pounds, although many are more than a hundred and a few catches have been over two hundred. They are beautiful fish: their backs blue and their sides silver. Often they swim so close to the surface that the sunlight flashes off their bright scales, causing fishermen to call them "silver kings."

Savvy local guides are important when fishing for tarpon. Some of the best fishing is in the Boca Grande Pass. Here most captains do what is called "controlled drift fishing," by carefully positioning their crafts up-tide and drifting through the channel. Lines are dropped to between forty and sixty feet. "The angler controls the depth of the bait at the captain's command," according to Sandy Melvin, a full-time Boca Grande guide, "to avoid hanging up on the irregular bottom and to keep the bait in sight of the fish." Then, when the tarpon is hooked, the captain maneuvers the fish out of the path of the other boats.

There is a tremendous thrill upon hooking one of these strong and agile fish. "The world suddenly comes apart," was the way an angler described it. The tarpon leaps through the air, then dives for the bottom. The pole bends and quivers. People on the boat yell encouragement. It's a good fight, and the captain joins in by using the boat as a drag. Even when the tarpon is finally brought along side, it will sometimes be thrashing so violently that the captain takes charge to prevent the fish from injuring the side of the boat.

The City Slickers and the Hammerhead Shark

Once in a while astonished anglers hook even larger fish than tarpon. One of the most unusual experiences happened to local guide Tater Spinks. Tater's clients were businessmen who had come to Boca Grande for excitement. At 5:30 on a morning in early June they were drift-fishing in the channel when one of them hooked a good-size tarpon. As the fisherman set his hook, a dark shadow suddenly engulfed the tarpon. Thereupon the angler found he was fighting a huge hammerhead shark! The animal was nearly as large as the boat and weighed far more. With a crash of water the powerful fish swam out of the channel and headed toward the open sea, carrying the boat with him. Tater and his clients refused to cut him loose, and, when one of them became exhausted, another eagerly took the throbbing pole. Still the monster kept on a westerly course. Gradually land disappeared. Morning wore into afternoon. Yet the great shark churned on, straight as a water-jet, into the reddening sky. Soon the sun set, yet the shark continued under a full moon. About their only link with civilization was radio contact with another boat. Eventually groups of tarpon passed them swimming in the same direction, their scales glimmering in the moonlight. Tater wondered what primal urge was leading two different species toward some rendezvous known only to them.

Finally, after more than seventeen hours, the hammerhead began to weaken, and by midnight the battle was over. The boat was eighteen miles out in the Gulf. Everyone was completely worn out. But they had to admit that they had come to Boca Grande for excitement, and that was what they had gotten!

Along the Village Docks

To visit the docks from where the fishing boats set out, drive back on Gulf Boulevard to First Street, then turn right a few blocks until First ends at Harbor Drive. Here is Whidden's Marina. Dating to the 1930s, it's one of the oldest marinas in the area. Around the bend on Harbor Drive is Miller's Marina, where you can eat at Harper's Restaurant on the second floor while enjoying a view of Charlotte Harbor. Charter boats are available all along here. During tarpon season, a six-passenger charter boat captained by an experienced guide—furnishing the pole, tackle, bait, and invaluable knowledge—will cost around $250 for a half day. Other times of the year, guided boats are available for shelling, snorkeling, or dinner cruises at rates that range from $50 to $140. Many captains advertise their services.

One last word about tarpon: if you believe you'll catch a tasty fish, you'd better stay on shore, unless you relish eating bones. The appeal of tarpon is the thrill of landing such a magnificent, fighting creature. Once the tarpon is brought boatside, the sport is over, and nearly everyone treats the fish as if it were a vanquished but worthy adversary. The barb is cut off the hook and it is withdrawn gently. Then the tarpon is revived by holding it under the belly and pushing it back and forth through the water. Finally, it's almost lovingly helped to swim off. Of course, those heartless people who want to boast to their

The former railroad station at Boca Grande is still a popular gathering place.

 friends and annoy their spouses can have the tarpon killed and mounted as a trophy. It costs around $450, plus $51 for a tarpon tag. Most fisherfolk (men, women, and children aged ten and older are welcome on the charter boats) prefer to keep the tarpon as a memory rather than a carcass collecting cobwebs on a basement wall.

The Loose Caboose

Continue along Harbor Drive as it becomes Bayou Avenue, ending at the public dock. Turn left from Bayou onto Fourth Street. In a few blocks you'll reach Boca Grande's most impressive building: the two-story former railroad station at the corner of Park Avenue. It has been converted into shops including the Loose Caboose, which offers light meals as well as scrumptious, homemade ice cream.

It's quite proper that the old depot is the village's signature building, for the railroad brought Boca Grande to life when the Charlotte Harbor & Northern Railroad reached the island in 1907. The passenger trains brought in tourists from as far away as New York City, attracted by Gasparilla Island's remoteness as well as its reputation for spectacular fishing. The CH&N Railroad became such a fixture at Boca Grande that the townsfolk even gave it a nickname:

the Cold, Hungry, and Naked line. But the railroad's main function was to freight in great loads of phosphate from areas near the Peace River to the thousand-foot loading dock at the southern tip of the island near the lighthouse. For a while Boca Grande was the fourth busiest port in the entire state. The railroad was an institution for half a century, but eventually the companies switched to Tampa and in 1979 the line was abandoned. Several years later the railroad bed was turned into the paved bike path that is so popular today. If you want to ride where steam trains once chugged, go to Island Bike 'N Beach at 333 Park Avenue, where you can rent a bicycle for $6 for one hour or $8 for two hours. The less athletically inclined will prefer the electric golf carts for $20 for two hours.

The Great Inn and the Humble Innlet

Park Avenue is the center of Boca Grande's quaint little downtown. Indeed, it's so quaint that the entire village has become a Lee County Historic District. But save some rhapsodies for the Gasparilla Inn (941-964-2201), which you can reach by going north on Park to Fifth Street, then two short blocks right. The Inn is the class of the island and has been from the moment it was constructed back in 1912. It is a magnificent two-and-a-half story structure with a portico graced by eight slender Doric pillars. It features an eighteen-hole golf course on a private island east of the hotel. This is a place for those who crave an association with high society. During recent years, the Bush clan—both Georges, Jeb (Florida's governor), and their wives—has celebrated Christmas holidays here. The restaurant and golf course, of course, are private.

For ordinary clods, the management offers The Innlet: homey, more relaxed lodgings at the foot of Twelfth Street. Rates here vary between $100 and $125 per night (941-964-2294).

The Battle of the Beaches: Manasota Key

Leaving Gasparilla, cross the picturesque causeway once more, and then head north through Placida on CR 775. Just before you reach the town of Englewood you'll come to SR 776. Drive west on SR 776 for half a mile to the junction with Beach Road, which is designated CR 776. Take Beach Road over a mile-long causeway across Lemon Bay to Manasota Key. The first bridge was a two-lane wooden affair constructed in 1927, costing all of $20,000. It was bitterly opposed by the few inhabitants of the key, who fumed that it would provide access for undesirable Yankees.

Their fears were horribly real, for the nearby town of Englewood was settled by people from Englewood, Illinois, at that time a suburb of Chicago. Even worse, the first public swimming area on Manasota Key was named Punta Gorda Beach, not because it was anywhere near that town but to attract prospective home buyers from the Chicago World's Fair of 1933. Although the fair is long gone, the name remains—as do descendants of the Chicagoans. Next to this beach, almost as if one stretch of sand were in competition with another, is Englewood Beach. Whatever, they're both wonderful places to enjoy a swim.

From here on north it's a disappointment. Although Manasota Key Road winds gently through an archway of trees, home developers have carefully managed to conceal almost any view of the water. Still, it's not a bad seven-mile drive, and there's more public swimming at the northern end. At this point take Manasota Beach Road east, crossing the Intracoastal Waterway and making two more abrupt turns before reaching Englewood Road (SR 776).

The Vanished Forest

Turn north on Englewood Road, which was originally cut through a vast growth of longleaf pine. Unfortunately for these trees, their wood was hard and resinous—prime building material. Thus, in 1918 the Manasota Lumber Company of New York established what was then the largest sawmill in Florida just east of Englewood Road. The sawmill was an imposing, four-story, wooden structure covering almost a full city block. From it, narrow-gauge railroad lines webbed out into the forest, enabling freight trains to transport a constant supply of pine logs to the mill. For five years a thousand men lived on the mill grounds, which were surrounded by an electric fence to keep bootleggers from disrupting the operation. When the trees were gone, the show was over. The owners sold out and moved on to devastate other forests. A few years later the entire mill went up in flames. Only the foundation stones were left, and they were hauled away for construction of a jetty at Venice.

Venice: Few Canals but Lots of Flowers

Northward, Englewood Road soon merges with US 41, which reaches Venice Avenue in five miles. Turn west on Venice Avenue and proceed through the heart of this little city of around twenty-one thousand inhabitants. Venice is a participant in the Main Street Program. The broad center parkway along Venice Avenue—lush with bushes, flowers, and trees—shows the program's influence. Nearly all the commercial buildings have been jazzed up to enhance the north Italian architecture that is the town's heritage. Almost every store is occupied. Antique-style streetlights line the way. An air of prosperity permeates everything. Especially appealing is Centennial Park, a square block of greenery with a public restroom that is a credit to the city and should be an example to others.

A Typical Florida Cycle

Venice owes its beginning to the Brotherhood of Locomotive Engineers, which in 1925 purchased the land from a wealthy New York surgeon. The Brotherhood was looking for a safe investment with a high potential for financial gain. Since the Seaboard Railroad had just reached the village and the Tamiami Trail was a-building, the location on the Gulf of Mexico, with its fine sandy beaches and warm climate, seemed ideal. As soon as the Brotherhood had consummated the deal, they began spending a million dollars a month preparing the site for settlement. After adopting a street plan that made Venice Avenue the principal thoroughfare, with a center parkway down which a bridle path meandered, the Brotherhood put up the Venice Hotel at 200 N. Nassau Street across from what is now Centennial Park. The hotel proved such an attraction that hardly was it completed when George Halderman landed his plane almost directly at its door, thereby claiming the distinction of piloting the first aeroplane ever to bounce down at Venice.

But happy times ended abruptly with the Great Depression. Sales ground to a halt, and the union's realty division went into receivership. The once-proud Venice Hotel became a dormitory for students of the Kentucky Military Institute. The town went into a decade-long decline that ended only with the advent of World War II. At that time, the army took over the Venice Airport and converted it into a large training base whose personnel sometimes totaled twenty thousand men. That breathed life back into Venice.

Now continue west on Venice Avenue, which, when it leaves the business district, is shaded by tall trees. The avenue ends at Venice Beach, grateful recipient of a major renourishment program a few years back. The public is invited to enjoy the fine swimming, and there are picnic tables, showers, and restrooms.

Facing the beach is The Esplanade, upon which you should turn north. On the Gulf side, you'll see the Best Western Sandbar, which calls itself a resort but to most observers is just a motel. It's directly on the beach, however, and the starting prices (which range between $115 and $179, depending on the season) are reasonable for

the location. Of course, if you've come to a beach resort to actually see the beach, it'll cost more. For reservations call 800-822-4853.

Fishing for Pelicans: The Venice Jetty

Beyond the Sandbar, The Esplanade once presented fine vistas of the Gulf. But now you'll have to settle for a Chinese wall of high-rise condos. After a few frustrating blocks, make a sharp left turn onto Tarpon Center Drive. This goes along Roberts Bay, where the fashionable Crows Nest Restaurant overlooks Venice's harbor. Just beyond the restaurant the road ends at the south jetty—a long, rocky breakwater that prevents sand from obstructing the flow between Roberts Bay and the Gulf of Mexico. From the parking area you can walk out onto the jetty, which anglers and strollers of all ages have made into a sort of social center.

The Venice Inlet is a popular location for fishermen as well as sightseers.

Although fishing from the jetty is popular, not everyone catches what he expects. Pelicans sometimes show up at the end of the line. Although it may seem amusing to hook a bird rather than a fish, it's not something you should look forward to. Pelicans often die if the hook remains in their mouths so it's up to you to remove it. Although a sign on the jetty gives cool, detailed removal instructions, it's doubtful that you're going to proceed in a cool fashion if you have a big, angry pelican flapping its powerful wings in your face. The sign tells you to call out for someone to hold the bird. But your call will probably be more like a shriek. If you're lucky enough to find a person to wrap his arms around the gyrating bird, you'll have to muster the courage to push your fishhook through the rest of its beak. Then you'll have to cut off the barb and pull it backwards until it's free. "Believe me," I was told, "hooking a pelican is not an encounter you're likely to relish!"

These Sharks Don't Bite

Now head back to Venice Avenue and go four blocks east to Harbor Drive. Turn south on Harbor. After a mile or so you'll skirt the Venice Airport, the World War II army base. On the Gulf side of the road is the Venice Fishing Pier, at the foot of which is

Sometimes very large fossilized sharks' teeth are found on Venice beaches.

a casual restaurant called Sharky's. It's a great place to enjoy lunch or dinner looking out on the sand, the pier, and the shimmering blue Gulf. The beach is ideal for swimming, particularly that portion north of the restaurant, which was revived during the extensive renourishment program several years ago.

There is no fee for using the beach, but it costs $1 to walk out onto the pier. There is a booth at the entry to the pier where you can rent a fishing pole and tackle for $7.50—bait costs extra. You don't need a license, for the pier carries a blanket permit. However, the permit does not cover hooking pelicans.

Simple as the booth is, it has a stock of items you've probably never seen before. These are fossilized sharks' teeth. Most of the teeth are black and under a half inch long. You can purchase a bunch of them in a plastic packet for less than a dollar. People who prefer to find them on their own usually rent a mesh basket for $4 and scoop through the sand. Occasionally very large teeth are found. Some, for sale at the pier booth, are more than five inches long and surprisingly heavy. Good specimens sell for $300 and up. People pay this price, but one can only speculate what buyers do with a shark's tooth.

Why are so many teeth found on Venice beaches? Actually sharks' teeth were deposited wherever oceans reached during the geological past. Some are found embedded in rocks as far inland as Iowa and

Caspersen Beach is a favorite place to find fossilized sharks' teeth.

The road to Caspersen Beach edges between dunes and sea oats.

Nebraska. But there are no waves in the cornfields to wash the teeth from the rocks. Venice, on the other hand, has an ample supply of waves willing to do the task. Furthermore, at Venice the Gulf slopes very gently, forcing the waves to deposit the teeth before running off to deep water with them.

You might wonder why the rest of the shark doesn't show up with his teeth. The answer is that sharks, whether ancient or modern, have no bones. Their bodies are composed of cartilage that quickly disintegrates when the shark dies. Another question might be: when will the supply of teeth run out? Probably never—at least in your lifetime—for an average shark, with his busy gobbling schedule, uses upwards of twenty thousand teeth during his ten-year life span.

If you would like to collect a few teeth, the best time to search is at low tide. The best place is in a shallow trough that closely parallels the shore. The best location is Caspersen Beach.

Toothville, USA: Caspersen Beach

To get to Caspersen, continue south on Harbor Drive for one and a half miles. The road leaves Venice and shoulders softly among low dunes. Sea oats pirouette in the breeze. There are no signs or commercial establishments, for this sand-spit has been left mostly in a natural state. The beauty of this short motoring segment may induce you to leave your car at the Caspersen parking lot and walk back down the road just for the joy of it.

The Caspersen Park is part of the Sarasota County system. County officials, perhaps as much for lack of money as concern about the environment, have kept the beach primitive. Nonetheless there is enough leftover junk to attract raccoons, and signs warn that they may seem cute, but they don't mind biting humans when they feel like it.

The beach has an otherworldly feel to it, although it's nice to know there are restrooms in the parking lot. Tooth-sleuths are usually here, many with rented sand scoops, poking along where the waves rustle against the shore. They're so intent that you'd think they were panning for gold, not for the little, black wedges that they could have purchased for a pittance at the fishing pier. But there's a fascination to gathering relics of monsters that may have cast ravenous eyes over this very spot twenty million years ago. What type of creature will be here twenty million years hence? What will we leave them to remember us by? How long do Coke cans last?

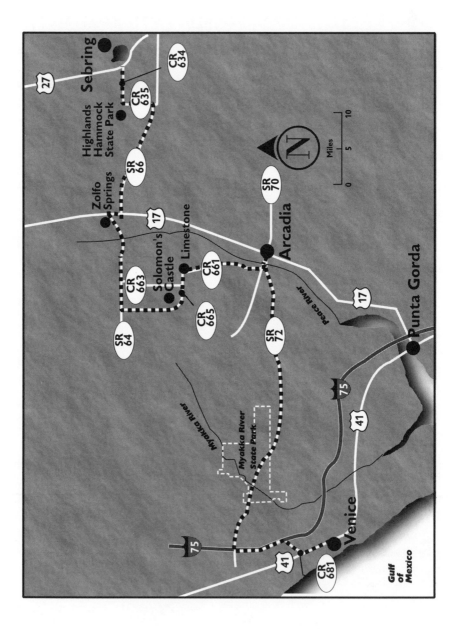

Cowboy Country
Venice to Sebring • 110 Backroad Miles

The Song of the Road: Overview

This exploration starts at Venice, then enters a vast flatland that reaches halfway across the southern portion of the state. Not far out on the road you'll pass through areas devoted to the unusual farming of saw palmettos. Next comes Myakka River State Park, where the world's largest airboat conveys visitors past a fascinating array of birds and alligators. Continuing eastward, you'll enter the Ninety-mile Prairie. Before fencing, cowboys conducted cattle drives over these grasslands that matched almost anything on the Great Plains. One of the wildest cattle towns was Arcadia, where you'll hear the story of Bone Mizell, a whiskey-swilling joker famous in these parts. Cattle are still important, as you will see during a visit to the Arcadia State Livestock Market.

On the northern outskirts of Arcadia is the Canoe Outpost beside the Peace River. Boats can be rented here either by the hour or for several days. The Peace River flows through a shady aisle of trees, and its banks are famous for the bones of mammoths and other Ice Age animals. Driving north through level country where ranches alternate with orange groves, you'll come to Solomon's Castle, created by a sculptor with a bent toward quirkiness. Here you can lunch in a Spanish galleon–style restaurant, where ancient cannons insure that everyone tips the serving wenches.

Finally, you'll reach a road designated as the Cracker Trail. In Florida the term "cracker" is not a put-down but refers to early cowboys who herded cattle with well-placed cracks of their eighteen-foot-long whips. The Cracker Trail runs through the hamlet of Zolfo Springs, where Pioneer Park offers more Peace River canoeing as well as a collection of buildings and a museum that will leave you with a much deeper understanding of what life was like for Florida's early settlers.

From Zolfo you'll follow the Cracker Trail eastward to Highlands Hammock State Park. Here you can enjoy a guided tour via an open-air tram or a stroll down one or more of the trails originally built by the young men of Franklin D. Roosevelt's Civilian Conservation

Corps (CCC). One of the CCC buildings serves as a museum and another as a place to buy refreshments.

This exploration ends in Sebring, whose central hub was laid out around a circle in honor of the mythical Greek City of the Sun. Sebring is also the location of the famous racetrack, where testing goes year 'round. You can overnight at a spectacular new hotel that overlooks the track. For those who relish a more peaceful atmosphere, there is the vintage Kenilworth Lodge, with a lobby adorned by an old pot-bellied stove that can get campfire-hot when the occasion arises.

On the Road Again

Setting out from Venice, drive northward on US 41. In a few miles you'll reach SR 681, where you should turn right onto Interstate 75. Head north on I-75, which you'll only have to endure for five miles before reaching the SR 72 junction. When you turn east on SR 72, you'll be back to country driving.

Prickly Prizes

This is a flat, lonely land where you'll sometimes see standing water. In many places there are extensive fields of saw palmetto. Although their dagger-sharp fronds are not the most friendly of exteriors, the plants have beneficial qualities—as the Indians long knew and modern man is beginning to appreciate. Saw palmetto berries, when crushed into powder or oil, can help in the treatment of prostate cancer. Some historians surmise that tales of the plant's value in restoring sexual activity to older men may have reached Ponce de León, for whom it may have become linked with the fountain of youth. After federal dietary supplement laws were relaxed in 1994, the powdered berries became a best-selling herb, not only in the United States but in Europe as well. Sales now total more than $20 million annually. Since south and central Florida are about the only places on earth where the plant thrives commercially, it has become popular with planters. It has also become popular with berry thieves, who descend on the prickly fields often enough that angry landowners are agitating for tougher trespassing laws.

Myakka River State Park

Nine miles past I-75 you'll come to Myakka River State Park, where there is an entry fee of $4 per car. The miniature strip of land across from the tollbooth contains prairie grass, which should be burned every so often, just as in nature. But before the park district can do this simple job, it must get the approval of a number of other agencies, including the weather service (to be sure the wind and other conditions are favorable) and the forestry department (to be sure the surrounding trees are not too dry). Thus, even bureaucracies must deal with bureaucracies. Somehow that's satisfying to know.

There is a curious sign at the admission booth warning that vultures, as well as humans, operate on the park grounds. These birds have obviously forgotten that their assigned task in nature is to feast on carrion, for they have somehow acquired a taste for the moldings on car windows, as well as similar savory trim on boat trailers. They are particularly hungry at breakfast time, so you are warned not to use the parking lot beside Upper Myakka Lake before ten in the morning.

Just beyond the entry gate is the barn-shaped visitors' center. Although it's small, there are good displays of a few of the animals, birds, snakes, and reptiles living in the park. The building was constructed during the Great Depression by young men of the Civilian Conservation Corps (CCC), who also laid out many of the park's roads, picnic pavilions, and cabins.

A Forest, a River, and a Beautiful Drive

Leaving the visitors' center, proceed along Park Drive, which runs for seven shaded miles along the length of the park. As you travel slowly down the road, you'll pass through a series of natural habitats. There are oak hammocks, where brawny branches intertwine like the arms of mighty wrestlers. There are fragrant pine flatwoods, where sunbeams slumber in calm pools on the forest floor. And there is the Myakka River, where you can pause at the bridge to fish or to simply watch the alligators watching you.

The Crest of a Hammock

Myakka's Canopy Walkway offers an unparalleled opportunity to explore the forest's crest. This eighty-five-foot structure is the world's first walkway through a subtropical hammock. Twenty-five feet above the ground, it reveals the secret lives of treetop plants and animals. If this isn't enough and you want to soar above it all, you can climb the seven-story tower.

Wonders of a Prairie

Back on Park Drive you'll come to an area where the trees give way to a wide prairie. This is an entirely different ecosystem from the forest. Wildflowers grow here amid the wire grass and bluestem. Prairie birds, such as colorful caracaras and grasshopper sparrows, often dot the open sky. At dusk they are replaced by owls gliding over the land like dark, hungry apparitions. You can see clouds forming on the distant horizon long before they drench the prairie. On certain days, lightning plays among the clouds and sometimes strikes the grass, where it explodes into flame. Wildfires such as these give life to the prairie by consuming the saplings that would convert it into a forest.

Not many years ago, park officials across America didn't understand the role of fires in nature. They were dismayed when flames consumed the vegetation. Smoky the Bear warned against fires, and the park service hurried to stamp them out. But, as officials watched once-beautiful prairies turn into forests, they began reevaluating this policy. They realized that prairies support an entirely different group of plants and animals than forests and that such diversity enriches the total environment. For this reason the park service itself now regularly sets the prairie to flame.

Continuing on Park Drive, you'll coast along Upper Myakka Lake, beloved by the auto-eating vultures. There are other birds here as well, for more than one hundred species visit the park during the course of a year. You can get an unexcelled view from the boardwalk extending into the lake. Onshore you may see deer and turkeys darting among the trees. If you're lucky, you may even spot a furtive bobcat.

The World's Largest Airboat

Now drive back to the sign pointing to the concession area. Bicycles can be rented here for $4 an hour. Canoes are also available at $10 for a two-hour paddle on the lake. But the park's most popular activities are the narrated airboat rides. These hour-long excursions cost $7 for adults and $4 for kids twelve and under. They leave regularly seven days a week during from mid-December to the end of May. For boat times and reservations call 941-365-0100.

The ride is not the roaring, wind-and-spray affair that you may have experienced on one of the earlier explorations. Although this is

One of the world's largest airboats takes visitors to Myakka State Park, past a multitude of alligators and exotic birds.

the world's largest airboat—carrying up to seventy passengers—it is also the world's slowest. It is used here because the lake is so shallow that the propellers of a normal boat would become entangled in hydrilla, that unwanted, immigrant seaweed whose visa has long since expired. The airboat's other disadvantage is that it has no reverse. But that's no real problem; in order to stop, the lumbering craft simply bumps into the pier.

Yet, just because it is so slow, the airboat affords close-ups of many birds. Coots paddle calmly by, apparently disdainful of this odd contrivance driven by an airplane propeller. White ibises, with their bright orange beaks, flutter past. Speedy osprey sometimes hop-skip over the lake as they scour the water with their talons. Perhaps the most unusual birds are the anhingas, which swim so fast underwater they're called snake birds. The anhingas catch their prey by spearing them with their beaks. They have cleverly solved the problem of how to release fish from their beaks in order to eat them: they toss them into the air and swallow them head first. But a botched toss presents a second problem, not yet solved. If the fish goes down tail first, the fin sometimes lodges in the bird's throat, choking it to death. In this matter nature has lent a hand, allowing the anhingas to snare a fish only once in every twenty or thirty tries. As for the lake, it doesn't miss the fish, for there are plenty of largemouth bass, catfish, and crappie.

A Jillion Wild Hogs

When the boat approaches the shore, the guide will point out the bare spots caused by the rooting hogs. These hogs were brought in by early settlers and left to run wild. They love it here, for the ground is soft and they have no problem rooting up food. The trouble is that this rooting destroys plants, resulting in areas of desolation. According to the guide, the number of hogs is more than a "jillion," which everyone will agree is certainly excessive. Ordinarily the park authorities would destroy the surplus hogs. But nowadays it is against the law to kill any animal within the park boundaries. So instead the park must hire a contractor to trap some of the hogs and cart them off. And what does the contractor do then? He kills them.

Alligator Heaven

But enough of flying things, diving things, and rooting things. It's the alligators that most people have come to see. Myakka Lake has lots—not exactly a jillion, but an estimated six hundred or so adults. Many reach up to twelve feet in length and weigh five hundred pounds. In the cooler months they love to doze on some sunny shore. Being cold-blooded, they need the sun's warmth to help them generate the ninety-degree temperature their stomach acids require for digestion. You'll notice that sometimes the alligators have their mouths open. This is not to display their teeth for tourists. Instead, it is to help the poor fellers cool off.

When passengers have had enough ogling of those onshore, the guide will head toward open water, where the hungry gators lurk just beneath the surface, with only their unblinking eyes above water. As the boat pulls slowly toward them, the eyes suddenly disappear in a mass of ripples. In a moment a similar set of eyes emerges many yards away.

Floridians have a strange relationship with alligators. Not many years ago they hunted them almost to extinction. But with the rise of the naturalist movement, Floridians adopted a live-and-let-live attitude. So much so that during the summer dry season, when Myakka Lake is only a few feet deep, sportsmen walk far out into the waters, ignoring the numerous gators. And the gators ignore them. But by sunset the fisherfolk are gone, because that is dinnertime for the reptilefolk. The saying goes that at night there are only two types of creatures on the Florida lakes: alligators and their next meals.

Scrawny Cattle and Stringy Cowpokes

From Myakka continue east on SR 72 toward the town of Arcadia. The road is narrow, with just enough space for trucks to make you appreciate how few there are. Emerging from the scrubby Myakka watershed, you'll be in rich pasture country. The grasses may look wild, but they have been specially planted for their adaptability to their particular type of soil, level of moisture, and amount of sun exposure. They are constantly fertilized and weeded and have ten times the nutritional value of the original vegetation, which was aptly named wire grass.

About the only thing tougher than the wire grass were the rough-cut cowpokes who roamed these plains for almost a century. Artist Frederic Remington, sent here in 1895 by *Harper's Weekly*, was shocked at what he found. He was well familiar with the picturesque cowboys of the West, but the cowboys of Florida were an entirely different breed.

The Florida cowpokes were sweaty and smelly. Their clothing was slovenly and disheveled. They wore muddy farmers' clodhoppers in place of Western riding boots. They seldom carried lariats but instead controlled their cattle with whips up to eighteen feet long. The crack of these whips resounded as loudly as a shotgun blast. Although the cowboys could easily have ripped the hide from a steer, they usually found the awful snap above its ear was sufficient to get the beast moving. The cowboys were thin, weather-seared hombres, tough as leather and deadly as rattlers. Each was an individualist who, as Remington wrote, "wends his lonely way through the ooze and rank grass."

The cowpokes rode ponies so scraggly that Remington wondered how they could carry their riders. But the ponies were surprisingly durable and well adapted to herd the cattle that were nearly as bony as themselves. These cattle were not the powerful beeves that thrived on the lush grasses of the Great Plains. And these mean-spirited critters' meat was as gristly as the wire grass upon which they fed.

The Ninety-mile Prairie

In those days this was part of the boundless, unfenced grassland known as the Ninety-mile Prairie, which ran from the Kissimmee Valley all the way west to the docks at Punta Rassa, Ft. Myers. Cowboys on the Ninety-mile Prairie had innumerable pests to contend with. Swarms of flies constantly harassed them and their skittish horses. And in the summer there were the mosquitoes, which thrived in the wetlands created by the rains and the prairie's poor

Cattle pastures occupy much of southern Florida's Ninety-mile Prairie. Egrets, like the one at this bull's feet, follow the animals closely to eat the bugs they kick up.

drainage. At night the tired men had to pile up dirt mounds to escape the dampness, then had to worry about rolling off into their water-filled ditch. They could hardly enjoy their slumber, for hungry bears often hovered close to camp. Far more numerous and dangerous were the panthers, stealthy and vicious. Even worse were the wolves, which attacked cattle in howling packs. When they were in the vicinity, the cowboys had to keep fires burning and shotguns ready. Often the night rang with the unnerving sounds of howling wolves, screaming panthers, hooting owls, and bellowing alligators. One prairie traveler noted that herding cattle on the prairie was as if a person "had offered to do duty in Hades."

The cattle drives centered on Arcadia after the railroad reached the town in 1886. By this time the land hereabouts had fallen into the hands of a few local ranchers. The spread along what is now SR 72 belonged to the Parker outfit. The story goes that Readding Parker distrusted paper money to the extent that he demanded his profits in gold doubloons, which he hid in a secret hole in the ground. When he died, the location was lost. But modern gold-seekers are still searching, even though some of them have reported unnerving sounds of Parker's ghost returning to protect what was his. To the south was the domain of Ziba King, a bull of a man who once killed a charging steer with his bare hands. He was also a fierce poker player. Yet he gave a great deal of land to churches and public institutions, and, when a nearby county couldn't pay its teachers, he donated the funds for six months' payroll. Ziba ultimately accumulated a herd of nearly fifty thousand cattle.

On the cattle frontier everyone looked forward to social shindigs. The rodeos at Arcadia were particular favorites. Here the rough ranch hands could show off their prowess with the whip, curling it out like a snake until it snapped a log. Other pokes raced their horses, shouting cattle calls as they went by in a flurry of dust and flies. Then there was bulldogging, where courage and skill were pitted against a bull's strength and fury. More excitement came with the bronco busting, whose champions always attracted admiring glances from the young ladies. Afterwards there was the much-anticipated barbecue feast, followed by a fiddler grinding out vigorous square dances. The gals had waited for this with great anticipation, even though the cowboys by this time reeked of cowhide and horseflesh.

The cowboys of yore are gone now, as are their scrawny cattle. The Ninety-mile Prairie is partitioned with barbed wire fences. The wolves have vanished, as have the bears. And the once fearsome panthers are reduced to less than three dozen pitiful, inbred relics hovering on the brink of extinction. The native Florida cattle have been replaced by exotic breeds whose very names bespeak of faraway lands: Brahma, Hereford, Angus. The trails have either disappeared or become paved roads, and the drives are done by truckers speeding along at sixty-five miles an hour in air-conditioned rigs.

The Juice Rockets

As you continue east on SR 72, an increasing number of orange groves begin alternating with pastures. The groves are relatively new to this area, having migrated here after a series of freezes devastated the groves farther north. This flat, wet prairie is not the most favorable to oranges, which prefer hilly, well-drained land. Nonetheless, these groves produce sufficient oranges to keep 120 large trailer-trucks a day hauling their cargo to the Peace River Citrus Company, whose bright silver juice evaporators rise eighteen stories above the prairie like slim rockets ready for launch.

To watch the company's operation, turn into the parking lot beside SR 72. The orange-laden trucks will pull onto scales in front of you, and their weight will determine what the grove owner will receive. Next the truck will drive to a platform carefully balanced like a giant teeter-totter. Machines tip the platform until the truck's front end is upward

A citrus truck is tipped and emptied at the Peace River citrus plant near Arcadia.
Orange juice is turned into concentrate in the rocketlike evaporators in the rear.

at a steep angle, causing the oranges to cascade from the trailer down to an area where samples are tested by a state official to be sure they meet legal requirements for sweetness, acidity, and maturity.

This done, a conveyor transports the oranges to the green storage bins you'll see at the top of the complex. At the proper time they go to the extractors, where they are squeezed to separate the juice from the pulp and rinds, which are converted into cattle feed. The rinds make the penetrating citrus odor that hovers over the plant. As for the juice, it is divided into two parts. One is sold almost as is. The other becomes concentrate. It's the making of concentrate that is the function of the "rockets," formally known as evaporators. Juice flows to an evaporator, where it is routed through hundreds of narrow tubes. The space around these tubes is filled with steam, which boils much of the water from the juice. But because the evaporator is under a partial vacuum, the boiling occurs at 160 degrees, not the usual 220. This lower temperature enables the juice to retain almost all its flavor, which canned juice does not. When the operation is over, a cap at the top of the cylinder opens to permit the steam to escape—which you'll see rising like smoke.

Arcadia's Oak Street is a lot quieter now than it was a hundred years ago, when cowboys made this one of the rowdiest towns in the entire nation.

Welcome to Cow Town: Arcadia

SR 72 ends at SR 70, where you should turn right. After crossing the Peace River, watch for a brown sign directing you down Oak Street to Arcadia's "historic downtown." Following the sign, you'll first enter the neighborhood where the well-to-do citizens built their residences. Many still grace this portion of Oak and of Hickory, one block north. Cattle baron Jasper Parker and his wife, Rhoda, constructed the two-and-a-half story home at 427 W. Hickory. Jasper died while still in his forties in 1896, just a year after moving in. His death left Rhoda to raise their daughter and five sons by herself. She lived for thirty more sad years. The home is now a bed and breakfast. Rates are $69 to $85. For reservations call 800-969-2499. The commercial section begins after you pass the Methodist Church.

Although it is said Arcadia was named for a lassie who baked "Boss" Hendry a birthday cake, the town's early history is far removed from ladies' niceties. Arcadia was long the hangout for roughneck cowhands who sought the town's pleasures while trying unsuccessfully to avoid its hangovers. Frederic Remington was watching one day as "two very emaciated Texas ponies pattered down the street bearing wild-looking individuals, whose hanging hair and drooping hats and generally bedraggled appearance would remind you at once of Spanish moss which hangs . . . to the limbs of the oaks out in the swamps." They had none of the glamour that he admired in Western cowboys. "The only things they did which were conventional were to tie their ponies up by the head in brutal disregard, and then get drunk in about fifteen minutes." The most slovenly, as well as the most drunken, was Morgan Bonaparte Mizell, whom everyone called Bone.

The Lovable Rustler

Bone was about the most dang-busted, ornery, soused, and lovable scoundrel in these here parts. When he wasn't stealing cattle, he was saucing it up in one of the humpty-dump saloons that made Arcadia the Deadwood of south Florida. Tall and gaunt, Bone seemed born to straddle a pony—or a barstool. He couldn't read or write, or add or subtract, or do about anything of value. 'Cept he was durn near the best cattle herder around—so good that none other than Ziba King made him one of his foremen. It was no small honor that Bone tried his best to live up to. 'Course, that was impossible, for Bone jest had to do things his own way.

The lack of schooling didn't cause Bone much trouble. Once when he was punching cattle and his horse broke down, he bargained for a new mount with a ranch hand nearby. When the price was settled on, Bone wrote out an IOU. Later his fellow cowboys chaffed at Bone's story. "Damn, you can't write," one of them grunted. "Hell," Bone retorted, "that old coot couldn't read, so we was even."

Time-worn conventions meant nothing to Bone. Once he told a couple he was fully qualified to marry them. When he couldn't come up with a Bible, he used a Sears and Roebuck catalog, which worked just as well. Although he claimed church attendance interfered with his drinking pleasure, he knew something of the Bible. When a pair of farmhands made some uncomplimentary remarks about his bumbling pace while under the influence, he retorted that he was simply Saul who went out a-hunting for his father's asses. "And lookee here," he chortled, "I've found two of 'em."

Bone was capable of bigger things than merely insults, like the time he had a run-in with a traveling circus that had pitched its tent along the railroad tracks. The big top was pretty near full when Bone staggered in, laughin' and carryin' on to beat all get-out. Although the Arcadian audience found his antics uproarious, the performers did not. Neither did the bouncers, who unceremoniously escorted Bone to the exit, and, without the slightest show of respect, gave him a rough heave-ho. That was a mistake, for even Bone Mizell had his dignity. And dignity demanded retaliation.

So Bone stealthily tied ropes onto the tent flaps. Then, when the next freight train pulled in, he secured the other ends to some of the cattle cars. The freight took a long time to load up, but Bone was happy to savor the situation. Eventually the whistle rang out and the train moved slowly forward. The ropes grew taut and the tent canvas began stretching. When the freight train began moving faster, the support stakes popped from the ground. Then the tent itself began to tremble. As patrons, performers, and animals began to dash out, the tent slid over them. The train whistle screamed once more as the powerful engine gained momentum. Everyone gasped as the tent was whisked off along the tracks.

Since there was no doubt that the prank was Bone's, the next morning he was hauled into court, where he was a familiar figure. The judge fined him $75. Bone gladly paid, and when he sauntered out, he chuckled that it was a bargain, for the prank had easily brought him a thousand dollars of satisfaction.

Everyone was accustomed to Bone's capers. Everyone knew he spent all his earnings on booze and rustled cattle mostly for something to eat. One story tells of Bone being approached by young Ed Welles, who remarked that his new wife was going to be alone that evening and he hoped there'd be nothing unexpected happening around his ranch. "Don't worry," Bone grinned, "I'm not workin' that side of the Peace River tonight."

But rustling was rustling, and Bone's perpetual borrowing of other men's cattle ultimately required some sort of legal action. So Bone was back in court and his case presented before a jury. Try as they might, they could find no good reason why he shouldn't be sent to prison. When the verdict was pronounced, many Arcadians protested, for it was common knowledge that Bone often shared his gains with one or more of the wealthy ranchers. Despite a petition asking for his release, the judge had no choice except to send him off to the state prison. Thereupon the citizens of Arcadia provided him a fine set of new clothes and a rousing send-off at the railroad station.

When Bone arrived at the state prison, he was welcomed by the officials, who gave the celebrity a guided tour of the institution. After that he was treated to a sumptuous meal, in exchange for which Bone regaled them with jolly tales of how he often outwitted the law. With Bone now having served time in prison, the officials led him to the railroad station, where he boarded the next train for Arcadia.

Today and Yesterday

The Arcadia of today is a far cry from the frolicsome place of Bone's time. All the good ol' boys are gone—the Parkers, Ziba King, and the other boisterous broncos who once made the town so lively. Even most of the Oak Street buildings that Bone and the boys knew have vanished, the result of a mysterious Thanksgiving Day fire in 1905 that converted the boozy bars and bosomy brothels into nostalgic cinders. This voracious blaze also gobbled up the court-house, causing the records of those convicted of shootings and general mayhem to vanish—and suspicions quickly surfaced that this had been the purpose of whoever set the fire.

Most of the current buildings reflect the 1920s, when eight rail-road trains a day rumbled into town. They stopped at the long brick depot, now privately rehabbed. The depot was one of Arcadia's show-places, boasting twenty-foot-high ceilings, polished oak floors, and wide overhangs to protect passengers from the sun and rain. At about the same time, an arcade building was constructed in a style hovering between Gothic and grotesque. You'll have no trouble recognizing this two-story pink landmark with arched windows and spiked pilasters at the melodious corner of Oak and Polk. Farther east on Oak, at the corner of US 17, is the courthouse, a resplendent brick structure that continues to be the pride of DeSoto County.

The Great Depression of the 1930s struck Arcadia a blow from which it never really recovered. The trains got fewer and fewer, and at last they stopped and the rails were torn up. Downtown continued on a steady downward slide until in desperation Arcadia joined Florida's Main Street Program. Today many of the buildings have been painted and cleaned up, and two dozen antiques and gift shops have begun to attract patrons.

But Arcadia, with barely seven thousand inhabitants, lacks the tax base for a real rejuvenation. Nonetheless the town has a secure place in this sparsely populated, agricultural community. Indeed, Arcadia is the only incorporated town in the entire county. Arcadia's rodeos are well attended, three-day events each March and October. If you are there during the rest of the year, you can visit the Arcadia State Livestock Market, a mile north of town on US 17, where cattle auctions are held each Wednesday after 12 noon. One or two thousand bulls and cows are sold here, and the action sometimes lasts until nine or ten in the evening. Admission is free and visitors can sit directly behind the buyers. Lunches are served after 1:00 P.M.

As for the downtown, it remains quiet. Unfortunate as that might be, the lack of a full-scale revival serves some visitors just fine. Dusty Oak Street, with its weathered canopies shading vacant storefronts, permits imaginations to recreate the grubby saloons from which there issues the dissonance of clinky pianos and clamorous ranch hands. Perhaps you'll be able to envisage Frederick Remington, sketchpad in hand, in the shadows watching Bone Mizell stagger along Oak Street as he peers down the neck of an empty whiskey bottle. One can almost discern the wail of a phantom locomotive murmuring a lament to the Arcadia that will never be again.

The Canoe Outpost

Now drive back west on Oak Street to SR 70 and take it over the Peace River. The Seminoles named the river after the hordes of wild peas that once festooned its banks. Americans transformed "peas" into "peace"—an ironic twist, since they brought only hostilities to the Indians. At the end of the Second Seminole War, the Peace River became the border of Seminole land, which ran east all the way to Lake Okeechobee. But army troops crossed the river freely during the Third Seminole War, which concluded in 1858 with the death or expulsion of all but a few hundred Seminoles and Miccosukees.

At the far riverbank turn north on CR 661 and proceed a short distance to the Canoe Outpost, which calls itself Florida's largest and oldest outfitter. You'll have to take its word about being the largest, but driving through the grounds you'll have no doubt it is the oldest. It could also be one of the junkiest. But canoeing and camping are not enterprises for the fastidious. The Outpost has many trips along the Peace River, hyped as Florida's most popular canoe trail. On one of these trips canoeists are transported to a point forty miles upstream. From there they drift-paddle downriver beneath a verdant umbrella of leaves and Spanish moss, spending a night camping on the riverbank. The cost is $65 for a canoe that holds two paddlers plus a passenger. Less ambitious paddlers can rent canoes at $15 for the first two hours and $5 per hour thereafter. For reservations phone 800-268-0083.

This area was once also popular with prehistoric mammoths, who left behind their tusks and assorted bones to remind us that they were here first. Some people have grown quite fascinated by the hairy beasts. During winter's low water, they rummage hopefully along the river shores for fossils.

As you continue north on CR 661, you'll find pastures mingling with citrus groves. The land is flat and sandy, and the road is very straight. There are few cars, for this byway does not go anyplace of importance, except, of course, to the local inhabitants. At a dot on the map called Limestone, the road makes a ninety-degree bend. This was a main street when Limestone was a railroad stop. But there's barely one train a day now, and it doesn't even slow down for Limestone, which consists of a church and a few scattered houses of indeterminate vintage.

Turning left at Limestone on CR 665 you'll come to a sign directing you to Solomon's Castle, certainly the oddest and downright silliest attraction in a state whose odd and silly attractions are world famous. In fact, it's so odd and silly that you have to see it.

Solomon's Odd and Silly Castle

Drive west over little-used CR 665 for about five miles, then down a private road to the castle's parking lot. Here you're likely to find cars with license plates from Maine to California, along with at least an excursion bus or two. It's a short walk to the "castle," which is a two-

Solomon's Castle is one of the more imaginative habitats in south Florida.

Howard Solomon's eyes twinkle as he stands before one of his creative projects made from common junk.

and-a-half-story, shimmering silver dream. It has turrets, towers, and battlements from which archers could defend the ramparts. There is even a pair of knights in mail guarding the entry. It's very formidable. But it's a complete illusion. For the silver walls are merely flimsy aluminum plates discarded by printers. And the knights are just artistically assembled pieces of junk metal.

The perpetrator of this delightful hoax is Howard Solomon, a recognized sculptor who settled here in 1972, attracted by the cheapness of the land and the solitude of this isolated setting. "There was nothing when I came here," Solomon told me. "My wife, Peggy, and I lived in a mobile home while we built the combination workshop and residential quarters." Even as the wood framing went up, Solomon began sheathing it with aluminum plates. "Once I started building it, people started coming." Soon he was asked to speak at the Kiwanis and other local clubs. Then he began giving free tours once a week. Next the folks in the Tampa–St. Petersburg area, fifty miles northwest, became interested. Newspapers took up the story, and he appeared on television in various markets around the U.S. This caused tour-bus operators to include him on their itineraries. Eventually he made the media in England, Germany, Italy, and Norway. "I haven't lifted a finger in promotion," he told me, then added with his characteristic dry humor, "People will buy tickets for anything."

Since there's no charge to see the castle's exterior, what's to induce you to purchase a $7.50 ticket for a narrated tour of the interior? The best reason is that, since you've come this far, why not? The attractions inside are metallic junk that Solomon has somehow turned into what can be loosely defined as works of art. Beer cans emerge as fish. A bunch of coat hangers becomes a surprisingly graceful giraffe. There is the model of a locomotive with clocks as wheel covers, which Solomon calls "a train on time." Along that line is a rifle with a clock in the stock, denoted as "a minuteman's gun for killing time."

 Solomon and his wife live in the castle, and the tour goes right through their kitchen, which is filled with more of Solomon's quirky artifacts. The castle's upper story contains not only their main living quarters but also four sets of rooms for overnight guests. These accommodations rent for $100 a night. For reservations call 941-494-6077.

You're also invited to take an eight-minute walk along Solomon's forest trail, which he warns will take sixteen minutes if you go around twice. And after the tour and the walk, you can lunch at a restaurant formed like a Spanish galleon. Solomon's daughter and her husband serve food here. It is quite tasty—and guaranteed to be free of papa's loose bolts or bottle caps. Was it risky opening a full-service restaurant so far from off-the-street patrons? "No gamble at all," Solomon noted. "After all, I know a captive audience when I see one."

The castle is open from 11 A.M. to 4 P.M. every day except Monday. However, Solomon raises the drawbridge during July, August, and September, when he is busy conjuring up more magical monstrosities.

The Cracker Trail

Having seen that Solomon's Castle is as odd and silly as promised, return to CR 665 and follow it north about eight miles to SR 64, designated as part of the Cracker Trail, which follows the general route once used by cowboys driving their cattle westward to the port at Bradenton. (The eastern portion of the trail terminated at the P. P. Cobb dock in Ft. Pierce.)

The Cracker Trail is a far cry from what it was in its rip-snorting, whip-cracking heyday. The herds were unruly. The bulls in particular were ornery, unpredictable critters. A cowboy related how a bull caught him off-guard and with one swipe of his horn ripped off his trousers, belt and all. But the most feared danger was of stampedes. A clap of thunder, the snarl of a panther, or almost any unexpected noise could do it. And when the herd began running it was beyond control. There was nothing the cowboys could do except flee for their lives. "If you try to cut across the herd," one cowpoke recalled, "they will run over you. It's a terrible and cruel thing. I have seen 'em run over anchored horses, and them horses would be stomped out as flat as a piece of paper."

When day was done, the herd would be penned behind a log rail fence. Then the smell of cooking would waft from the chuck wagon, where the cook was preparing venison or turkey or the meat of other animals killed along the way. There were plenty of biscuits and sweet potatoes swimming in syrup. And coffee was a staple, strong and black. When dinner was over and the horses had been rubbed, watered, and fed, the cowboys would gather around a pine knot fire and recount their adventures of the day. Finally they'd spread blankets on the ground, cover themselves with mosquito netting, and drift into the soundest of slumbers.

Often the men spent four months on the prairie. It became a way of life and they hated to return to civilization. "Unshackled and free," was the way one of them put it. But drives ended when barbed wire began cutting up the prairie. The last great herd went through here in 1937.

Continuing east on SR 64, in a few miles you'll reach a creek that must have caused cattlemen considerable difficulty, for they named it Troublesome. But it's no problem now. A few miles farther on you'll cross the Peace River, then enter Zolfo Springs.

"One Last Goodbye": Zolfo Springs

About the only thing of interest in tiny Zolfo Springs is Pioneer Park, off of SR 64 just before the US 17 junction. The park is surprisingly large, especially for a village of less than a couple thousand. Fishing is available here in the Peace River, with the boat launch near the springs that Italian railroad workers called "zolfo," after its sulfurous odor. There is a children's playground, nature trails, and a small outdoor zoo where injured animals are rehabilitated. Facilities are available for sixty-two campers, with centrally located restrooms and showers.

There's plenty of old stuff too, as you'd expect from the park's name. On the grounds is a mill where stalks of sugarcane were

This old outhouse in Pioneer Park reminds us that the "good old days" had their drawbacks.

squeezed by a mule-turned grinding stone. There is the actual blacksmith shop where Clarence Bryant shoed horses for more than half a century. And William and Mary Jane Hart raised seven children in the log cabin with the outhouse in the rear.

One of the park's most striking objects is the Baldwin steam engine, similar to those which formerly dispatched cascades of smoke and cinders over Zolfo Springs, Arcadia, and the other towns along the line. Beside the locomotive is a plaque to Bone Mizell. This helps recall that such an engine figured in Bone's best-known incident.

It happened that a young man from a wealthy Northern family was spending some time with Bone and the boys when he suddenly died. They dug his grave out on the prairie beside that of a ranch hand. When the young man's parents learned of his death some time later, they requested the remains be sent to them. Bone put remains in a container and dispatched them by rail. But he made one little switch, which inspired Ruby Leach Carson to write *The Ballad of Bone Mizell*, which concludes:

> So instead of that Yank with his money and rank
> Who had been 'round and seen lots of fun,
> I jes' dug up Bill Redd and sent him instead
> For ole Bill hadn't traveled 'round none.

Steam locomotives, like this one in Zolfo Springs' Pioneer Park, were shot at by cowboys.

Bone's antics continued until 1921, when he boarded the train for the last time. He got off at Ft. Ogden, eleven miles south of Arcadia. Here he took a long, satisfying swig of whiskey, lay down on one of the station benches, and simply died—a smile on his face, so the story goes. Yet even in death Bone had one more trick to play. He was buried at the Joshua Creek Cemetery, a few miles east of Arcadia, but somehow his marker was placed on the wrong grave.

Pioneer Park also contains a fine museum, which is open Monday through Saturday 9 A.M. to 6 P.M. and Sunday 1 P.M. to 5 P.M. Admission is just a dollar. All the items on display were used by people who actually lived around Zolfo Springs. You'll find the lantern that B. F. Holland carried on his early morning chores to the milking barn. And a photo shows old Bob Lanier's home with his prized Curved Dash Olds parked out in front where everyone could marvel at it. There's a well-worn, handmade quilt, a butter churn, and spinning wheel. And, for those who want to see a really early pioneer, there's a jumbo mammoth rib discovered by Eagle Scouts in 1963.

In one corner you'll find an ancient pump-organ with the ivory worn off several keys. It must have resounded to melodies from the finger-smudged songbook opened to "No More Goodbyes," in which the chorus goes:

No more goodbyes, that's the glory of the Lord.
Yes, in that home beyond the skies,
Where the endless ages roll,
Shall be no more goodbyes.

However, there is one last goodbye, and it's ours.

Donald's Slaughtering House

Leaving Pioneer Park, turn south on US 17 to the village center at the corner of SR 66. This junction is highlighted by a row of empty buildings and a gas station sporting an ancient Pure Oil sign. There is also a weather-worn sign for Donald's Slaughtering House advising you to bring your live hog to Donald's place in Arcadia, where he'll cause it to become deceased, then cut it up for just ninety-nine cents a pound. Since I didn't happen to have any live hogs with me, I passed the sign by. But I got to wondering if Donald was still in business, what with suburban sprawl and the conversion of farms into housing. So later I gave the number a call. When a woman answered, I asked if this was Donald's Slaughtering House. She retorted that it was a sandwich shop and no one was getting slaughtered at that time. But she knew Donald and had gotten calls like this before. He was still slaughtering, and she gave me his new phone number. So, if any of you have live hogs and want Donald's number, write to me in care of the publisher and I'll send your name on to Donald as a public service.

SR 66 is the Cracker Trail, as if you couldn't have guessed. Following it east, you'll pass some trailer parks where the RVs are packed hood to hookup—ignoring the vast Ninety-mile Prairie that certainly has enough space to give them more breathing room. The Cracker Trail may have a romantic aura when viewed from a historical distance, but, frankly, some find it a rather unexciting drive. Perhaps they would like me to concentrate on other phenomena, like the cattle egrets. Every egret seems to have a steer with which it chums. As the big animals munch around, they kick up the grass and insects pop out. To the egrets, they are ready-made dinners, a kind of self-service McDonald's. Although they are called cattle egrets, the birds also enjoy the company of horses. But a careful per capita count will reveal that a majority of the egrets do, indeed, find the cattle to be better providers.

Another item of limited interest may be the signs. "Beef, What's for Dinner" predominates at first. Then you'll notice a plaque bravely announcing "Citrus, The Best Thing Growing." Beef does not take that lightly, however, for several more of its signs quickly follow. But citrus fights back. Soon it's an even battle. You may wonder about the outcome, for a dozen or so miles out of Zolfo you'll leave the signs behind and turn left onto CR 635. To relieve your suspense, I'll tell you that citrus finally wins, for ahead lies the fabulous ridge country, where oranges reign unchallenged. But, before we get there, let's take a brief detour to Highlands Hammock State Park.

The Tree Troopers: Highlands Hammock State Park

After traveling five miles north on CR 635, you'll reach CR 634, where you should turn west a short distance to Highlands Hammock State Park. If you're debating whether to pay the $3.25 per car entry fee, you should be made aware that Highlands Hammock boasts some of the most beautiful tall-tree trails and scenic catwalks in Florida. It is one of the four parks forming the state's original system in 1935. It also has Florida's only museum dedicated to the young men of Franklin Roosevelt's Civilian Conservation Corps (CCC.) The museum is in a former CCC building just down the road from the admission booth.

The museum, which is open seven days a week from 9:30 A.M. until 3:30 P.M., helps recall an era few of us can comprehend—the gray years of the Great Depression, when millions could find no jobs; when unemployed couples lost their homes; when shabby men sold apples on the streets to survive. The young men of the CCC came from families on relief. There were nearly two thousand camps across the nation, twenty-one in Florida.

Many museums are full of dusty relics about which the attendants know very little. But this museum seems alive, for during the 1930s it was the recreation center for the two hundred or so lads who turned the subtropical hammock into something that ordinary citizens could enjoy. Here the CCC boys could relax after long hours clearing paths through the dense forest or building catwalks and foot bridges over the swampy areas.

The CCC volunteers were mostly seventeen and eighteen years old, many away from home for the first time. Their enlistment was for six months. But during the Depression there was nothing to return to, so a large percentage reenlisted for more than one term. It was not a choice most of them relished, however, for the work was

Visitors to Highlands Hammock are about to enjoy a narrated tour aboard this tram.

grueling, particularly during the summers, when the long days were torrid and muggy and the forest seldom permitted cooling breezes to circulate. Their supervisors were tough Army men who tolerated no slackers. The Army called the young men Tree Troopers and emphasized that their training in carpentry, surveying, and plant husbandry would be invaluable later. The youths were not impressed, however, and referred to the CCC as the Colossal College of Calluses.

But gripe as they might, when it was over most realized the value of their training. Five decades after the camp had been closed and the buildings left to rot, surviving members of the National Association of CCC Alumni donated memorabilia and otherwise helped establish this official museum. Across from the museum is the log building where the boys could buy sundry items and whatever luxuries they could afford with their meager $5 a month pocket money—all that was left after the government sent the rest of their $30 a month pay to their needy parents. This is now a snack shop hardly altered from the CCC days.

The CCC recreation hall was used for everything from the unit's own swing band to boxing matches, raucous skits, and general goofing around. Today music retrieved from old 78 rpm records again enlivens the hall. Photos show the CCC youths at play as well as at work. Each camp had its own athletic team. Baseball games between camps sometimes took on the intensity of a World Series.

Amid Green Grandeur

That such a hammock formed in the midst of the surrounding pine forest is due to the fact that a favorable land contour collected enough moisture to encourage the growth of huge oaks, hickories, and other deciduous trees. You can take your car on the three-mile Loop Drive that wends among these grand trees. Or you can board the park tram and receive a narrated tour. The tram leaves from in front of the museum Tuesdays through Fridays at 1 P.M. and Saturdays and Sundays at 1 and 2:30 P.M. (June through September it operates weekends only.) Bikes can also be rented.

The Loop Drive gives access to eight hiking trails, each passing through different ecosystems. The names are descriptive: the Big

Youth of the Depression-era Civilian Conservation Corps built raised boardwalks through the dense jungle at Highlands Hammock State Park.

Oak Trail, the Hickory Trail, and the Fern Garden Trail. The most popular is the Cypress Swamp Trail, which features a CCC-style raised boardwalk.

Whatever trail you take, pause at some point to listen to the forest. You'll discern subtle sounds you probably were never aware of. You'll hear the claws of squirrels as they scamper from limb to limb. You'll hear leaves fall. You'll hear breezes nudge through the trees almost as if the forest were breathing. For the plants do breathe, exhaling oxygen as they combine atmospheric gasses and water to form the sugars that are their food.

While you're in a contemplative mood, look closely at the trees. Start at the base of the nearest tree, down where the roots emerge from the mysteries of the soil. Notice the patterns of the bark, running like woody rivulets up the trunk. Follow one of these slowly, dodging the twigs and pausing to let busy ants pass. When you come to the first limb, run your eyes along it until you get to the very end. Then float like fluff to the limb of another tree. Continue upwards until you rest amid the topmost leaves, where you can almost feel them sipping the sunshine.

Sometimes it's strange how an experience like this can turn out. As I was craning my neck, a little boy tugged at my sleeve and asked what I was doing. I told him I was looking at the tree. "Kin I look too?" he asked hesitantly. "Of course," I answered. So we were both gazing upward as his slightly older sister arrived. When she asked her brother what he was looking at, he paused, thoughtful, and answered, "I guess nothin'." "Oh," she retorted with near-adult exasperation, "then come along with me. We can look at those things anywhere." When they were gone, I shrugged. She was right. But will they?

Sebring

 From Highlands Hammock take CR 634 east three miles until it ends at US 27/98, which runs along Lake Jackson. Although you're within Sebring, the main part of town is across the lake. Sebring is famous for its racetrack, which is where the next chapter begins. If you're spending the night here, you might like the Inn on the Lake, located about a mile south from CR 634 on the federal highway. Rates begin at $60 and top out at $90, which gives you a balcony with a good view of Little Lake Jackson (800-531-5253). There is also a brand new resort hotel, Château Élan, at the racetrack (863-655-1442). And within the main part of town is the renovated Kenilworth Lodge, a local landmark ever since its construction by George Sebring in 1916 (800-423-5939).

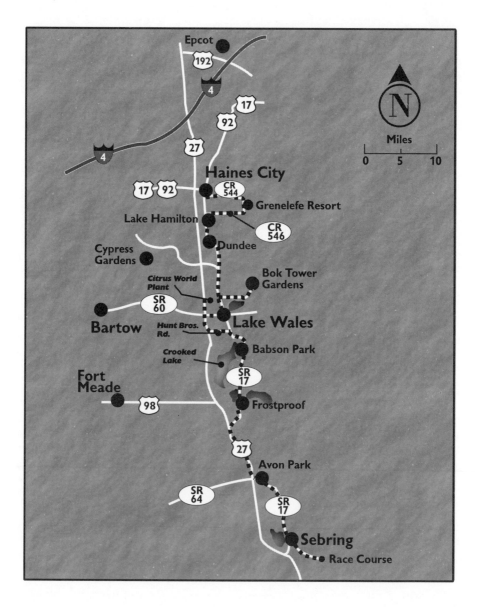

The Fabulous Citrus Ridge

Sebring to Haines City • 57 Backroad Miles

The Song of the Road: Overview

This backroads exploration follows SR 17, which locals call by its traditional name, the Scenic Highway, given in the days when roads were differentiated by descriptions rather than by numbers. Traveling its many curves, you'll be greeted by pleasing vistas as it threads a long, narrow range of hills whose well-drained soil is ideal for raising citrus. Indeed, orange trees ride every dip and rise along this land formation that some call the Citrus Ridge, others the Lake Wales Ridge. To most, it is simply the Ridge.

You'll begin at Sebring, ironically known more for its racetrack than for its fine orange groves. After viewing the track, as well as the spanking new high-rise hotel on the grounds, you'll go to downtown Sebring, where the Circle of the Sun warrants inspection. Then it's north through the groves along the Scenic Highway. At Avon Park you can visit the block-long Jacaranda Hotel, a refurbished monument to the 1920s. If it's lunchtime, you can stop in the same dining room where the world-champion St. Louis Cardinals of yore once supped.

Leaving Avon Park, you'll soon enter the village of Frostproof, where you'll learn of the mysterious monster of Clinch Lake. You'll also pass the extensive citrus-processing plant of Cargill, where oranges are converted not only into concentrates but also fragrances, cattle feed, and industrial solvents. Just out of Frostproof you'll be treated to one of the most expansive views in peninsular Florida. At the same time you'll learn of the numerous pests that citrus growers must battle, as well as the problems faced by the migrant orange-pickers.

Continuing through the orange groves, you'll reach Babson Park, named for Roger Babson, who had the good fortune to predict the stock market crash of 1929. He also founded Webber College, whose campus overlooks Crooked Lake. From here the road leads to the town of Lake Wales, home to one of the nation's largest citrus-processing plants, belonging to the Florida's Natural Growers co-op. The company has an attractive visitor's center across from the plant. Lake Wales' downtown is a stunning example of a successful Main

225

Street rejuvenation. You can also visit the city beach and enjoy a pleasant drive around Lake Wailes while you learn why the lake is spelled differently from the town. A visit to Lake Wales is not complete without driving up Iron Mountain to the beautiful Bok Singing Tower and Garden.

The last segment of this backroads trip continues north on the Scenic Highway through the citrus hamlets of Dundee and Lake Hamilton to Haines City. Although there are still many groves, the soft hills are more and more likely to support newly built homes and golf courses such as the Grenelefe Golf and Tennis Resort, where you can stop for lunch before continuing on to Haines City. Haines City has a resurrected downtown, but much of the city is becoming transformed into a cluttered companion of greater Orlando. So it's here we'll end our last backroads exploration.

On the Road Again

Approaching Sebring on US 27, turn north on SR 17. In a mile you'll reach the stoplight at Kenilworth Boulevard, marked by the historic Kenilworth Lodge. Turn right onto the boulevard and drive six miles east. Along the way the route becomes Airport Road. Much of the distance is through orange groves, for you're on top of the low ridge that produces some of Florida's finest fruit. As the road descends to flat country, the groves end, for citrus trees prefer the good drainage that the sandy ridge provides. Sod farms take their place. Just ahead is the Sebring International Grand Prix Race Course. That such a facility was established in this isolated location was due mainly to the inspiration and hard work of one man, Alec Ulmann.

The Russian Racer

Ulmann grew up in Russia. His initiation into car racing came in 1908, when he witnessed the winning auto stumble into Moscow after traveling more than four hundred miles from St. Petersburg. "That settled me into a lifelong appreciation of and love for automobile racing," Ulmann wrote in his engaging book, *The Sebring Story*. His family fled Russia during the Communist Revolution and settled in Switzerland, where Alec rode to school on a motorcycle he rescued from the junkyard. He eventually made it to the United States, culminating his formal education at the prestigious Massachusetts Institute of Technology. After he secured a job with the Goodyear Tire and Rubber Company, he was able to attend racing events, such as the

This display sign honors winners of the grueling contests at the Sebring International Racecourse.

Indianapolis 500. "It was a constant source of disappointment for me," he wrote, "to see American racing forced by promoters into the dead end of round or oval racing." A trip to the Le Mans race in France in 1950 showed him what he wanted for the United States: an event where ordinary sports cars endured the same harsh road conditions that the average driver might encounter. The track he envisioned would have a lot of curves. And when a car broke down, the driver would either have to repair it (using the commonplace tools carried in most cars), or, if he managed to get his car to the mechanics' pit, only one man could help him. The event would last for twelve hours, many of them at night. For these reasons it would be even more an endurance race than one of speed.

Ulmann's involvement in the transportation industry led him to search out old airfields where surplus World War II planes could be stored. When he came to Sebring, he realized that the virtually unused concrete runways of old Hendrick Field were ideal for race cars. Using his position as chairman of the Sports Car Club of America, he set the wheels in motion for the first Sebring race. Held on New Year's Eve in 1950, it was conducted, admitted Ulmann, "in the total ignorance of international regulations." Only a few spectators attended, for there were no bleachers or public address system.

The Grand Prix Raceway—Sebring Version

There have been many changes from Ulmann's day. Now nearly one hundred thousand spectators watch the Twelve Hours of Endurance Race held every March. Most patrons are long-time attendees happy to pay the $200 two-day admission price. Its importance brings worldwide media coverage, with the winning car receiving invaluable prestige. Another important event is the Trans-Am Race in October. Don't feel bad if there's no race during your visit to Sebring. Without the crowds, you're able to drive freely through the gates and around most of the public area. Just resist the urge to burn rubber on the track itself.

On the track grounds is a classy new hotel called the Château Élan, overlooking the notorious Hairpin Turn, where some of the most dramatic moments of the races occur. The Château offers rates designed to attract a broad clientele (863-655-6252). Even though you may not choose to stay here, you should at least walk through the lobby to the outdoor patio, from which you can often see test cars maneuvering on the track. The hotel restaurant also serves breakfasts, lunches, and dinners.

Circle of the Sun

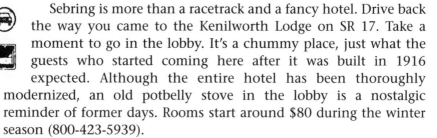
Sebring is more than a racetrack and a fancy hotel. Drive back the way you came to the Kenilworth Lodge on SR 17. Take a moment to go in the lobby. It's a chummy place, just what the guests who started coming here after it was built in 1916 expected. Although the entire hotel has been thoroughly modernized, an old potbelly stove in the lobby is a nostalgic reminder of former days. Rooms start around $80 during the winter season (800-423-5939).

Now go north on SR 17 to the center of town, which you'll easily recognize by the central circular park. The park was laid out by George Sebring, who founded the town in 1911. Because George was a deeply religious man, some local historians see the circle as a representation of heaven's perfection. Others believe Sebring was responding to a movement for city layouts more imaginative than the usual grid-work pattern. Some insist that the circle came about because George had recently read an article about the ancient city of Heliopolis, with a circular layout devoted to the sun god. Whatever his purpose, this unusual shape has made the town's central business section distinctive.

This circular park was laid out in 1911 by George Sebring. The original bank building is in the background.

Many of the buildings on the circle were constructed just after the town's founding. The town's most impressive original building—which you might have known would be the bank—is at 300 North Circle (corner of Commerce Avenue). It dates back to 1913. There bank officials waited smugly in their offices on the north side of the building for the bustling real estate company in the south portion to send property-buyers in to secure mortgages. But perhaps the realtors sent too many, for the bank became excessively involved in real estate and went under during the great bust in 1929. During the next half century the building was used as the city hall.

At 113 South Circle (corner of SR 17) is the Withers Building, where the village drugstore was located. Aaron Withers arrived with the original surveying crew and stayed on to become the town marshal and first fire chief. Next door is the Zeall Building. John Zeall was a salesman with George Sebring's real estate company. For many years this was the village clothing store. At 104 North Circle, Walt and Mamie Zackary operated a clothing and dry goods store. The grocery, run by Englishman Tom Whitehouse and his wife, Emma, was located at 313 South Circle.

To Sebring's first citizens, the circle must have seemed the hub of the world. Florida's famed Scenic Highway, now relegated to mere number 17, ran around it from north to south. The other axis was Center

Avenue. Center was anchored on the east by the Atlantic Coast Line, whose impressive depot (sparkling like new) now hosts Amtrak trains, and on the west by Lake Jackson, where George Sebring built a grand mansion on the site now occupied by the public library.

George was a square-jawed man of fifty-two when he supervised the town's founding. That it carried his name was nothing new, for he had already founded another Sebring, this one in Ohio, location of the pottery company that had made him wealthy. He came to Florida to found a community where "preachers, evangelists, college professors and Christian workers . . . will find a place to rest . . . and a pleasant climate in which to spend the evening of their lives"—so runs the quote in Stephen A. Olausen's excellent book *Sebring: City on the Circle.*

Sebring and Salvation

George's predilection toward religious people led him to favor members of the Salvation Army. One of these was John Newcomb, whose memoirs (and those of his son Harold) can be found in the Sebring Library. John, his wife, Hannah, and their two young boys arrived in Sebring when it consisted of a few shacks almost lost amid the Lake Jackson pines at what is now the foot of Center Avenue. There was barely space in their cramped quarters for a wood-burning stove, two small wooden beds filled with moss for the kids, and a double bed for John and Hannah. The roof leaked such quantities that each bed had a makeshift rain-shield overhead. The vermin were so numerous that everyone had to check constantly for body lice.

Despite the rigors, son Harold found it an exciting place. "There was so much to see in a town a-building," he wrote, recalling the "teams of horses and mules and slip scrapers tearing up the young growth and roots to make space for the Circle and breaks through the woods to smooth the way for future streets." Houses and stores were being constructed at almost the same time, providing the kids with wood framing to climb. The air resounded with pounding hammers, rasping saws, and the crack of teamsters' bullwhips as they drove the work animals.

Soon the Newcomb family moved into a real house, and, as more settlers flocked in, Harold and older brother Freddie welcomed new playmates. The town pier was their gathering place. Here they'd play "I Dare You," which often involved swimming under the pier, dodging the pilings. The adults too seemed to find their way to the pier, where the sunsets over Lake Jackson made everyone gasp with delight. They'd sing songs, mostly religious. John had a fine tenor voice, and Hannah accompanied him on a five-string banjo. "To go down on the pier and hear a large group of people singing with joy and feeling," Harold recalled, "was something not to be forgotten."

Today there is a new pier at the foot of Center Avenue. The entire lakefront at this point has become the Cultural Center, showplace for this bustling city of twelve thousand. Included are the public library, the Historical Society, the Highlands Little Theater, and the Museum of the Arts.

Triumph and Tragedy on Lakeview Drive

Some of the city's choicest residences can be seen as you drive north on Lakeview Drive, which runs in front of the library. At first the homes are older and modest, but as you continue, they become slightly newer and more impressive. After a mile and a half you're definitely among Sebring's upper set. Watch for the home at 2107 with the red tile roof and five-foot-high wall. It formerly belonged to Rex Beach, who, during the first half of the twentieth century, was one of America's foremost adventure writers. Several of his books, including *The Spoilers*, have been made into major movies. During this time, he was Sebring's most exalted resident—so much so that Lake Jackson was subtitled "Rex Beach Lake" on city maps. The chamber of commerce always took important visitors proudly past his residence. Today, when I asked receptionists at the chamber about him, not only did they not know the location of his home, they did not even know who he was. Such is the fleeting nature of fame.

But Rex Beach does not deserve to be forgotten. He grew up in Tampa and attended college in Winter Park, where he worked in the laundry to pay his tuition. Muscular and athletic, he even tried his hand at professional football. Then, seeking adventure, he migrated to the Alaska mining frontier, where, although the nuggets eluded him, he met Gretta, a kindred spirit who became his wife and lifelong companion. "She was very attractive," he wrote in *Personal Experiences*, "in fact she was quite the loveliest creature I had ever seen." He loved the saucy tilt of her chin and her deep dimples "that looked as if they had been poked into her cheeks by a mischievous finger." He claimed that meeting her was the event from which all others in his life were dated.

Returning from Alaska, he wrote his first novel, *Pardners*. Later, after he completed *The Spoilers*, his reputation as a major outdoor novelist was secured. In 1926, after years of successes, he and Gretta came to Sebring, where they bought the home on Lakeside Drive. It was a joy. One window of Rex's writing room looked out on palms and tropical shrubs where mockingbirds and cardinals nested. The other fronted on Lake Jackson. He found the lake a temptation that sometimes interfered with his writing: "the damned thing is full of bass and they fin their noses daring me to toss a plug and see what happens."

He also bought a large amount of land and began an additional career as gentleman farmer. He was so successful raising gladioli that he made a second fortune. But the money was less important than pleasing Gretta. "She loves flowers," he wrote, "and when I return home from toil I carry so many glads and Easter lilies that I look like an open grave." During the Depression years, he and Gretta devoted much time and money to local causes.

His wealth and good works could not protect him from tragedy, however. In his early seventies, he began going blind. Then he got cancer of the throat, possibly caused by his ever-present cigar. When his beloved Gretta died, he fell into deep despair, realizing that not only was his lifelong sweetheart and buddy gone, but now he, who had always espoused the rugged life, would not even be able to care for himself. In 1949 he took out his hunting gun, aimed it at his last quarry, and ended his life to the roar of a bullet.

On the Road to Avon Park

Turn right at the Rex Beach house onto a short street with a long name: Sten-E-Wah-Hee. Go two blocks to Home Avenue, then two blocks right on Home to SR 17. Turning left onto SR 17, you'll ascend a low hill. It's not much today, but to settlers trudging to Sebring it presented an inspiring view of their future on Lake Jackson.

Dinner Lake, once the site of a large sawmill, is on the distant right. "The sawmill was a great attraction," wrote Harold Newcomb, who knew it well as a boy, "with its steam engine which was fueled by the pine slabs, the big saw screeching through the virgin pine logs and the smell of fresh-cut pine mingled with the wood smoke." Harold and the other boys enjoyed sliding down the fragrant pile of sawdust. Afterwards they roamed along the lake shore, gathering turtle eggs with which to placate their mothers when they showed up late and dirty for the evening meal.

The route before you lies over the gentle contours of the sandy ridge that forms the state's soft spine. During Indian days a meandering path wound through pinelands rich with wild turkeys and other small game. The Indians traveled easily through the ridge's shady depths. But when the white settlers came with their heavy vehicles, they found it far more difficult. One lady recalled that it took almost six body-straining hours to cover the ten miles from Avon Park to Sebring "with all five children pushing most of the way." Travel improved greatly when the Scenic Highway was built in 1918. It wasn't perfect—being only nine feet wide and laboring over each hill like a tired turtle—but at least it had a surface of bricks, not sand.

The Citrus Ridge

The road brought settlers, and the settlers brought their sawmills, and the mills chewed up the pines. Then they were gone. But they were not missed, for now the Ridge was open to orange groves. This was ideal country for citrus. The climate was warm. The rains were plentiful. And the hilly, sandy soil ensured good drainage. Furthermore, trees on the Ridge withstood high winds better than those in the flatlands, whose anchorage was weakened by the wet soil. The Ridge was also less susceptible to the rare freezes, since the cold air tended to sink to the flatlands. So citrus trees were planted by the hundreds of thousands.

This orange grove may soon become a residential development.

Oranges come in several varieties. Navels are excellent eating. They also mature early in the winter, when freezes are less likely. Parson Browns bear mid-season fruit. But the juicy Valencias are by far the most popular. And that's what they mostly grow around Sebring and Avon Park. Oranges are almost everything here. "To say that the citrus industry is important in Highlands County," the Sebring Chamber of Commerce writes, "is at best an understatement." In a town of just eleven thousand people, up to three thousand are employed in the citrus industry, and that number doubles during the October–May harvest season, when migrant workers are added.

Although citrus is the undeniable king, many parts of the Ridge seem to be at the beginning of a transition. The rolling, elevated land that is so favorable to citrus is also appealing as homesites. Already signs are starting to pop up along SR 17 advertising prime grove land for sale in tracts as small as five acres. It's not difficult to picture the verdant groves displaced by the dull brown roofs of suburbia's cookie-cutter homes.

The Ridge: Born from the Sea

The Ridge is an unusual phenomenon. It was formed quite recently, at least as geologists compute time. During the last inter-glacial period, the earth's warming caused the polar ice to melt, releasing such huge amounts of water that the oceans rose several hundred feet, flooding all of Florida except the center, where a long beach topped by extensive sand dunes formed. When the glaciers returned to Northern climes, the ocean level dropped, leaving the sandy hills known today as the Ridge.

The waters receded about ten thousand years ago, and since then portions of the Ridge have eroded into hollows occupied by scores of lakes. You can glimpse several as you travel the road to Avon Park: Lake Letta, Lake Lotela (named, perhaps, for pioneers' wives or daughters). We travel so fast these days that we forget how personal a segment of land is to its inhabitants. Did you miss Dead Man's Curve, where SR 17A meets SR 17 as it makes a ninety-degree right turn? What frightful incident occurred here? History books don't tell us. Rex Beach's gladiolus farm was several miles east of here on the floor of a drained lake.

Avon Park

Rounding another turn, SR 17 enters Avon Park, with a population of eight thousand. Lake Verona, with a small sand beach and an adjoining park, is on the right. This was the site of the locally famed Verona Hotel, completed in 1889 by Oliver Crosby, the town's founder. Crosby was a dreamer who arrived on horseback before there were roads or even hunters' shacks for shelter. When it rained, he simply got wet. "Night after night," said Crosby in Leoma Maxwell's *The First Hundred Years of Avon Park, Florida,* "we slept in damp clothes and soggy feet, without shelter." As for bugs, Crosby continued, "the mosquitoes I found too numerous and aggressive . . . but it is a poor pioneer that will grumble about little things like these." Crosby believed he could create a thriving town here, with the Verona Hotel as merely the first step. It was a two-and-a-half-story building, with a veranda where guests could enjoy a fine view of the lake. But it was wooden, and light was furnished by highly flammable kerosene lamps. Thus it made a fine blaze when it burned to the ground. By then, however, Crosby had lost his entire fortune, including the hotel, when the great freeze of 1895 destroyed crops and sent almost everybody trudging back north. Crosby too had departed—minus his dreams and his self-esteem.

Without the Verona, the site was turned into a park, which it remains today. In 1939 the Tin Can Tourists convened here with 180 trucks and trailers and a menagerie of kids. They were not the most welcome of guests, as this poem suggests:

> Cars from the North, the East, the West,
> Bring weary tourists seeking rest. . . .
> They're singing songs and making plans
> And piling up the empty cans.

The "Belle of the Ridge"

Even without Crosby, Avon Park kept the dream of becoming a major Ridge town. To outdo archrival Sebring, with its heralded circle, in 1918 Avon began turning its main street into what was proclaimed the Mile-long Mall. In order to broaden the street and add a landscaped center strip, Avon had to move several buildings. The mall was a tremendous undertaking for the little town, but it seemed to work the miracle wished for when out-of-town investors constructed the Jacaranda Hotel. Occupying an entire city block, it

Avon Park's Jacaranda Hotel has been a landmark since 1926.

was a massively impressive structure resembling a three-story fortress. Yet its interior was homey, and its fine dining room became an added attraction. The hotel gained national fame when the world champion St. Louis Cardinals baseball team resided here during the 1926 and 1927 spring training seasons. On the team was Grover Alexander, now in the Baseball Hall of Fame. The Cardinals, boisterous as they were, were welcome guests in Avon Park, and Alexander even managed the local girls' baseball team.

But the Great Depression ended the hotel's glory years and brought catastrophe to the owners, particularly the chief investor, John Raab, who left Avon Park as destitute as had Oliver Crosby more than three decades earlier. Since then the Jacaranda has had many owners. The latest is South Florida Community College. Using student labor, the rooms have been modernized and the lobby rehabilitated without destroying its 1920s charm. Students majoring in the culinary arts work in the kitchen, helping make the Jac's lunches and dinners what the college's promotional literature calls "Southern delights."

The Jacaranda, even with its moderate revival, is symbolic of the misfortunes Avon Park has experienced over the years. It began with

Oliver Crosby, who, even before he was ruined by the deep freeze, had difficulty bringing telephone service to town. He built a line west to the connection at Ft. Meade, but cowboys in the flatlands took great pride in popping off his glass insulators for target practice. So the line had to be abandoned. A far greater blow came in 1923, when Highlands County was created and the prize of county seat went to Sebring. During World War II, military activity gave a lift to Avon Park, as well as neighboring Sebring. But when it was over, Sebring had a fine airfield and Avon Park was left with a deserted bombing range. Although parts of the range are now open to hikers, it's hardly an attraction comparable to Sebring's raceway.

SR 17 continues down the Mile-long Mall. Not much has gone on ever since US 27 bypassed the town. The railroad station still stands. Once this was the most exciting place in town, but the trains don't stop here anymore—they speed on to Sebring. The station has been given a new coat of paint and is now used for historical society displays.

The mall extends to US 27, where you should turn north. The land is flat; you're not on the Ridge any longer but at its base. Continue for six miles until SR 17 branches off, and follow it once more. Soon you'll pass the Sun Pure plant, where rocket-shaped cylinders heat raw orange juice under pressure to convert it into concentrate. The company recently purchased an even larger facility in Ft. Pierce's Indian River grapefruit belt, making it one of the larger fruit processors in Florida.

The Sand Swimmers

With its scrubby pines and occasional oak hammocks, the area might look as it did in the days when panthers and black bears lurked in the shady recesses. They'll never return, but a few of the original animals still manage to survive. Two of them are unusual legless lizards known as sand skinks and blue-tailed mole skinks. They have adapted to the sandy environment that provides no traction by actually swimming over the sand using their tails. They can exist only in the Ridge environment, but most people never see them because they're only four inches long and hide beneath the sand. "They're not as glamorous as some other [animals]," apologizes a U.S. environmental official, "but they have a role to play in the ecosystem."

This scrubby area, once rejected by citrus growers, has suddenly become such a highly desirable piece of property that the state has recently purchased 150 acres of it. That was about all that remained of the original six hundred thousand acres that made up what is called the Lake Wales Ridge Ecosystem. On it are rare plants and animals, such as skinks and Florida scrub jays, some found nowhere else on earth. Even so, you probably won't want to stop and wander through this tangled maze of thorny growth and shifting sand. No need to apologize. Even the most devoted environmentalists understand: "For most people," says Mary Huffman, who was instrumental in the state's purchase, "scrub is an acquired taste."

Orange Juice and Paint Oil

As the road ascends the Ridge once more, the orange groves begin again. In several miles you'll reach the little town of Frostproof. Although its population is hardly above three thousand, it hosts an extensive orange-processing facility belonging to the Cargill Company, one of America's largest agricultural organizations. During the harvest season, constant truck caravans haul just-picked Parson Brown and Valencia oranges to the plant, where they are converted into concentrate for foreign export.

But much more than juice comes from the oranges. After the juice is removed, the peels, pulp, and seeds are chopped up. This gloppy mass goes through giant presses that squeeze out the liquid, which is then made into everything from industrial solvents to the oil used in paints. What remains is routed into a huge dryer, where it is converted into low-cost cattle feed that's rich in carbohydrates. Sometimes parts of the peel are set aside for making marmalade or candy or perfumes. The seeds can be separated out and pressed to make cooking and salad oils.

The Story of a Name: Frostproof

Although Frostproof's name recalls the days when cowboys used to drive their herds up the Ridge whenever frost browned the grass in the flatlands, the first permanent settlers decided to call it the more high-class sounding Lakemont, in reference to the surrounding lakes and hills. The horseman carrying the application to the postal authorities at Ft. Meade had other plans, however. So when the townsfolk received their post office, they were astonished to see it designated as Frostproof. The name remains, although it has not kept occasional frosts—or even a few deep freezes—at bay.

The Reluctant Monster of Clinch Lake

Frostproof may have its very own monster, according to Allen Morris in *Florida Place Names*. Morris found evidence of an Indian legend that claimed a ferocious beast lived in Clinch Lake, a few blocks west of the Scenic Highway. When a relatively sober eyewitness saw the mighty beast in 1907, it was thirty feet long and presumably slobbering for sacrificial maidens, or at least a fisherman's foot. The fact that it hasn't made its terrifying presence known for nearly a century has greatly detracted from its aura. Its reappearance certainly would be a gift for local tourism. Even a few minutes of thrashing and slobbering would suffice. Perhaps the monster is pouting somewhere in the depths, longing for the days when it could really scare people, not just be a curiosity freak. To get to the lake, take First Street three blocks west from the Scenic Highway. You'll end at the city dock. Here, perchance, you may come upon the monster, slobber and all. But don't count on it.

Wall Street on the Ridge

The Scenic Highway is Frostproof's main street. Along it, north from the Cargill plant, are some old buildings, somewhat updated. The center of Frostproof is Wall Street. It's not exactly New York City, but it does boast the Citizens Bank, locally owned and in the same building since 1920. Frostproof also has a restaurant with the irresistible name of Utopia. Can Manhattan say the same?

Migrant Workers

Frequently in Frostproof you hear discussions relating to the Hispanic workers who make up thirty percent of the area's population. Many begin appearing throughout Florida at harvest time, for two hundred million boxes must be filled with oranges during the next eight months. The work is exhausting, and about the only source of labor is the migrants, mostly Mexicans. Astonishingly, of the upwards of one hundred thousand agricultural laborers in Florida, an estimated sixty percent are here illegally, according to an article in *Citrus Industry Magazine*. Their living and working conditions are often below what Americans consider minimal but above what they must accept in their own countries. It might seem an easy solution to simply pass a law raising wages, but this might price American citrus out of the world market, where there is strong competition from Brazil.

The soft hills of the Ridge present endless vistas of orange trees.

Numerous as the migrants might be, travelers are hardly aware of them, for they generally live away from the main highways. But watch the groves during harvest and you'll see them driving vehicles and on ladders picking the fruit. Although mechanical tree shakers and other devices may eventually displace most of them, for now they are absolutely essential. Many people believe it's time to give them legal status, and there is a movement in Congress to grant those who work in the United States at least six months a year for five of the next seven years the right to apply for legal permanent residence.

The Hazlehurst Archipelago

A mile north of Frostproof, SR 17 comes to Lake Moody, which lies in a gentle swale surrounded by citrus. Here is the Ridge at its finest: the velvet-soft hills verdant with lush citrus trees, the breeze perfumed with the fragrance of orange blossoms. This is the rounded summit of the Hazlehurst Terrace, former dunes that once stood as lonely islands above the interglacial seas. There are only two other places in peninsular Florida this high: Iron Mountain (crowned by the Bok Tower a dozen miles north) and the hilly country near Starke, not far from the Georgia state line.

Unseen Assassins

The scene that is so tranquil to us is not so tranquil to the grove owners. The area is not immune to freezes. Brief freezes can be handled, for citrus can take temperatures that dip briefly as low as twenty-four degrees without serious damage. When freezes are expected, the trees are sprayed with water, which forms an ice jacket that is surprisingly effective at keeping really frigid temperatures from penetrating the fruit. But a hard freeze will wreck the fruit.

Growers have far greater worries than freezes, however. There is deep concern regarding Mediterranean fruit flies. The damage is done by the larvae-maggots, which destroy the fruit. When the flies are discovered, the state declares total war. The area is quarantined so no fruit can be taken out. Ground spraying begins immediately, soon abetted by planes overhead. It's costly and often lasts a month or longer. But it works.

More dangerous is the root weevil, which arrived in Florida from South America. It destroys the citrus rootstock slowly but persistently and is now found in every citrus-producing county. It's impossible to eradicate the pests with any known poison, and their only enemies may be fire ants. But colonizing the groves with such aggressive insects is not an alternative that delights any grower, much less his workers.

Even the "evil weevils" are not the worst danger, though. The really scary threat is the dreaded citrus canker, which forms lesions on the fruit, causing it to fall to the ground prematurely. There is no known preventive, and the only control is to burn the infected tree and all those within a third of a mile around it. During one canker epidemic in the 1980s, more than twenty million trees were uprooted and burned. Even that does not always work, for the canker can be spread on the shirt of someone who has barely brushed against an infected tree. Or a mower can send the canker sailing into the air currents. Hurricanes can blow it far and wide. Among Florida growers there is an almost paranoid fear that a canker epidemic could actually wipe out the state's entire crop in a single season!

The Dance of the Sandhill Cranes

These concerns need not be ours as we move along the Scenic Highway, for we hope Florida's Citrus Research Center will come up with solutions. So just enjoy the grand vista as you drive on toward Babson Park. If you're here during the October–May harvest season, you'll probably see long trailers parked just off the road, heaped with oranges, waiting for trucks to haul them to processing plants.

In the days when the hills were covered with pines and the

Trailer trucks carry huge loads of oranges to the processing plants at Frostproof and Lake Wales.

marshes were undrained, thousands of sandhill cranes made their nests around here. The cranes stood four feet high with bright red heads and plumage of light slate. "For about three weeks in the spring during mating time," marveled Orren Ohlinger, who often horsebacked between Babson Park and Frostproof, "these birds would gather in massive flocks and stage an unbelievable, beautiful dance. . . . Wings flapped and all the fancy steps that only sandhill cranes know made a scene of such wild loveliness as only a few have seen." The cranes largely vanished after their nesting areas were destroyed. Then other not-so-colorful critters appeared. It was not unheard of in this yet-unfenced land for an angry bull to chase a vehicle down the road. Even a cow could pose problems. "If a cow was switching her tail to swat flies and had her head down, she was probably stable for a moment," noted Louise Quinn in *Crooked Lake—Babson Park Rediscovered*. "But an erect head and a motionless tail meant to slow down or prepare for a quick detour." Above all, you didn't want to run into a hog, which was just the right height to cause a wagon to overturn.

The Crooks and the Frills

Crooked Lake, which comes up on your left, once designated not only the body of water but the village on its shores. The name had a kind of devil-may-care ring to it that appealed to the young men of the village, who called themselves the Crooks. They dated the Frostproof Frills, reaching them by way of a handcar borrowed from the railroad. Together the Crooks and Frills would continue on their jolly handcar excursion to the roller-skating rink at Avon Park. Returning, they'd feast on watermelon snitched from farms. But the village elders, planning to start a bank, didn't relish a name that had "crook" as part of it. So they decided to become Babson Park, a reassuring title associated with the respected economist Roger Babson, who had established his winter headquarters here. This could not have displeased Babson, for he was a flaming egotist.

The Strange World of Roger Babson

Roger Babson was a national figure, having served as assistant secretary of labor. In 1923, he decided to move his cold-season activities down to orange blossom country. He viewed Crooked Lake as an investment as well as a business location. Thus, he constructed some apartments and commercial buildings as well as a single-story structure beside the Scenic Highway that became his office.

Babson was a very unorthodox individual. When he was fresh out of college, his own father threatened to fire him from the family bank for his crazy ideas. He tried a scheme to retread auto tires by coating them with crushed stone. He promoted glass beads coated with fish shells as imitation pearls. But he did have some good ideas. When he couldn't get tenants for his buildings, he donated them to a college he formed, named after his young granddaughter, Camilla Webber.

Babson's reputation was firmly enhanced in 1929, when, just weeks after he warned of an impending financial catastrophe, the stock market crashed. Thereupon he was heralded as a financial genius. Babson soaked up the adulation that followed. He began envisioning himself as some sort of superior creation. Thus, when the president of Webber College dared to say "Good morning," he snapped back that it was not a good morning until he said so! He was not even averse to insulting Franklin Roosevelt. When the president offered him an important position in his administration, Babson retorted that he would consider working for the most powerful man in the world. FDR was flattered until Babson added that he was referring to Joseph Stalin, the dictator of the Soviet Union. The offer was promptly withdrawn.

Webber College

As for Webber College, it opened as a girls' school in 1927 with a curriculum devoted to teaching young women how to compete in the business world. One way, according to Babson, to help scatter-brained females understand punctuality was to have them punch time clocks whenever they came and went. Nonetheless, the educational concept gave the students confidence in their own abilities. It also caused them to reevaluate the lofty estimate they had once held of males. Louise Quinn relates some of the pithy sayings that made the campus circuit:

> If you flatter a man, you frighten him to death; and, if
> you don't, you bore him to death.
> If you permit him to make love to you, he gets tired of
> you in the end; and, if you don't, he gets tired
> of you in the beginning.

But the girls found that witticisms couldn't replace actual men, so in 1971 Webber College began admitting them, and today slightly more than half of the five hundred students are male. The curriculum has been greatly expanded to include courses on such subjects as international tourism. As a result, the student body represents nearly fifty countries.

This grim monument left by Roger Babson greets students at Webber College.

Although the memory of dour old Roger Babson has grown faint, he provided everyone with a somber reminder of his presence. Characteristically, it is in the form of a gravestone-shaped marker near the library commemorating an apparently equally obstreperous English ancestor named John Rogers, who was burned at the stake in 1555 for translating the Bible and preaching the destruction of people and nations who didn't honor the Lord as Rodgers defined him. Not so gruesome is Babson's former office beside SR 17, now called Old Main and occupied by the college president. But the commercial buildings that Babson had no use for and donated to the college have been replaced by sleek modern structures occupying choice land along Crooked Lake.

That's One Big Juice Plant

From Babson Park, SR 17 arches westward past Crooked Lake, then makes a sharp turn north as it approaches Lake Wales. Watch for Hunt Brothers Road. The Hunt family is one of the most influential citrus growers on the Ridge. Their extensive groves are east on Hunt Brothers Road. Frank Hunt is president of Florida's Natural Growers, a division of Citrus World, which operates a huge processing plant nearby. Its visitors center is a must-see for those who want a better understanding of Florida's citrus industry. To reach it, drive a half mile west on Hunt Brothers Road to US 27, then three miles north. The Florida's Natural plant (on the right side of US 27) processes twenty million boxes of oranges yearly. (For comparison, the large Cargill plant in Frostproof handles sixteen million.)

The visitors center on the left side of the highway is an impressive, new facility where, after complimentary glasses of orange juice, you'll be invited to see a film showing how the juice is processed. Exhibits trace the development of Florida's citrus industry, including the formation and growth of the cooperative that became Florida's Natural.

The co-op was created many years ago by an amalgamation of local growers' co-ops seeking to combine their assets in order to build a grapefruit-canning plant. When the art of making frozen concentrated juice was developed in the 1950s, the co-op became one of the largest concentrate processors in Florida, eventually changing the company's name from Citrus Canners to Citrus World. As consumers' tastes turned toward fresh juices, the co-op began producing the Florida's Natural brand, which today is one of the two largest-selling premium fresh juices in the United States. Only Tropicana is larger.

The co-op is not made up of individuals but of twelve separate organizations representing eleven hundred growers from Lake Wales, Sebring, Frostproof, Haines City, and other central Florida locations. Representatives of each of these twelve organizations comprise the board of directors, which sets the general policies that the on-site management team must follow.

Florida's Natural's extensive advertising stresses that its juice is from Florida oranges exclusively, which distinguishes it from others, particularly Minute Maid, which often uses a mix of Florida and Brazilian oranges in its concentrate. "We own the land," runs a Florida's Natural slogan, "we own the trees, and we own the company. It's a difference you can taste." Their ads often feature scenes from Lake Wales that stress the company's roots in small-town Florida.

Now head back south on US 27 a mile to SR 60. Turn east onto SR 60 and in another mile you'll come to SR 17 once more. By remaining on SR 60 you can see Lake Wales' other large processor, Citrosuco, which processes barely about half as much as Florida's Natural. There is nothing unusual about this plant—except that the company is part of a large Brazilian conglomerate. And that's something in itself.

The Brazilian Invasion

The arrival of the Brazilians happened suddenly in the mid-1990s. Although Brazil had recently edged out Florida as the world's largest citrus producer, its market was primarily in Europe. The Brazilians desperately wanted to sell their juice in the United States, but stiff tariffs kept them out. Therefore, the two largest Brazilian companies bought out several American processing plants. One of these was Citrosuco. The other Brazilian giant, Cutrale, purchased the plants of Minute Maid north of Interstate 4. In short order, the Brazilians controlled a significant portion of U.S. processing facilities. "We're very concerned," a Florida grower told the Associated Press, his concern centering on the leverage the Brazilian companies now might have to cut citrus tariffs.

The Gem of the Ridge: Lake Wales

When you turn left onto SR 17, the Scenic Highway, you'll be in the town of Lake Wales, which calls itself the Crown Jewel of the Highlands. Despite the hyperbole, there *is* an atmosphere about the place that makes Lake Wales seem more important than

This appealing arcade lies between Lake Wales' two main streets.

would seem warranted by its modest population of eleven thousand. You can learn more about what made the town special at the historical museum in the former Atlantic Coast Line depot at 325 South Scenic Highway. It's open every day except Sunday, and the admission price is more than reasonable: it's free.

Four blocks beyond the depot is Stuart Avenue, one of Lake Wales' two main streets. A block beyond is Park, the other main street. Turn right onto Park and cross the tracks to the parking lot that was once the railroad freight yard. From here walk back across the Scenic Highway to a pair of eye-catching outdoor murals at the corner of Stuart and SR 17. One shows the railroad being constructed through the pine forest. The other depicts downtown as it was in 1931.

A building whose side accommodates one of the murals is the old Scenic Theater, one of the nation's earliest structures put up specifically to show movies. Within its cavernous interior four hundred patrons could sit—about half the town's entire population at that time. Even today its low twin towers and mission-style parapet are impressive. But the flicks and popcorn are gone, for the interior has been converted into offices with nary a singing cowboy on staff.

Across Stuart is the Bullard Building, constructed in 1919 by B. K. Bullard, one of the town's founders. In its heyday it was the center of almost all town activity. It was here that farmers and townsfolk

Lake Wales' attractive downtown is marred by the deserted, multi-story Dixie Walesbilt Hotel, a relic of the 1920s.

collected their mail, got their meat, and purchased their clothing. In the evenings they would party at the bowling alley on the second floor. Slightly farther west is the Rhodesbilt Arcade Building, with several restaurants and a block-long arcade that connects with Park Avenue. Walking east on Park, you'll pass some of the buildings pictured in the mural. At the end of the block, at the corner of SR 17, is a two-story structure with a Greek-style entry that was the Lake Wales State Bank. Messieurs Stuart and Bullard were among its principal officers. The bank was a wonder hereabouts, for it was one of the few that didn't go under during the Great Depression.

Park and Stuart Avenues, as well as some of the adjoining streets, are now part of a federally recognized historic district that includes seventeen vintage downtown buildings. Most are one- and two-story structures, all trim, neat, and prosperous. But then there is that vacant, ten-story monolith that looms over the downtown like a nightmare. It was constructed in 1926 as the posh Dixie Walesbilt Hotel. The only alternative to an expensive reconditioning of the neglected yet historic structure would be to tear it down, a proposition that frightens nearly everyone.

Pulling on the Same Rope

It wasn't just the grand hotel that couldn't make it in the years following the Great Depression. The entire downtown went into a tailspin, worsened in the late 1950s by the completion of US 27, which skirted the city. This not only diverted the tourist trade but led to the growth of strip shopping centers that further siphoned trade from the downtown. Eventually what was once the "crown jewel" was more like a chipped rhinestone.

The turnaround began in 1973, when a local attorney contacted the University of Florida for help. The university sent down experts from the Architectural School who drew up revival plans. Seed money was obtained from a special tax on building owners as well as from the general revenue fund. The initial spending involved improving the area's appearance with such projects as new sidewalks, streetlights, planters, and creative landscaping. This was a start. But the way back was difficult. "The biggest problem," one civic promoter told me, "is the cynicism you encounter: the attitude that it can't be done. It's difficult getting everyone to pull on the same end of the rope."

A decisive moment occurred in the 1980s, when Lake Wales became one of the first towns to join Florida's Main Street Program. First, a Community Redevelopment Administration was set up. This enabled the town's Main Street Board to initiate a tax-increment program whereby, as the business section began to revive and property values rose, the increase in tax revenue was allocated strictly to downtown improvements. Today, with this flow of tax-increment money, the board is able to grant owners up to $4,000 to improve the facades of their buildings. "We're even expanding our area," a Main Street Board member told me. "Right now we have fifteen owners on the waiting list."

Most visitors are not aware of the ongoing effort in keeping the downtown alive. And that's the way it should be.

Overnight with George and Effie

From the downtown, drive a few blocks north on the Scenic Highway to Sessoms Avenue, then a block east to Third Street. On the northeast corner is the home of George Tillman. Next door is the almost identical residence of C. L. Johnson. These men, along with Stuart and Bullard, were the four town founders.

Tillman was the first to visit this area when he roamed through it in 1902. He was impressed by the beauty of the ridge country with its rolling landscape and hidden lakes. It was still virgin territory, with not a town or village within miles. Deer and bear were plentiful, and the wail of bobcats during mating season echoed eerily through the pines. Returning to civilization, Tillman conveyed his feelings to Johnson and Bullard, who had come to Florida as representatives of the Sessoms Investment Company. After touring the region with Tillman, they agreed that, with proper promotion, the land would be exceedingly valuable. So in 1911 they formed the Lake Wales Land Company, bringing in E. C. Stuart, who already had holdings nearby. When the Atlantic Coast Line extended rails to Lake Wales that same year, the town's future was assured.

Four years later George Tillman built the commodious two-story home that bespoke of his high position as a co-founder of the bank as well as of the Citrus Growers Association, which eventually blossomed into the Citrus World cooperative with its huge plant on US 27. George and his wife, Effie, lived in the home for many years. It was one of the first in the area with indoor plumbing—although, of course, the servants were advised to continue patronizing the convenient backyard outhouse. In this home the Tillmans watched their four children grow from rambunctious tots to sedate marrieds with families of their own. George died at the age of seventy-two. Effie remained in the house until she passed on nearly three decades later.

 Today the Tillmans' refurbished and modernized home is a bed and breakfast. Guests are impressed by the period furniture and the dazzling heart-of-pine floors. They like to relax on the spacious verandah looking towards Crystal Lake, much as George and Effie did as they dreamed their dreams for their future. Room rates are $85 to $140 per night. For reservations call 800-488-3315.

The City Fishing Pier

From the Tillman house, Sessoms Avenue leads one and a half blocks east to North Wales Drive, where a right turn will take you to the body of water for which the town is named. But there is a slight difference. The lake is spelled Wailes, christened thus by a government surveyor seeking favor with his superior of that name in Washington. Apparently the gratuitous "i" displeased George Tillman, who thought it conveyed a disturbingly plaintive feeling, and it was he who was responsible for the letter's demise.

The city fathers did an admirable job of protecting the lakefront from being disfigured by developers, bequeathing us an extensive public park that runs around the lake's entire western perimeter. A scenic foot trail lets hikers and strollers enjoy the vista. The city pier juts into the water near the foot of North Wales Drive. Fishing is allowed, although you can't sully the lake by cleaning your catch here. You may also be disappointed that you can't indulge in horseplay on the pier—so warns a sign. The sign, which also prohibits diving, recalls one of the tragedies of early Lake Wales. This took place when the young and handsome Henry Starnes, the popular elementary school principal, dove into the lake, not knowing how shallow it was. He hit his head on the bottom, ruptured his spine, and died two days later. Ironically, Starnes had just rehearsed his students for a play entitled *At the End of the Rainbow.* "The children are perfect in their parts," he had told some friends. "My work is done. I can now rest."

Follow Lakeshore Boulevard as it heads north, then east along the lake. At Tower Boulevard, you'll come to a second city park. This was once the site of a large turpentine still.

Bok Tower

No visit to Lake Wales is complete without a sojourn to the Iron Mountain and Bok Tower, which you can easily reach by driving north on Tower Boulevard. (If you skipped the lake drive, take SR 17 north to Burns Avenue, which is well marked, then drive a short distance east to Tower Boulevard, where you should follow the Bok arrow.) The park is open daily from 8 A.M. to 6 P.M., with the last admission at 5 P.M. The entrance fee is $6 for adults and $2 for kids five to twelve. That's rather stiff, but you'll be awed by the beautiful tower with its melodious carillon bells, extensive gardens, and inspiring view from the highest point on the peninsula.

After passing through the entry gate, you'll still be nearly a mile and a half from the tower. Much of the land is planted with citrus. The soil is bright rusty-red, the effect of the ferric oxide that gave Iron Mountain its name. The winding road gives you a chance to see the tower from different angles. Rising more than twenty stories from the hill's summit, it's built of pink and gray Georgia marble and crowned by eight stylized statues of herons. As you get closer, you can make out Gothic windows with turquoise-colored designs of pelicans, flamingos, geese, and other native wildlife. Once you're parked, stroll the shady path to the base of the tower for an up-close look. The best view is from the reflecting pool on the north side.

Almost as impressive as the tower is the extensive landscaped area around it. There are trickling streams, fern gardens, huge

The Bok Tower and Garden atop Iron Mountain is a place of beauty.

banks of rhododendrons, and large trees of about every species that grows in Florida. The trees are home to numerous tribes of squirrels. Most will regard you quizzically as they try to determine whether you're going to ignore them, feed them, or just be one of the nuisance characters who tries to scare them. In the pool you'll see colorful wood ducks, swans, and a water snake or two. Birds of many species and colors flutter from tree to tree. Foxes, raccoons, and even bobcats have found this habitat quite to their liking. That there are so many animals is not surprising, for when Edward Bok began developing this pine-clad hill in 1922, he thought of it as an animal sanctuary. The tower came a few years later.

The Dual Personalities of Edward Bok

Edward Bok was not the meek, rose-petal individual that the graceful tower and tranquil gardens suggest. On the contrary, he was a tough, aggressive businessman—the son of Dutch immigrants—who began his career as a young boy hawking ice water in downtown Brooklyn. At the age of twelve he promoted himself into writing a column for a local newspaper, gleaning his stories from a cadre of schoolmates he roped into acting as reporters. Nine years later he had the guts to start his own magazine. Soon he hit the big time when Scribner's took him on as a hard-hitting columnist. It wasn't long before Cyrus Curtis, owner of the highly respected *Ladies' Home Journal*, hired him. Such was his get-up-and-go that he climbed to top editorship in 1889. He was only twenty-five years old.

Under Bok's dynamic leadership, the *Journal* blew away the musty assumptions that women craved only bland pieces on romance and housekeeping. Bok solicited exciting, first-rate writers like Mark Twain and Rudyard Kipling to bring his readers into a gutsy new world. He even cajoled Teddy Roosevelt into writing a column, keeping his name mum, for he happened to be president at the time.

Although Edward Bok drove the *Journal* staff relentlessly, even ruthlessly, he had another side that rejected the snarling, competitive world in which he was such an effective player. "The one was bottled up in the other," he wrote in his autobiography, *The Americanization of Edward Bok*. So when he retired in 1919, he entered this far different world. It was then that he began planning what became the Bok Tower Gardens, which was formally dedicated by his friend, President Calvin Coolidge, ten years later. Yet even here Bok's twin personalities were apparent: whereas the garden expressed his pensive side, the tower—protruding boldly above the countryside—expressed the domineering side that could never be stilled.

Edward Bok died less than a year after the tower was dedicated. Today only the gentler side of the man is remembered, for the park has become a place for reflection and the enjoyment of nature. The only attempts at amusement are serenades by giant carillon bells each afternoon at three o'clock. Recorded chimes sound at thirty-minute intervals throughout the day. There is also a fully stocked gift store and a large sandwich shop with outdoor tables looking toward the tower.

Moon Food

Returning to SR 17, head north once more. In a few miles you'll come to Chalet Suzanne Road. Turn west and almost immediately you'll be at the road leading to the famed restaurant and inn. The same family has owned Chalet Suzanne for more than sixty years, and the bumpy, brick entry lane must date at least that far back. Strung out along the way are overnight guest suites, some of which look like dwellings out of *Alice in Wonderland*. As for the restaurant, *Gourmet* magazine calls its meals "glorious." When I stopped for one of its glorious lunches, I found that the cheapest item on the glorious menu was soup and sandwich costing $19. Although I passed it up—for "glory" must be savored, not part of a quick meal—I'm sure it would have been a stellar experience. Indeed, Chalet Suzanne's reputation is so lofty that its Romaine soup was carried by astronauts on their way to the moon—and that *is* lofty.

"The Top of Florida"

The Scenic Highway continues through citrus groves, most of whose owners belong to the local association that is part of the Florida's Natural co-op. In a few miles the road reaches the village of Dundee, where it makes a sharp left through the abbreviated business section, whose main activity seems to center around Melanie's Restaurant. Dundee chose its name after a well-known Scottish town in order to advertise its highland location. This promotional effort was not particularly successful, for even today Dundee's population is less than three thousand.

Once the Scenic Highway has made its dutiful detour through the town, it resumes a northward course. Paralleling the railroad, it hurries through another tiny citrus village called Lake Hamilton, which proclaims itself the "Top of Florida." Then the road breaks out once more into the groves. Although the groves may seem boundless, the long arm of Orlando is slowly reaching out to grasp and destroy them. The only question is, What will these scenic hills become? One alternative is golf courses, for which they are ideal.

Golf Balls vs. Citrus Balls

For a forecast of the future, take a five-mile side trip east on CR 546, Kokomo Road. At first you'll be among the groves, but as the road curves north you'll be engulfed by the fairways of the Grenelefe Golf and Tennis Resort. It's as if you're suddenly in a large park. The grass is clipped, the trees are spaced and trimmed, and clumps of flowers brighten the vista.

Although Grenelefe caters mainly to business groups, tourists are welcome. So drive into the grounds and follow the "Guest Registration" signs past fairways and two-story guest lodges to the main building. If you just want a burger or something to drink, walk through the lobby to the Lancelot Lounge. For a more complete meal, continue down the hall to the Camelot. Both are casual places looking out on the swimming pool. If you'd like to stay overnight without golf privileges, a room will run somewhere around $190 during the winter and $140 during the summer.

Leaving Grenelefe, continue on north CR 546 a short distance to CR 544, then turn west. One of Grenelefe's three golf courses is on your left, and the links of the Diamondback Country Club are on the right. As you go up a barely perceptible incline, the groves start again. Watch for the YTONG Company, which manufactures lightweight concrete building products. The fact that this German firm has located here was the result of an ongoing search for clean industries by the Haines City Chamber of Commerce.

The Rebirth of Haines City

When CR 544 reaches Tenth Street, turn north seven blocks to US 17/92, Hinson Avenue (Haines City's main thoroughfare), where you should head west. The town of thirteen thousand is a community on the go, and that spirit is clearly communicated by the multi-story building that dominates Hinson. It was constructed in the 1920s as a hotel by local grapefruit king Ralph Polk. But the good times didn't last and eventually the building became as much a derelict as the similar skyscraper in Lake Wales. It has recently been upgraded and now accommodates a Baptist college on the lower levels—although some wags contend that the upper floors would be more convenient for God.

Haines City suffered the same twentieth-century decline as its sister Ridge towns, Lake Wales and Sebring. But that's a past episode. The Main Street Program has revitalized the Sixth Street business section, which runs north from Hinson Avenue. Here you'll find period buildings skillfully converted into beauty parlors, antiques shops, and a restaurant or two. Sixth Street ends at Railroad Park, where carriages and horse carts once gathered when that all-important train chugged into the depot. At first the railroad had refused to stop at the town, then known as Clay Cut. But when the astute city fathers changed the name to Haines City, which just happened to match that of the railroad executive in charge of operations, a station magically appeared.

Gateway to a New Future

Although Haines City's traditional motto was "Gateway to the Scenic Highlands," its meaning today is far different from that of yesterday. Then it was designed to attract tourists to the Citrus Ridge.

Railroad Park in Haines City has hosted town functions for many decades.

Now Haines City is at the hub of the fastest-growing area in central Florida. The chamber of commerce expects the annual growth rate to exceed thirteen percent for the next several years. "Gated communities are lining the hillsides where citrus groves formerly filled the air with orange blossom aroma," says a chamber booklet. Five major subdivisions are currently under way, and a "mammoth" new industrial park is already under lease. Two more golf courses and country clubs have just opened. A modern medical complex, as well as a Wal-Mart Supercenter, have gone up. The police department is expanding. New bridges and overpasses are being built. And the city is preparing to annex an additional five miles on US 27. The land around the YTONG plant on CR 544 is earmarked for more factories. The exuberant chamber is planning a major new visitors center. In short, suburban sprawl has reached this part of the Ridge in all its glossy splendor.

Journey's End

It's here our southlands explorations end. I hope you've had fun during our nine expeditions. Together we've wandered the lesser-used byways. We've poked along both coasts, roamed the sugar fields, crossed the Everglades, and drifted among the fragrant citrus groves. Although these backroads seem a permanent part of Florida, in reality nearly all are under stress. What is a country byway today may be a suburban boulevard tomorrow. So drive them slowly, even lovingly. Enjoy them while they still exist. They may be far different the next time you pass their way.

Bibliography

Ahl, Janyce Barnwell. *Crown Jewel of the Highlands: Lake Wales, Florida.* Lake Wales, FL: Lake Wales Library Association, 1983.

Akerman, Joe A. *Florida Cowman: A History of Florida Cattle Raising.* Kissimmee, FL: Florida Cattlemen's Association, 1976.

Alden, Peter, et al. *National Audubon Society Field Guide to Florida.* New York: Knopf, 1998.

Baum, Earl L. *Early Naples and Collier County.* Naples, FL: Collier County Historical Society, 1973.

Beach, Rex. *Personal Exposures.* New York: Harper, 1940.

Beater, Jack. *Pirates and Buried Treasure on Florida Islands.* St. Petersburg, FL: Great Outdoors Publishing, 1959.

Bloch, Michael. *The Duchess of Windsor.* New York: St. Martin's Press, 1996.

Board, Prudy Taylor, and Esther B. Colcord. *Historic Fort Myers.* Virginia Beach, VA: Donning Co., 1992.

Bok, Edward. *The Americanization of Edward Bok.* New York: Scribner's, 1920.

Brown, Loren G. "Totch." *Totch: A Life in the Everglades.* Gainesville, FL: University Press of Florida, 1993.

Burgess, Robert F., and Carl J. Clausen. *Florida's Golden Galleons: The Search for the 1715 Spanish Treasure Fleet.* Port Salerno, FL: Florida Classics Library, 1982.

Carr, Archie. *A Naturalist in Florida.* New Haven, CT: Yale University Press, 1994.

259

Carr, Archie. *So Elegant a Fish: A Natural History of Sea Turtles.* New York: Scribner's, 1976, 1984 (revised).

Carson, Rachel. *The Edge of the Sea.* New York: Signet, 1955.

Cortes, Josephine O. *The History of Early Englewood.* Englewood, FL: Lemon Bay Historical Society, 1976, 1993.

Dickinson, Jonathan. *Jonathan Dickinson's Journal.* Port Salerno, FL: Florida Classics Library, 1985 (reprint of original 1699 edition).

Dodrill, David E. *Selling the Dream: The Gulf American Corporation and the Building of Cape Coral, Florida.* Tuscaloosa: University of Alabama Press, 1993.

Douglas, Marjory Stoneman. *The Everglades: River of Grass* 50th Anniversary Edition. Sarasota, FL: Pineapple Press, 1997.

Federal Writers' Project. *The WPA Guide to Florida.* New York: Pantheon, 1984 (originally published in 1939).

Garbarino, Merwyn S. *The Seminole.* New York: Chelsea, 1989.

Gregware, Bill, and Carol Gregware. *Guide to the Lake Okeechobee Area.* Sarasota, FL: Pineapple Press, 1997.

Hanna, Alfred J., and Kathryn A. Hanna. *Lake Okeechobee.* Dunwoody, GA: Norman S. Berg, 1973 (originally published in 1948).

Hutchinson, Janet, ed. *History of Martin County.* Hutchinson Island, FL: Martin County Historical Society, 1975, 1998 (reissued).

Jamro, Ron, and Gerald Lanterman. *The Founding of Naples.* Naples, FL: Friends of the Collier County Museum, 1985.

Jewell, Susan D. *Exploring Wild Central Florida.* Sarasota, FL: Pineapple Press, 1995.

Johnson, Carey. *Boca Grande—the Early Days: Memoirs of an Island Son.* Placida, FL: Barrier Island Parks Society, 1990.

Jumper, Betty Mae. *Legends of the Seminoles.* Sarasota, FL: Pineapple Press, 1994.

Kaplan, Eugene H. *Southeastern and Caribbean Seashores* (A Peterson Field Guide). Boston: Houghton-Mifflin, 1988.

Katz, Cathie. *The Nature of Florida's Beaches*. Melbourne Beach, FL: Atlantic Press, 1994.

Kaucher, Dorothy. *They Built a City*. Lake Wales, FL: no publisher given, 1970.

Kay, Russell. "Tamiami Trail Blazers: A Personal Memoir." *Florida Historical Quarterly*, Vol. 49 (January 1971): 278–287.

Larson, Ron. *Swamp Song*. Gainesville, FL: University Press of Florida, 1995.

Lockwood, Charlotte. *Florida's Historic Indian River County*. Vero Beach, FL: MediaTronics, 1975.

Lodge, Thomas E. *The Everglades Handbook: Understanding the Ecosystem*. Delray Beach, FL: St. Lucie Press, 1994.

Lyon, Eugene. *The Search for the Atocha*. Port Salerno, FL: Florida Classics Library, 1979.

Mahon, John K. *History of the Second Seminole War: 1835–1842*. Gainesville, FL: University Press of Florida, 1967, 1992.

Matthews, Janet Snyder. *Venice—Journey from Horse and Chaise: A History of Venice, Florida*. Sarasota, FL: Pine Level Press, 1989.

Maxwell, Leoma B. *The First Hundred Years of Avon Park, Florida*. Sebring, FL: Avon Historical Society, ca. 1980.

McCarthy, Kevin M., ed. *The Book Lover's Guide to Florida*. Sarasota, FL: Pineapple Press, 1992.

McCarthy, Kevin M., and William L. Trotter. *Twenty Florida Pirates*. Sarasota, FL: Pineapple Press, 1994.

McGoun, William E. *Southeast Florida Pioneers: The Palm and Treasure Coasts*. Sarasota, FL: Pineapple Press, 1998.

Morris, Allen. *Florida Place Names*. Sarasota, FL: Pineapple Press, 1995.

Newcomb and Baker Collections. Unpublished memoirs in Sebring Public Library, Sebring, FL.

Orlean, Susan. *The Orchid Thief.* New York: Random House, 1998.

Perry, John, and Jane Greverus. *The Sierra Club Guide to the Natural Areas of Florida.* San Francisco: Sierra Club Books, 1992.

Peterson, Olive Dame. *A. E. Backus: Florida Artist.* Stuart, FL: Gallery of Fort Pierce, 1984.

Quinn, Louise. *Crooked Lake—Babson Park Rediscovered.* Kissimmee, FL: self-published, 1990.

Richards, Lucie. *Memories of Eden: A Young Girl's Letters about Life in South Florida Frontier from 1880 through 1888.* Compiled and edited by Raymond Richards Brown. Jacksonville, FL: Eden Grove Trading Co., 1996.

Shroder, Tom, and John Barry. *Seeing the Light—Wilderness and Salvation: A Photographer's Tale.* New York: Random House, 1995.

Tolf, Robert, and Russell Buchan. *Florida Weekends: Where to Go, What to Do.* New York: Crown, 1990, 1994.

Ulmann, Alec. *The Sebring Story.* Philadelphia: Chilton, 1969.

VanLandingham, Kyle S. *Pictorial History of Saint Lucie County 1565–1910.* Ft. Pierce, FL: St. Lucie Historical Society, 1988.

VanLandingham, Kyle S., and Alma H. VanLandingham. *History of Okeechobee County.* Orlando, FL: Daniels, 1978.

Waitley, Douglas. *The Last Paradise: The Building of Marco Island.* Marco Island, FL: Marco Island Eagle, 1993, 1999.

Waitley, Douglas. *Roadside History of Florida.* Missoula, MT: Mountain Press, 1997.

Weisman, Brent Richards. *Unconquered People: Florida's Seminole and Miccosukee Indians.* Gainesville, FL: University Press of Florida, 1999.

Wilkinson, Alec. *Big Sugar: Seasons in the Cane Fields of Florida.* New York: Borzoi, 1989.

Will, Lawrence E. *Okeechobee Hurricane and the Hoover Dike.* Belle Glade, FL: Glades Historical Society, 1978 (originally published in 1961).

Youngberg, George, Sr., and W. Earl Aumann. *Venice and the Venice Area.* Venice, FL: Feather Fables Publishing, 1969, 1995.

Zeiss, Betsy. *The Other Side of the River: Historical Cape Coral.* Cape Coral: no publisher given, 1986.

Index

If you enjoyed reading this book, here are some other books from Pineapple Press on related topics. For a complete catalog, write to: Pineapple Press, P.O. Box 3889, Sarasota, FL 34230 or call 1-800-PINEAPL (746-3275). Or visit our website at www.pineapplepress.com.

Florida Island Hopping: The West Coast by Chelle Koster Walton. The first tour guide to Florida's Gulf Coast barrier islands, including a discussion of their histories, unique characters, and complete information on natural attractions, shopping, touring, and other diversions. ISBN 1-56164-081-6 (pb)

Florida's Finest Inns and Bed & Breakfasts by Bruce Hunt. From warm and cozy country bed & breakfasts to elegant and historic hotels, author Bruce Hunt has composed the definitive guide to Florida's most quaint, romantic, and often eclectic lodgings. With photos and charming pen-and-ink drawings by the author. ISBN 1-56164-202-9 (pb)

Guide to Florida Historical Walking Tours by Roberta Sandler. Put on your walking shoes and experience the heart of Florida's people, history, and architecture as you take an entertaining stroll through 32 historic neighborhoods. ISBN 1-56164-105-7 (pb)

Hemingway's Key West Second Edition by Stuart McIver. A rousing, true-to-life portrait of Hemingway in Key West, Cuba, and Bimini during his heyday. Includes a two-hour walking tour of the author's favorite Key West haunts and a narrative of the places he frequented in Cuba. ISBN 1-56164-241-X (pb)

Historic Homes of Florida by Laura Stewart and Susanne Hupp. Seventy-four notable dwellings throughout the state—all open to the public—tell the human side of history. Each home is illustrated by H. Patrick Reed or Nan E. Wilson. ISBN 1-56164-085-9 (pb)

Houses of Key West by Alex Caemmerer. Eyebrow houses, shotgun houses, Conch Victorians, and many more styles illustrated with lavish color photographs and complemented by anecdotes about old Key West. ISBN 1-56164-009-3 (pb)

Houses of St. Augustine by David Nolan. A history of the city told through its buildings, from the earliest coquina structures, through the Colonial and Victorian times, to the modern era. Color photographs and original watercolors. ISBN 1-56164-0697 (hb); ISBN 1-56164-075-1 (pb)

Visiting Small-Town Florida Volumes 1 and 2 by Bruce Hunt. From Carrabelle to Bokeelia, Two Egg to Fernandina, these out-of-the-way but fascinating destinations are well worth a side trip or weekend excursion. **Volume 1** ISBN 1-56164-128-6 (pb); **Volume 2** ISBN 1-56164-180-4 (pb)